THE GIRLS FROM AMES

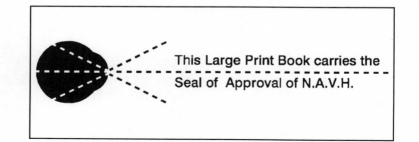

This Large Print Book carries the
Seal of Approval of N.A.V.H.

THE GIRLS FROM AMES

A STORY OF WOMEN
AND A FORTY-YEAR FRIENDSHIP

JEFFREY ZASLOW

THORNDIKE PRESS
A part of Gale, Cengage Learning

Detroit • New York • San Francisco • New Haven, Conn • Waterville, Maine • London

GALE
CENGAGE Learning™

Copyright © 2009 by Jeffrey Zaslow.
Photos courtesy of: Teness Herman: pp. 78, 162, 226, 295, 354, 482, 500, 537; Karla Blackwood: pp. 30, 115, 246, 312, 326, 369, 479; Jenny Litchman: p. 530; Marilyn Johnson: pp. 73, 369; Kelly Zwagerman: p. 161; Jane Nash: pp. 78, 285, 405; Angela Jamison: p. 130; Cathy Highland: p. 226; Diana Sarussi: p. 295; Karen Leininger: pp. 185, 256, 423; Sally Hamilton: p. 226.
Thorndike Press, a part of Gale, Cengage Learning.

Thorndike Press® Large Print Biography.
The text of this Large Print edition is unabridged.
Other aspects of the book may vary from the original edition.
Set in 16 pt. Plantin.
Printed on permanent paper.

LIBRARY OF CONGRESS CATALOGING-IN-PUBLICATION DATA

Zaslow, Jeffrey.
   The girls from Ames : a story of women and a forty-year friendship / by Jeffrey Zaslow.
    p. cm.
   "Thorndike Press Large Print Biography."
   ISBN-13: 978-1-4104-1669-8 (hbk. : alk. paper)
   ISBN-10: 1-4104-1669-0 (hbk. : alk. paper)
   1. Women—Iowa—Social conditions. 2. Women—Iowa—Ames—Biography. 3. Female friendship—Iowa—Ames. I. Title.
   HQ1206.Z27 2009b
   305.4092'2777546—dc22
   [B]   2009010165

Published in 2009 by arrangement with Gotham Books, a member of Penguin Group (USA) Inc.

Printed in the United States of America
1 2 3 4 5 6 7 13 12 11 10 09

The Ames girls, circa 1981 — Karla, Sally, Karen, Diana, Jenny, Sheila, Jane and Angela

*For all those who've known
the gift of friendship . . .*

CONTENTS

INTRODUCTION

At first, they were just names to me.

Karla, Kelly, Marilyn, Jane, Jenny.

Karen, Cathy, Angela, Sally, Diana.

Sheila.

They arrived, unheralded, in my email in-box one morning in June 2003. The email came from Jenny, who offered three understated paragraphs about her relationship with these women. She explained that they grew up together in Ames, Iowa, where as little girls their friendship flourished. Though all have since moved away — to Minnesota, California, North Carolina, Maryland, Pennsylvania, Arizona, Massachusetts, Montana — they remain a powerful, loving presence in each other's lives. Now entering their forties, Jenny wrote, they're bonded by a lifetime of shared laughs, and by more than a few heartbreaking memories.

After I read Jenny's email, I sent her a

quick reply, thanking her for writing. Then I printed out her message to me, bundled it up with a couple of hundred other emails I received that day, and put it in the bottom of a filing cabinet, where it remained untouched for three years.

Jenny had contacted me because I write a column for *The Wall Street Journal* called "Moving On." The column focuses on life transitions, everything from a child's first crush to a dying husband's last words to his wife. Though the *Journal* covers the heart of the financial world, my editors have embraced the idea that we must also tend to the hearts of our readers. And so they've given me freedom to do just that. There are a thousand emotionally charged transitions that we all face in our lives, and most come without a road map. That's the territory of my column.

Jenny decided to tell me about the girls from Ames (and yes, they still call themselves "girls") after reading a column I'd written about the turning points in women's friendships. The column focused on why women, more than men, have great urges to hold on tightly to old friends. Sociologists now have data showing that women who can maintain friendships through the decades are healthier and happier, with stronger marriages. Not all women are able to sustain those friendships, however. It's true that countless grade-school girls arrange themselves in pairs, duos, threesomes and foursomes, vowing to be best friends forever. But as they reach adulthood, everything gets harder. When women are between the ages of twenty-five and forty, their friendships are most at risk, because those are the years when women are often consumed with marrying, raising children and establishing careers.

For that column, I spoke to women who had nurtured decades-long friendships. They said they felt like traveling companions, sharing the same point on the timeline, hitting the same milestones together — thirty, forty, fifty, eighty. They believed their friendships thrived because they had raised some expectations and lowered others. They had come to expect loyalty and good wishes from each other, but not constant attention. If a friend didn't return an email or phone call, they realized, it didn't mean she was angry or backing away from the friendship; she was likely just exhausted from her day. Researchers who study friendship say that if women are still friends at age forty, there's a strong likelihood they'll be lifelong friends. "Female friends show us a mirror of ourselves," one researcher told me.

That column ran in *The Wall Street Journal* on a Thursday, and by 5 A.M. that morning, emails from readers had begun filling my inbox. Every few minutes, well into the weekend, I'd get an email from yet another woman proudly telling me about her group of friends:

"We've gotten together twice a year ever since we graduated high school in 1939 . . ."

"We met in Phoenix and call ourselves Phriends Phorever . . ."

"We've had lunch together every Wednesday since 1973 . . ."

"My girlfriends and I joke that when the time comes, we'll all just check into the same nursing home . . ."

"I'm only 23, but your article gives me hope that I will hold on to my friends for life . . ."

One reader told me about her grand-mother's eight friends, all from the class of '89 — that's 1889! They stayed remarkably close for sixty-five years, and even when they reached their eighties, they still called themselves "The Girls."

And then there was the letter from Jennifer Benson Litchman, an assistant dean at the University of Maryland School of Medicine. Jenny from Ames.

In some ways, Jenny's story was like so many of the others. She shared a few details about how the eleven Ames girls met, some as early as infanthood in the church nursery, and how they feel bonded forever. But her short, tossed-off note didn't fully reveal how extraordinary those bonds have become — I'd learn all that later — and she didn't even tell any of her friends she had written to me. Jenny ended her email by saying that she appreciated my take on female friendship. She also paid me a compliment: "You really seem to understand women. Your wife is very lucky indeed."

My wife would have to speak to how lucky she is or isn't, but I can say this: I do feel an almost urgent need to understand women. That's mostly because I am the father of three teenagers, all daughters.

I have seen my girls pout and fret and cry over friendships in turmoil, and I have seen how their friends have buoyed them at their lowest moments. At times, their sweetest friends have turned into stereotypical mean girls. At other times, former mean girls turn into friends. As a parent witnessing it all, I often feel helpless and exasperated.

Having observed how my mother, sister and wife built lovely friendships over the years, I naturally hope that my daughters can be as fortunate. When I think about their futures, I want them to feel enveloped by people who love them, and I know they'll need close, loving friends at their sides. (I'm also aware that men's friendships are completely different. I've been playing poker with a group of friends every Thursday night for many years. About 80 percent of our conversations are focused specifically on the cards, the betting, the bluffing. Most of the rest of the chatter is about sports, or sometimes our jobs. For weeks on end, our personal lives — or our feelings about anything — never even come up.)

There have been many self-help books designed to help women find and navigate friendships. Scholarly books have been written, too. And of course best-selling novels have won huge audiences by focusing on the sisterhood among fictional women.

But as a journalist, I know there's great power in honest stories about real people. So, over time, I found myself intrigued by the idea of asking one articulate group of long-standing friends to open their hearts and scrapbooks, to tell the complete inside story of their friendship. I had a real sense that a nonfiction narrative — the biography of a friendship, meticulously reported — could be a meaningful document for female readers. Perhaps it would also help me understand my daughters, my wife and the other women in my life.

And so in the summer of 2006, I returned to that filing cabinet, and went through all the emails from women describing their friendships. I read them again, building a short stack of possibilities. I contacted many of the letter writers, and they were all very eager to share their thoughts.

They told me that when women think about their friends, they find themselves pondering every part of their lives: their sense of themselves, their choice of men, their dependence on other women, their need for validation, their relationships with their mothers, their dreams for their daughters . . . everything.

Many of these women shared beautiful anecdotes with me. They all said their friends could certainly fill a book. But once I called Jenny and spoke to her for a while, I had a sense that she and the ten other girls from Ames had a sweeping and very moving story to tell. That was confirmed when I eventually met each of them. They were born at the end of the baby boom and their memories are evocative of their times. Born in the middle of the country, they now live everywhere else, but carry Ames with them. Their story is universal, even common, and on that level it can't help but resonate with any woman who has ever had a friend. And yet some of their experiences together are so completely one-of-a-kind — haunting and touching and exhilarating — that I found myself feeling spellbound as they talked to me.

The Ames girls were intrigued by the idea of a book about them, but understandably, several were hesitant at first. It is not an easy decision to reveal your life to a journalist (and eventually to the world), and I tried to move slowly and respectfully with them. Turning their lives into an open book, I said, would be a journey for them and for me. I wanted to know vital details of their interactions, the good and the bad. I'd ask them about the times they showed each other great care and compassion. But I also wanted them to reflect on the times they disappointed each other or were purposely unkind. How did they overcome those moments and remain so close for so long?

A few of them feared that my reporting for the book might bring up old ghosts or highlight long-ago misdeeds or challenge their assumptions about themselves. I asked them to take that risk with me. Yes, I hoped that the finished book would honor and strengthen their friendships. But I couldn't guarantee that everything would go smoothly and that no one would get hurt.

We began with tentative steps. One by one, often in long phone conversations after they tucked their kids into bed, they talked to me about their loving feelings for each other, the rougher times between them, and about how their story, if told well, could benefit other women of all ages. I decided to take a year-long leave from my job at the *Journal,* so I could travel around the country spending time with them. I immersed myself in their lives, asking them to think back, to think hard, to force themselves to remember everything as clearly and honestly as they could. Why did they choose each other? Who were they then, and who are they now? They all turned out to be so articulate, so able to find perspective and broader truths. Because of that, compiling their story became a remarkable experience for me as a journalist.

As we got to know each other, the Ames girls became more comfortable with me. In time, they let me read hundreds of pages of secrets locked in their old diaries. They shared stacks of letters and emails they had exchanged. They introduced me to their parents, children, siblings, husbands and old boyfriends. They even pointed me toward women outside their group who saw them as a clique and didn't much like them.

Born in 1962 and 1963, they spoke vividly about what it was like to be girls in the sixties and seventies, young women in the eighties and new mothers in the nineties. They offered up countless examples of how close female friendships can shape every aspect of women's lives.

Almost all of the Ames girls are scrupulous savers, chronicling their lives together in scrapbooks and photo albums, holding on to whatever memorabilia marked their friendship. That was a huge help in piecing together their story. Because I had their diaries, letters, concert ticket stubs and notes passed in homeroom, I was able to track many of their interactions to the exact day and even the exact hour. I felt like an archaeologist, sifting through crumbling prom corsages, looking for meaning.

Of course, there were plenty of challenges.

When I'd tell people about this project, some wondered whether it was an appropriate task for a man. Could a man ever really understand women's friendships? It was a fair point. And I admit that I sometimes asked the Ames girls questions that were silly, obvious or naïve. I'd catch them trading glances, and I knew that they were thinking: "This guy doesn't get it, does he?" And yet I also think that being a man gave me a wider canvas. I was often inquisitive in ways a female interviewer would not have been. I made no assumptions. I asked. I rephrased. I tried to comprehend. On some fronts, my outsider's curiosity helped enrich the story you're about to read.

In the end, the girls and I agreed that to make the project work, it had to be based on a great deal of trust between all of us. We worked to build that trust, interview by interview, recollection by recollection, sometimes with tears, sometimes with great laughter.

Karla, Kelly, Marilyn, Jane, Jenny, Karen, Cathy, Angela, Sally, Diana, Sheila.

Theirs is the story of eleven little girls and the women they became. I feel privileged to have this opportunity to tell it.

A GUIDE TO THE AMES GIRLS

(Childhood Photos on Left, High School Graduation Photos on Right)

Marilyn: the doctor's daughter; earnest, risk-averse, a bit of an outsider in the group; closest to Jane. Now she is a stay-at-home mom in Minnesota.

Karla: adopted at birth; lively and lovable, but as a girl, not always sure of herself; first to have a child (her daughter Christie). Now she's a stay-at-home mom.

Sheila: the dentist's daughter; considered the sweetest of the girls growing up; an incorrigible flirt. She left Ames for Chicago to help families with ill children. Never married.

Kelly: free spirit of the group and the most likely to surprise them with her words and actions. Now divorced, she is a high school teacher in Minnesota.

Jane: smart, studious, bonded with Marilyn, and the only Jewish member of the group. Now she is a psychology professor outside of Boston.

Diana: known as the beauty of the group. Now married with three daughters, she works at a Starbucks in Arizona.

Cathy: last of seven siblings, which made her more worldly (and a bit sassy) as a girl. Never married. Now she works as a makeup artist in Los Angeles.

Sally: smart, funny, but at the periphery of the group in early years; brought into the friendship by Cathy. Now she is a teacher and the only one remaining in Iowa.

Karen: the auto dealer's daughter. Longtime nickname: "Woman." Now she is a stay-at-home mom near Philadelphia.

Jenny: one of the archivists of the friendship; close to Sheila; last to have a child. Now she is the assistant dean at the University of Maryland School of Medicine.

Angela: newest member of the group; arrived in town in ninth grade, when her father came to manage a hotel in Ames. Now she runs a PR firm in North Carolina.

1
THE GIRLS
IN THE PHOTOS

The old photos are spread all over the kitchen table, and in so many of them, going back so many years, the eleven girls are completely mashed together. This is how they loved posing. Arms all intertwined. Or giving each other the tightest group hug. Or they'd line up, chest-to-back-chest-to-back, all scrunched up, KarlaSallyKarenDiana-JennySheilaJaneAngelaMarilynCathyKelly, as if they were one living, breathing organism with eleven separate smiles.

There's a photo of them in their school lunchroom, spent milk cartons in front of them, and they're laughing and leaning into each other, arms draped over every available shoulder. In another photo from their teen years, taken from overhead, the girls are lying flat on their backs on a carpeted floor. Their heads are pressed together in a circle, with each body pointed outward, like rays from the sun. It wasn't enough for

them to be head-to-head-to-head, all of
them beaming; some decided to hold hands,
too.

They were just as tactile as they got older.
In a photo taken when they were in their
twenties, Kelly is pregnant, and the other
girls have their palms on her belly. In
another photo, from their thirties, they're
all squished on a bed at Karla's house, their
legs overlapping.

The "girls" are forty-four years old now, and these images of their younger selves are a reminder that in certain crucial ways, nothing has changed. The pictures are laid out tonight on this kitchen table at Angela's home in Wake Forest, North Carolina, and as the girls look through them, there is an ease with which they touch each other. A hand will nonchalantly rest on someone else's arm. Over on the sofa, a head will drop casually onto someone else's shoulder. They're comfortable sitting close together, four of them on a couch meant for three, almost on each other's lap.

This summer visit to Angela's is the latest Ames girls reunion, and ten of the eleven girls are here. That's everyone except Sheila, though as far as the ten of them are concerned, she's here, too. For one thing, Sheila is in photos all over the table, looking up at them with that full-on smile of hers. For another thing, as they explain it — well, they can't quite explain it. She's just here with them, that's all.

They've been gathering like this all their adult lives. Every year or so, they fly or drive somewhere to be together, and once they arrive, it's as if they've stepped into a time machine. Being in each other's company, they feel like they are every age they ever were, because they see themselves through thousands of shared memories.

Yes, they're all forty-four. But in their heads and hearts, they are also twelve and fifteen and seventeen and back in Ames.

As twelve-year-olds, they'd sit in a circle, combing each other's hair.

As fifteen-year-olds, they knew what it was like to kiss the same cute boy. Kelly knew and Karen knew and Marilyn knew, but didn't tell anyone.

As seventeen-year-olds, they were slightly wild and unwittingly cliquey, and every weekend, the eleven of them would squeeze into two cars, and off they'd drive, in search of eleven boys.

Growing up in the corn-and-college town of Ames, home to Iowa State University, they were exposed to so many of the same influences — the rural values of family and hard work, the focus on higher education, the constant presence of alcohol among their peers. Day after day, they shared the not-always-appreciated joys and often-exaggerated complaints about small-town life. But no matter what, the girls loved the place then and love it more now. It's a town of just 53,000 — about half of whom are transient Iowa State students — and it can be traveled end to end in fifteen minutes.

That's a small space, yet it offered the girls a microcosm of how the wider world worked. All around Ames sit cornfields, with a farmhouse here or there, and not much else off into the horizon. But in the town itself there was an energy, with adults falling in love and doing meaningful work, or making mistakes and paying the price, or taking the time to teach the girls life lessons they've never forgotten. For the girls, who often say they feel like sisters, Ames was their shared womb.

As friends there, they certainly weathered disagreements and disappointments. They traded harsh words and cold shoulders. They annoyed and angered each other. But they always vowed to remain that group of eleven, even after they left Ames and built new lives. What they could never have predicted in Ames were the exact numbers to come: They ended up moving in or out of seventeen different states. Between them, they found nine first husbands and two second husbands, and brought twenty-one children into the world. They have buried five parents.

They've come together for this four-day weekend at Angela's not just to reminisce and review all that ground; they've also come to share tentative predictions and yearnings about what's ahead in each of their lives. Sometimes two or three of them will disappear into a corner of Angela's house for a private connection. Other times, all ten will sit and talk as a group. A few of the girls are facing serious moments of transition. It is a relief, they say, to have these hands to hold, these ears to hear them, before they embark on their uncertain futures.

Karla's change is imminent. She has decided to move with her husband and kids from their home in Edina, Minnesota, to a new home they are building in Bozeman, Montana. Moving day is later this summer. To an outsider's eyes, this may seem like no big deal; families move from one place to another all the time. But the Ames girls know that in Karla's case, this is a move accompanied by painfully raw emotions, and their hearts ache for her. Karla's decision to go is actually a way of attempting a new life after the life she and her family had together was forever altered. "Come sit with me. Let's talk," Jane says to Karla. And they do, well into the night.

After this weekend, Kelly's life will also take a different path. Her divorce is just now final, after two years of struggling that left her without primary custody of her kids.

She talks freely of how she envies some of the other Ames girls and their marriages. "I want to find a relationship as powerful and meaningful as the ones you have," she says to them. "And I will."

Marilyn has come to the reunion with a copy of a letter she wrote and mailed out just a week ago. It's a letter to a truck driver she spoke to just once on the phone, in a conversation that lasted only a few minutes. She has never met him, and knows almost nothing about him, except for a flash of memory from long ago, and a few things she has since learned through a Google search. She has the letter in her purse but hasn't yet shown it around. Maybe later in the weekend, she'll take it out. "When the time is right," she tells a few of the girls, "I have something I'd like you to read."

Cathy, meanwhile, is at her own turning point, because she's on the cusp of changing her career. For many years, she has been a successful Los Angeles–based makeup artist, touring the world with Janet Jackson or working with the casts on sitcoms such as *Frasier*. Lately, however, the thrill of being what she calls "a face-painter" to the stars has passed, and she has decided to use other gifts — her dry sense of humor, her insights into people, her grasp of words. She plans to try to make it as a screenwriter.

Over the next four days, the Ames girls will pay little attention to the outside world, leaving their cell phones in their suitcases and their kids in the care of their husbands. They will spend time laughing so hard that they'll have to make emergency trips to the bathroom. They'll also cry over the deepest sorrows imaginable — matters they never contemplated back when they were girls.

"That couch out on the porch, for some reason, that has become the crying couch," Cathy says at one point. "You sit down there, you start talking, you start crying."

Angela's house is perfectly appointed and spacious, with an understated Southern charm and comfortable furniture everywhere. But the girls don't spend most of their time inside. Instead, they are drawn to that open-air back porch. The simple resin-wicker furniture faces into the backyard, where Angela's seven-year-old daughter has a swing set. Just on the other side of the tree line, there's a large tobacco field, dusty and sun-baked this time of year. And beyond that, 1,163 miles to the west, is Ames.

For the girls sitting together on the crying couch — holding cups of coffee in the morning, glasses of wine at night — Ames, or at least the Ames of their memories, feels

36

far closer. They can actually reach out and touch it. All they have to do is touch each other.

How did it all start? When, exactly, did the eleven of them begin to bond? The answer, as they explain it, has a quasi-cosmic touch: It's almost as if they remember each other before they remember each other. Or more accurately: They have memories in common that date back to the days before they even met. Most of them didn't know each other as preschoolers, but in their own homes, they were sometimes having the exact same experiences at the same exact moment.

They'd all watch this local Ames TV kids' show, *The Magic Window,* which for forty years was hosted by a woman named Betty Lou Varnum. In every episode, Betty Lou would introduce a craft-making segment by announcing the materials needed. These were always kid-safe items that could be found around the house. But the kids had to find everything fast, really fast, or Betty Lou would go on without them.

"OK, children," she'd say, "you're going to need an egg carton, string, two paper clips, cellophane tape, a pair of safety scissors, a piece of green construction paper . . ."

At that instant, all around Ames, the frenzy began. "It was like 'Game on!' " Cathy says. "You had maybe a minute to round everything up. I'd yell to my mother, 'Mom . . . MOM! I need an egg carton. I need string. Hurry! I need two paper clips. I need scissors. . . .' "

Cathy can now deliver a perfect comic routine of how she'd scamper around the house doing Betty Lou's bidding, and when she does, the other girls laugh in recognition.

Most of the girls don't recall being formally introduced to each other. There was no magic moment, no feeling of love at first sight, the way some of them recall meeting their husbands. But that's common when it comes to early childhood friendships. There are often just hazy memories of playing in the same vicinity in a class or on a playground (child-development researchers now call it parallel play), and then liking each other's company, and then, almost always without fanfare, crossing that line from acquaintances to friends.

Jenny and Karla were born days apart in Mary Greeley Hospital, and were infants together in their mothers' arms at the same church. It's possible that one of their parents said, "Jenny, this is Karla; Karla, this is Jenny." But the girls wouldn't remember that. What they do remember is being four years old together at Barbara Jean's Academy of Dance, and the costumes they wore. For one number, they actually wore itsy-bitsy-teenie-weenie-yellow-polka-dot bikinis — a live-action kid version of the 1960 novelty song. They also did a tap dance together in red satin Eskimo costumes, and they remember the soft white fur around their necks.

Most of the other girls didn't begin meeting face-to-face until kindergarten or first grade. Cathy, Sally and Sheila went to St. Cecilia on Lincoln Way, the local Catholic school, and their friendships took root because of proximity and happenstance. As an adult, Cathy has spent time marveling about this. She admits that if she hadn't met her Ames friends until adulthood, it would have taken more time to connect — or they might not have connected at all. After all, the friends she has made in Los Angeles tend to be nontraditional, having kids later in life and working in the entertainment industry or other creative jobs.

In Ames, the girls often landed in each other's lives by virtue of alphabetical order or group homework assignments. Cathy became friends with Sally in first grade because their teacher at St. Cecilia made the match. Cathy had a broken arm and had missed the first week of school. When she showed up at the class, the teacher said, "Why don't you go sit next to Sally?" The teacher figured Sally and Cathy were the two tallest girls. And Sally was smart, so she could help Cathy catch up on the missed work. From that pairing, a lifelong friendship was born.

Sheila became Cathy's friend because they lived near each other. The two of them ended up walking home from school together every day. That brought Sheila into Sally's life, too.

Sheila, whose dad was a dentist, had this spark about her that went beyond her sparkling white teeth. She was completely cute, with big brown eyes and that always-animated smile of hers. She was also tiny back then, which made her a favorite of the nuns at St. Cecilia. The sister who taught first grade liked to invite Sheila to join her up front when she read stories to the rest of the class. "Sheila would be sitting there, cuddling on the nun's lap, and we'd be sitting on the floor, feeling jealous," says Sally.

In second grade, their teacher got pregnant. (This particular teacher was not a nun, or at least, not anymore.) Given that the Immaculate Conception had been faintly addressed in religion class, the teacher decided she'd better explain her situation to her students. So she brought in a book titled *I Wonder, I Wonder,* which, in the most innocuous way, touched on how sperm meets up with an egg. The pregnant teacher read it cheerfully to the class as they sat on the big rug in the corner. For Sally and Sheila, however, the book only increased the wondering. They had always assumed pregnancy was a direct result of heavy kissing, and the book wasn't about kissing at all. Luckily, Cathy had an array of answers, courtesy of information provided by her six older siblings. She gleefully offered up the F word.

"That's the word they use. That's the main word," she told Sheila as they walked home from school the day *I Wonder, I Wonder* was recited to the class. Sheila had never heard the word before, didn't have any idea how babies were created, and her eyes grew wider and wider as Cathy explained all the details. Sheila kept asking, "How do you know all this? Who told you this?" It seemed dangerously exciting just thinking about it. That day, she and Cathy made up a rhyming song with this new vocabulary. For weeks afterward, they sang it as they walked home from school.

These days, when the Ames girls spend time with women they didn't meet until adulthood, they can act sophisticated, mature and worldly. They can't do that as easily with each other, of course, because in the back of their minds, they have a full log of all the goofy things they said and did when they were young.

Jenny hasn't forgotten all the odd excuses Karen would give in elementary school because she was too afraid to have a sleepover. "I can't sleep at your house because I haven't been baptized yet," Karen said one afternoon.

Jenny was confused. "What does not being baptized have to do with it?"

"Well, when a Catholic hasn't been baptized, they have to spend the night in their own bed in their own home," Karen told her. "Otherwise, if they die in their sleep on a sleepover at some other kid's house, they won't go to heaven."

Jenny, a Methodist, felt bad that Karen would be risking an eternity in hell by agreeing to a sleepover. She let it be. But she asked her mom about it, and her mom explained that Karen just had sleepover anxiety; it had nothing to do with Catholicism. Karen stuck to the baptism story for months, but Jenny was kind enough not to call her on it.

Eight of the eleven Ames girls spent their elementary years in public school. Most met up with Cathy, Sheila and Sally when the three of them came from St. Cecilia to Central Junior High, one of the two public junior highs in Ames. (Only Marilyn, Jane and Angela went to Welch Junior High.)

The girls got to know and understand each other in part through their quirkiness. Cathy had aspirations to be a model when she grew up — a hand model. She'd hold up her right hand and move it around oh-so-elegantly. Then she'd showcase her left hand. The other girls couldn't stop laughing as she regaled them with predictions for her future life as a highly paid hand model. They imagined her as a spokesmodel for, say, hand lotion or engagement rings, touring the planet in protective gloves.

Karla, meanwhile, had become adept at creating a world very close to the one described and photographed each month in her *Seventeen* magazines. She turned her bedroom closet into a magazine-worthy showcase closet. She had hooks for necklaces, hooks for purses, shoes arranged in a particular order — like a fireman's boots, ready for action. The other girls would come over and stand at the closet, oohing and ah-hing, as if *Seventeen*'s closet committee had actually come to Ames to certify that Karla's layout met their specifications.

The girls were always observing each other closely. They were constantly wondering, speculating, judging, measuring. They wanted to know everything about hygiene, acne, puberty, sex, and they learned by monitoring each other. That led to a lot of blurting and blushing on their road to discovery. Kelly, by far the most strident of the girls, was relentlessly curious, always willing to ask the question everyone else was thinking.

During the winter of eighth grade, some of the girls went on an overnight church retreat together. Back then, Marilyn always slept on her stomach, and she liked to keep her hands warm by tucking them neatly under herself. Kelly looked at her for a few minutes and then just had to ask: "Marilyn, what are you doing?"

All Marilyn could sputter was "Well, I'm not doing *that!*"

By junior high, the girls had begun establishing nicknames for each other. Jenny, whose last name was Benson, became "Jenny-Benny." Karla, whose last name was Derby, became "Kerby." Diana Speer became "Spi-ana" or "Spi." And then there was Karen, whom they always called "Woman."

Woman got her nickname from her father, the chattiest, friendliest auto salesman in Ames. She was the youngest of his five kids, and starting when she was a toddler, he loved to call her "my little girlfriend."

He'd introduce her to other adults: "This is my little girlfriend." In her earliest years, Karen was OK with that. She'd smile bashfully when people would tell her dad, "Well, Hugh, your little girlfriend is very pretty."

However, when Karen entered third grade, she'd had enough. That September, parents and students were invited to an open house at school. As she and her father walked to the school, Karen found the courage to say: "Dad, when we meet my teachers, I don't want you calling me your little girlfriend." Her dad listened to her, thought for a moment, and replied, "OK then. I understand. I'll just call you my woman." Once the other Ames girls got wind of that father/daughter exchange, she was their woman, too. That's what they still call her today: "Woman."

All of the girls were basically middle class or a little above or below that. In fact, that described pretty much the entire town. There were no snobby neighborhoods with mini-mansions. There were a few snooty people here and there, but between the Ames girls, any class differences were noticed and noted, and then everyone moved on. When shopping for school clothes, not all of the girls' parents could afford to drive them 350 miles east to Chicago, or 180 miles north to Minneapolis, where there were more fashionable stores. But there weren't many complaints among those who didn't get to go.

These days, young girls are more class- and status-conscious, measuring every article of clothing, and every earring, that their friends have on. The Ames girls somehow stayed mostly clear of that. There was actually an urge to downplay what they had. Marilyn, always aware of being the daughter of a doctor, knew that her family was likely the most comfortable financially. Her home was bigger than most, and on a large piece of land. But her family wasn't showy at all. Marilyn was mortified the day Karen came over and noticed the shampoo in her bathroom. It was regular shampoo, just like Karen had at her house. "Why don't you have fancier shampoo?" Karen asked Marilyn. Marilyn thought she was implying that a doctor's daughter should have more luxuriant hair products. (For her part, Karen was just being curious about brands.) The comment sat with Marilyn, leaving her wondering whether the other girls also thought about the products her family had or didn't have, and talked about them behind her back. In truth, though, most of the girls were oblivious when it came to parents' paychecks or economic status.

The girls didn't talk much to each other about their parents' jobs, but when they did, they were often quizzical. There were certain occupations that were easy to figure out. Karen's dad, of course, sold families their Chevys. Sally's mom was a music teacher. Kelly's father was the junior-high guidance counselor, and her mom was an administrative assistant at Iowa State. And several of the girls had Marilyn's dad as their pediatrician and Sheila's dad as their dentist. But some of the girls' fathers held jobs with secret code words and clear expectations about how the girls should talk about them.

Diana's dad was a well-known swine nutritionist at Iowa State. City types would assume he was creating weight-loss programs for pigs, but as Diana explained it to everyone, "He wants them bigger, fatter, faster." Actually, that wasn't exactly it. Her dad was really researching ways to build muscle weight, as opposed to fat, and to do it rapidly and cost-effectively. He always instructed Diana and her friends to say "swine" rather than "pigs" or "hogs." To his ears, and in people's minds, "pig" sounded unclean; "hog" sounded uncouth. And so, when he'd bring piglets into Diana's grade-school classrooms for show-and-tell, the operative word was "swine."

Cathy's dad, meanwhile, was a soil scientist at Iowa State. Her father considered "dirt" to be a dirty word — a four-letter word. Dirt is what you get under your fingernails when you work in soil. "I study soil, not dirt," he'd say.

"Well, soil is also a four-letter word, Dad," Cathy replied.

Cathy and her siblings were discouraged from using the word "dirt" in the house, but behind their dad's back, they jokingly called him "Dr. Dirt." One day, some of the Ames girls came over to work on their soil-gradation projects for science class. Cathy's dad helped them, explaining the difference between the D word and the S word, as Cathy rolled her eyes.

Karla and Sally both had fathers who worked for Iowa's Department of Transportation, which was based in Ames. Karla's dad was a civil engineer who designed bridges. Sally's father was a materials engineer, he handled materials inspection. Both helped build many of the highways now criss-crossing Iowa. They had their own language protocol, too. Whenever the Ames girls were around Sally's dad, if they were ever referring to a roadway, they had to use the word "concrete," not "cement."

"Cement is a binder. It's a component of concrete," Sally's dad would say. "Highways are made of concrete."

Concrete, not cement. Swine, not pigs. Soil, not dirt. The Ames girls took it all under advisement, giggling, but mostly they just focused on their own young lives.

If you're a kid hanging out with a bunch of other kids in a small town (or even a large city), you don't ever stop what you're doing and say, "Hey, wait a second, how did we all get here?" And so, it took years — in some cases, well into adulthood — for the Ames girls to learn the details of how they all ended up being raised within a few square miles of each other.

Several of the girls' parents, not surprisingly, first came to Ames to attend or work at Iowa State. Karla's dad and Diana's dad both enrolled at the university in 1942. Kelly's dad, being so much younger, didn't enroll until 1963.

A few of the families ended up in Ames by happenstance. Ames sits in the center of Iowa, forty miles north of Des Moines, and people heading due north or south often have little choice but to pass the town on Interstate 35.

Sally's parents were born in North Dakota, and in March of 1956, when her dad was ready to graduate from college there, he drove to a job interview in Peoria, Illinois. On the way, he happened to stop in Ames. It had been cold and snowy that day in North Dakota, but Ames was warmer and brighter. He liked what he saw, found a job in Ames as a civil engineer for the Iowa Highway Commission and stayed the rest of his life. In a town with brutal winters and sloppy, slushy springs, Sally's dad was one of the few residents who actually moved there for the weather.

Jenny's family, meanwhile, was in Ames because of an incident that happened on July 4, 1944. Her dad was nine years old then, living in southern Iowa, and that day, Jenny's grandfather was out driving and came upon a car accident. There had been a police chase, and the officer's car ended up attached to the mangled bumper of the car driven by a robber on the run. When Jenny's grandfather stopped to help, the policeman asked him to lend a hand lifting one car's bumper off the other. He obliged and immediately felt something snap in his neck. From that instant of exertion, he suffered a subarachnoid hemorrhage, or bleeding onto the surface of his brain. By the next day, he was in a coma — barely living proof that no good deed goes unpunished. He was forty-three years old, and doctors gave him a one in ten thousand chance of surviving a year.

He lived, however, remaining in a coma until 1947. Without his income as a county agent for the U.S. Soil Conservation Service, his family struggled. "We only ate what friends, neighbors and farmers brought to us," Jenny's father would tell her. "I know what it's like to have a can of beans for seven people."

Even after Jenny's grandfather came out of the coma, he was blind and couldn't speak, so Jenny's grandmother had to support the family. She ventured to Ames in 1949 with her incapacitated husband, taking a job as social director at Iowa State, with tasks such as overseeing sorority rush and selecting party chaperones. She ended up holding the job for decades. Jenny's father went to Ames High, where he befriended Sheila's dad. Jenny's grandfather eventually recovered his sight and speech, and lived until 1976.

That's the story of how Jenny ended up calling Ames home, but few of the girls were aware of that. When they were young, they were most apt to ask her dad, "Can Jenny come out to play?" They wouldn't have thought to ask him, "So what brought you to Ames?" Only in adulthood have the girls come to recognize and appreciate the thousands of different destinies and decisions, going back generations in their families, that brought them all together.

In junior high, the most thrilling weekend activity in Ames, at least for thirteen-year-olds, was the basement make-out party. Most homes in town didn't have finished basements like middle-class homes have today. The basements then were cinder-block dungeons with bugs and dusty storage boxes. But in those damp basements, back in the early 1970s, the Ames girls got lessons about a changing world.

At a party on the last day of seventh grade, the boys and girls played spin the bottle, and the little pecks being issued weren't enough of a sexual charge for some of the faster kids. So a suggestion was made. All the boys would put their names in a hat.

Each girl would pick a name. Then the matched couples would go off to some quiet or dark corner to make out more heavily in private. All of the girls knew, going in, that one of them would end up getting a certain boy's name. When they agreed to the game, they implicitly agreed to making out with him. Or did they?

Kelly and the other girls looked across the room at the boy — the only African-American in attendance. He was a nice kid and sort of a friend, but what if they got his name? Would they kiss him? Would they let him slip his hand under their shirts to touch their breasts? Ames was a town with hardly any black people, and Kelly recalls feeling frightened by the possibility and, at the same time, excited by it.

The hat was passed around and Kelly picked a name. She opened her slip of paper, and it was like winning the jackpot; she had gotten Scott, one of the cutest, most popular boys in school, a kid with dark hair set off by sweet blue eyes. The girl who ended up getting the black boy's name was not one of the eleven Ames girls. That girl opened up her slip of paper, her eyes met the boy's, and with hardly a pause for a breath, off she went with him. The two ended up pawing and kissing in their corner, just like everyone else.

A part of Kelly felt relieved that she didn't pick that boy's name. But she also felt great admiration for the girl who did. That was really something, how the girl just took the boy's hand and off they went to make out. Even today, when Kelly gets together with the Ames girls, she tells them she still wonders: What would she have done if she had pulled that boy's name? What would the other Ames girls have done? Kelly briefly dated a black man later in her life. But how would she and the other girls have responded with that slip of paper in their hands, in that junior-high moment, in a basement that was damp with sexual and racial tension?

By high school, the girls had coalesced firmly into that group of eleven. Not every girl was close to every other girl in the same way. There were definite pairings — Jane/Marilyn, Kelly/Diana, Cathy/Sally, Jenny/Sheila — but like a corporate flow chart, all were linked to one another through someone else. Each girl had a distinct way of interacting with each of the other ten, meaning there were ninety-nine different one-on-one relationships between them. All sorts of variables played into how they got along:

Who was irritable because of menstrual cramps? Who felt she'd been given short shrift by one of the others? Who had a boy at the moment?

Still, what happened in the group almost always stayed in the group. Every time they confided in each other without spilling details to their families or acquaintances, they were laying the foundation for a deliberate loyalty that would serve them well in adulthood. Sure, when some of the eleven weren't around, the others might talk about them — they still do — but they rarely bad-mouthed one another to those beyond their group.

As a clique, they had a reputation for being flirts — more social than academic, and more apt to tease boys than to please them. In reality, though, most of the Ames girls were very good students. And a couple of them actually pleased more than they teased.

They were mostly well liked at school — they were definitely one of the "popular" groups — but everyone knew they were a closed society. It was the eleven of them, period. If any of the 620 other girls at Ames High hoped for an invitation into the inner circle, the eleven girls were too wrapped up with each other to notice. In their recollections today, they swear that no other girls really wanted to join them. But they admit that they may have been clueless about the urges of outsiders. (Friendship researchers today would refer to them as a closed clique, as opposed to an open snowball group, which keeps growing as it welcomes members.)

As a group, the girls sometimes seemed like they had an overabundance of attitude and self-confidence. After Rod Stewart's "Da Ya Think I'm Sexy?" came out in 1979, their sophomore year, they loved to strut around singing it. But most of them, as individuals, were insecure. They didn't really want to ask that question and they didn't want to hear the answer.

They were not stereotypical mean girls, except within the group a few times. Still, some fellow classmates found their cliquishness irritating. Other girls assumed that the eleven of them phoned each other every morning before school to see what they'd all wear that day. One outside observer, Nancy Derks, was a member of the female jock crowd. She would notice one of the eleven girls wearing a hat in the hallway, and she knew, she just knew, she'd soon see the rest of them meandering down the hallway in hats. Or if one was wearing sweatpants, they'd almost all be in sweats. Or if one was all dolled up in a dress, there'd be the ten others wearing dresses. "They're conformists," Nancy would say. (In the final days of high school, she and a friend would hatch a simple scheme to get back at the eleven girls for all their perceived prissiness and conformity.)

The girls deny always moving in lockstep — in their own heads, they were very much individuals — but they did come to realize that being part of a group meant being defined as a group, for better or worse.

Once, when a few of the eleven girls dated boys from nearby Marshalltown, Iowa, the Ames boys were jealous and upset with them. Marshalltown High, the archrival of Ames High, had the bobcat as its mascot, and some kids in Ames dismissed Marshalltown athletes as "bobcat shit." (It was a term coined by a group of boys that included Jenny's and Jane's brothers.) That led certain Ames boys to start calling the eleven girls "the Shit Sisters." Soon enough, others at Ames High picked up on it. The girls later toned down their moniker to the Shisters. But today, when their kids ask why they refer to each other as "Shisters," it's hard to give a G-rated explanation.

In any case, their Marshalltown fixation

was fleeting. Mostly, the girls were loyal to Ames and its boys. On many nights, they organized their social lives around Ames High football games, and fashioned their fantasies around the Ames athletes. Several of the girls maintained meticulous scrapbooks about the football team's exploits. They even did this in their junior year, when the team went 0 and 11. Karla was diligent. In her scrapbook, she neatly pasted newspaper clippings about the team and every photo she could find of the boys in action.

The girls saved stacks of the notes they passed in class. These folded-up sheets of notebook paper were often devoted to specific interactions with male classmates, giving their correspondence a definite immediacy. Sally, who was often shy around boys, was better able to express herself in writing, such as this play-by-play note to Jenny, written one day at the library:

Jack just now walked over to the table next to me. You're right. He does look excellent today: red Adidas shirt, Nike shoes with a red stripe, Lee jeans and a little bit of comb sticking out of his back pocket. I wasn't sure if I liked him anymore but I just decided that I do.

Now he's sitting at a different table

with some guy, facing me. There's a stupid pillar in the way, damn it! Now he just burped, but that's OK because he said "excuse me." Besides, it's a normal human function. Well, enough about him. Time to go to lunch. Bye. Love Sally.

Jenny has held on to notes like this for three decades now, little moments preserved in time.

In certain ways, the girls were not unlike Ames girls of previous generations. As teens, several of them read a memoir titled *Blooming: A Small-Town Girlhood* by Susan Allen Toth. The author grew up in Ames, and her book offered an evocative look at life there in the 1950s. She described Ames High back then as an institution dominated by boys' athletics. "Boys played," she wrote. "Girls clapped."

In the 1970s, Ames girls were still clapping. But the broader world wasn't quite as innocent, and neither were they. The longtime Ames High cheer — a spirited repetition of the words "Ames High aims high!" — was rejiggered by mischievous students. At school sporting events, both girls and boys couldn't resist cheering "Ames High gets high!" School administrators were un-amused, but powerless to stop it.

Still, despite a growing drug and drinking culture, Ames mostly remained unchanged, and several of the girls were reassured by Toth's lyrical memoir. She described mid-century Ames as "a quiet town . . . but against that backdrop of quiet, a girl could listen to her heart beating." Jenny saw the book as confirmation that Ames was still a quiet, wondrous place. Kelly, on the other hand, found the book far too sweet. "Where's the dirt?" she'd ask. "That woman is writing about how much she loved the Ames Public Library. OK. Fine. I love it, too. But the book is too much nostalgia and not enough dirt."

That was typical Kelly, of course. She was always the most opinionated. In fact, she was the "most" on a lot of fronts. She was the most likely to ignore her parents' curfew, the most athletic, the most focused on women's rights, the most vocal about her views on political issues, whether in school or in the nation. She was also the most forward with boys. She was unafraid of them. She enjoyed them.

From the start, Kelly's role in the group was often to do or say things that the other girls marveled at or shook their heads about.

"That's Kelly," they'd say. In some ways, they envied her lack of inhibition. But they also saw it as their job to rein her in from time to time.

Like Kelly, each of the girls had an identity in the group. Diana was the fresh-faced blonde whom boys compared to supermodel Cheryl Tiegs. She never seemed too full of herself, which the other girls appreciated. Still, they couldn't help but feel like afterthoughts whenever they entered a room with her.

Sheila was the cutie-pie, the big flirt with the big white smile, a walking advertisement for her father's dental practice. She had wavy brown hair and these thick eyelashes that helped make her a natural beauty who required no makeup. She also had this effortless, genuine charm that enabled her to connect with people, from little kids to the oldest person in the local nursing home, where she volunteered.

Jenny was the former tomboy who became more and more feminine. She was a chronicler of the group, an organizer of their activities, and the girls' constant chauffeur, driving a 1947 Willys surplus jeep she got from her dad.

Angela was the bouncy, vivacious newcomer; she didn't arrive in Ames until ninth grade, when her dad came to town to manage a local hotel. She wasn't part of the group right away, because the nerdier girls at school had quickly befriended her. Angela knew that she was being embraced by those in need of a friend, and she was OK with that at first. But she was cooler than those more desperate girls. She met Jane on the junior-high basketball team. Then she got to know Jenny in geometry and honors English class because they were seated alphabetically: Bendorf, Benson. Through Jenny and Jane, her entrée into the lives of the other ten was secured.

Karen/"Woman" was the girl who had gorgeous long hair down to her rear end. She also had three popular older sisters, and a mother who was a realist about teen behavior by the time Karen came along. Her mom knew all about the secret keggers staged each weekend deep in the cornfields at the edge of Ames. She'd advise Karen and her friends to coat their stomachs with milk before drinking beer.

Sally, back in those early years, was the in-the-background friend, an extremely bright girl who was sometimes dismissed by the others for not being cool enough, for not flirting with boys enough, for being too much of a follower. She got into the group because of her longtime friendship with Cathy. Though she wasn't always certain about her status among the others, she wasn't going to change herself to fit in. Cathy liked to say Sally was "authentic."

Cathy was the self-confident, sassy member of the group, who viewed herself as Sally's protector. She was the pioneer in some respects, with all this inside knowledge gleaned from her six older siblings. She was the first of the girls to highlight her hair. Sally helped her do it with a home highlighting kit.

Marilyn and Jane were the two intense and studious ones, each of whom desperately wanted a best friend and found it in each other. Both had similar short haircuts and dressed conservatively. Their parents, like a good many of the other Ames girls' parents, were cerebral and cultured. Marilyn's dad, the doctor, and Jane's dad, a renowned anthropologist at Iowa State, were both men with great presence and much to say, and Jane and Marilyn were captivated by them, eager to listen and learn. It was Jane who brought the more reserved Marilyn into the broader group.

And then there was Karla, the lovable, funny, full-of-life friend who laughed so hard and long at the movies that everyone in the theater would turn around. She was tall, regal and beautiful, but because of her uncertain self-esteem, she never seemed to realize it.

So that's who they were. And by their teen years, they were absolute confidants who assumed they'd be friends forever. Once high school ended, and most made plans to move away, they maintained their bravado about remaining close. In their hearts, however, they struggled with the uncertainty of splitting up.

Late one night in the summer of 1981, Jenny sat with her father, a fellow night owl, on the front porch of their house on Hodge Avenue. It was too dark to see each other's face, but they always liked it that way. It made it easier to talk.

Jenny would soon leave for the University of South Carolina. "The girls are all heading separate ways," she said, "and I'm going to miss them so much." She told her dad she was OK with that, because she knew they'd always be in each other's life. "I just know it," she said. "I just do."

For years, her dad had watched and admired the loving chemistry between the eleven girls. But he was an insurance executive who spent every day monitoring statistics and actuarial tables. He was aware that in any group of people, odds can be determined for almost every outcome and every tragedy that might befall them. He told Jenny she needed to be realistic.

"Listen, honey," he said, "these were beautiful childhood friendships. But adulthood is different. Who knows what life will be like ten or fifteen years from now? Don't be surprised. Your friendships might not survive the road ahead."

"No, no. We'll all be together," Jenny said. But she was listening.

Her father explained himself. "You've got to look at the odds. Odds are you won't all be friends as years go by. And it's unlikely that everyone's life will go smoothly." His actuarial instincts overtook him, and he couldn't resist being specific: "My guess is, in fifteen years, one of you girls will be estranged from the group. Two of you will be divorced. One of you will still be single. One of you may be dead. You have to expect that. Because that's just how life works."

Today, Jenny and her dad both have a vivid recollection of that conversation — where they were sitting, how her dad's words hung in the air, in the darkness, and how she sat there thinking he had to be wrong.

2
MARILYN

Marilyn has her camera out, and she's walking around, snapping away. She has decided to be an unofficial photographer for the reunion at Angela's. It's a role that suits her. She's able to be part of the group and, at the same time, to stand away from it as an outside observer.

It always has been this way. Marilyn loves all the girls, more now than ever, but at times she feels an ambivalence regarding her connection to them. From early on, some of the others had her pegged as the squarest of the Ames girls. Sure, she was often right there with them at the high-school keg parties — she even hosted some — but she also saw each decision as a test of her conscience. She never wanted her parents to be disappointed by her behavior. She felt an obligation to be studious, respectful, appreciative — to stay safe. When some of the other girls would arrange sneaky escapades, misleading parents about their plans or whereabouts, Marilyn was adept at deflating the moment by voicing her reservations and reminding them of the dangers. This was true even though her mom and dad were among the most lenient and nonjudgmental of all the parents.

The girls found themselves being different around Marilyn. Even here, at the reunion, when she is in the room, they sometimes seem more proper, more careful about what they say or do. There's this continued earnestness about Marilyn that seems to keep the others in check. "You were always the one talking about doing the right thing, and you still are," Kelly says to Marilyn when the two of them get to talking. "It's your nature to confess. That was never part of my nature, but I've always tried to understand you."

When she was young, Marilyn would do almost anything for Jane, her closest friend of all, but Jane knew that Marilyn's allegiances to family superseded everything. Marilyn was especially connected to her dad, a pediatrician who reminded people of TV's Marcus Welby. He was a beloved figure in Ames, and he was even more than that to Marilyn. He was her absolute hero. Certainly, she grew up identifying herself as one of the Ames girls, and she reveled in her bonds with Jane. But when she defined herself, right down to her core, it was as "Dr. McCormack's daughter."

Jane understood this better than the other girls. She spent so much time with the McCormacks; she loved them, too. She also knew details about Marilyn's family life and history that the other girls did not. As Cathy recalls: "I always knew something had happened, but I didn't know what it was." Now, as adults, all of the girls know almost everything, and it helps them to better understand Marilyn.

"Pretend I'm not here," Marilyn says to a few of them as they lounge on Angela's porch. She lifts her camera. "Beautiful. You all look beautiful."

To understand lifelong friendships, sometimes you have to go back to a time before any of those friends were even born. And so in a way, Marilyn's connection to the Ames girls can be traced back to September 25, 1960.

That day, her parents decided to drive her four older siblings to a friend's farm sixty miles north of Ames. It was meant to be a fun excursion on a bright Sunday morning, a chance for the kids to ride a tractor, check out the inside of a barn, and pass by thousands of acres of cornfields. Dr. McCormack was always trying to expose his kids to the wider world, to help them appreciate nature. This was just another one of those adventures.

The McCormacks' oldest child, Billy, then a few weeks shy of his seventh birthday, had been sitting in the third row of the station wagon, the row facing backward. That allowed him to smile and wave at all the Sunday morning drivers on the road behind them, while the corn whizzed by out the side windows.

When they left Ames, Marilyn's mom was in the front seat. But at about the halfway point, she decided to take a nap and switched places with Billy. He got in the front passenger seat, put on his seat belt — the car hadn't come with seat belts, but Dr. McCormack had them installed — and they continued driving.

The family was on a gravel road about a mile from the farmhouse when a fifteen-year-old boy in his parents' car appeared out of nowhere and slammed, broadside, into Dr. McCormack's car. Because it was September, the cornstalks were near their tallest point, obstructing the view at that intersection. An experienced driver, familiar with the dangers on rural roads, would have known to be cautious at such an intersection. But the boy had his foot hard on the gas; police later estimated he was traveling ninety miles an hour.

Each member of the McCormack family was seriously injured in the collision. Sara, age five, had a forehead wound. Three-year-old Polly had a ruptured spleen. One-year-old Don was bleeding profusely from the back of his head. Mrs. McCormack had a shattered collarbone. Everyone had multiple lacerations. The boy who had driven the other car was also badly injured.

The McCormacks' front passenger door had taken the brunt of the impact. As a result, Billy, still buckled in the front seat, was the most severely hurt. Dr. McCormack, his hands and arms bleeding from windshield glass, his ribs cracked from the steering wheel, pulled his son from the car, and called upon all his medical knowledge to try to save him. For an hour, he hunched over the boy on that gravel road, attempting to stop the bleeding, to make sense of the internal injuries, to talk to his son. Ambulances arrived, and some of Dr. McCormack's medical colleagues sped in from Ames to offer their help. By the time they got there, Billy had been pronounced dead at the scene.

A story about the accident ran on the front page of the next day's *Ames Daily Tribune.* The top of the page was dominated by a photo of two horribly damaged cars smashed together. It was hard to tell which car was which, given all the twisted metal. The headline: "Accident Fatal to Ames Boy."

The story mentioned that tall cornstalks at the intersection were a factor, and that the boy in the other car was driving illegally. He had a school permit, allowing him to drive only on a direct route from his house to school. There was no explanation given for what the boy was doing on that rural road; the scene of the accident was about two hours from his home.

The three younger McCormack children recovered, and Mrs. McCormack forced herself to focus her emotional energy on being grateful for that. Most of the time, she did not allow herself to feel guilty for switching seats with Billy just before the crash. Her reasoning was this: Had she died in the front seat, she would have left Dr. McCormack to raise all of their children alone. As she saw it, her life was spared because her surviving children needed a mother. And so the accident left her doubly

71

committed to motherhood.

At first, Dr. McCormack had great trouble coping with his son's death. He asked that all photos of Billy be removed from the family room of their house; it hurt too much for him to look at them every day. He couldn't bring himself to talk about Billy, either, and it upset him when well-intentioned people asked questions about his son or shared a memory of him. Years later, he'd become known in Iowa medical circles for his comforting bedside manner and his pioneering efforts to help people accept and live with loss. His hard journey to that role began with Billy's death.

All grieving families struggle to find relief from their pain, and at some point in the months after the accident, Dr. and Mrs. McCormack developed a sense of what might help them. Their family felt so terribly out of balance. Maybe their three surviving children needed another sibling. Maybe they needed another child to love. Dr. McCormack, then thirty-five years old, decided he would try to reverse his vasectomy.

Back then, such operations were primitive and usually didn't work, but the decision to try gave Dr. McCormack a sense of purpose. In the summer of 1961, he flew to

Marilyn and her father, Dr. McCormack

Rochester, New York, to have his first operation. It failed. In the spring of 1962, he flew
to Eureka, California, to meet another
surgeon, who was then doing experimental
work in vasectomy reversals. Dr. and Mrs.
McCormack told no friends or loved ones
what they were trying to accomplish. They
explained the out-of-town trips as business
meetings.

That 1962 operation seemed to work. The
couple waited. That summer, Mrs. McCormack became pregnant.

On April 8, 1963, Marilyn was born.

Marilyn knows well that she was brought into this world to deliver life to a family still grieving death. From childhood on, she saw this as both a responsibility and a gift. And today, as she looks back, she realizes that the gripping circumstances of her birth helped shape her friendships.

It's understandable that she often thought of herself as an outsider among the Ames girls. When the others were making questionable decisions — about drinking or having secret parties or ignoring schoolwork — she'd sometimes feel too guilty to participate. She never wanted to disappoint her parents or lie to them. How could she? Before she was born, they had wanted her so badly. She'd have to be an ingrate not to honor that.

At times, that made her seem prissy and subdued. A prude in a page-boy haircut. Some of the other girls would roll their eyes when they talked about her. But she stood firm. "I feel lucky to be alive," she'd tell herself, "and so I need to take life seriously."

In the diary she kept all through junior high and high school, she sometimes wondered why she was even part of that group of eleven girls. Some of them were too wild.

Their behavior with boys and alcohol didn't always feel right to her. On too many weekends, the Ames girls were hanging out with guys who seemed to have nothing intelligent to say. She got tired of sitting around, listening to boys brag about drinking too much and throwing up; they called it "the Technicolor yawn," and thought they were so clever. Marilyn briefly dated one boy who set out to prove how macho he was by cutting the seat belts out of his car. He figured girls were turned on by guys who lived dangerously. Actually, Marilyn thought he was cute for sure, but after too many remarks like that, she knew he was a loser. And that made her question her friendships, too: Why did some of the other Ames girls seem so happy hanging out with dim bulbs like that?

Marilyn also was unhappy that the other Ames girls weren't being inclusive socially. Other girls at school didn't like it. She'd vent about the Ames girls' cliquishness in her diary. "I hate being identified with them!" she wrote at one point.

And yet at the same time, she saw something she admired in each of the girls — an open heart or a sense of playfulness or a contagious urge for adventure. She had an ability to notice people's positive traits. In that respect she was like her dad, who would say he could find the good in anyone. And so she remained with the group, even though at times she'd hold herself off to the side.

It's not surprising that she felt closest to Jane Gradwohl, who in her own way, as the only Jewish girl in the group, knew what it felt like to be a bit of an outsider. Jane and Marilyn were part of the eleven, but also in their own two-person orbit. They had met as ten-year-olds in a local theater production of *Hansel and Gretel*. Jane was cast as Gretel, and Marilyn was jealous and annoyed. She got over it.

By eighth grade, Marilyn and Jane were confidants. They were a good match, too: Both were a little slower than the other girls socially, a little nerdier, more academic. Like others among the Ames girls, they came from families where matters of culture and the arts were regular dinner-table conversation. (Jane's father, the anthropology professor, got his Ph. D. from Harvard; her mom was a social worker.) So Marilyn and Jane, especially, felt comfortable talking to each other about classical music or ancient Greek architecture or silent movies. They sometimes felt like black-and-white throwbacks in a town teeming with Technicolor yawns.

As their friendship blossomed, they both felt the need to mark their connection. Early in high school, they bought each other a matching star sapphire necklace. One necklace was engraved: "MM Love, JG." The other read: "JG Love, MM." They were always trading notes in which they gushed about their feelings for each other. Looking back at it now, they find the mushiness almost embarrassing. Jane has a scrapbook from high school, and glued into it is a Hallmark card Marilyn had picked out for her. Hallmark had written: "Our relationship is so strong because we are completely truthful with each other in every word and thought, and because we trust each other as equals in every aspect of life."

They had their own playlist of background music by Cat Stevens, Dan Fogelberg, Hall and Oates, Bread — each song reminding them of a shared laugh or an unrequited crush.

Marilyn told Jane about the first boy to kiss her on her ear and her neck. "It felt so warm and tingly," she explained. "I could fall asleep holding him. I really could." Later, when the boy told her, "I don't like you sexually, but we can be friends," she cried to Jane.

Jane and Marilyn, then and now

There were times when the phone rang and Marilyn's heart would jump; maybe it was the boy she was hoping to hear from. Invariably it turned out to be Jane on the other end, but Marilyn's disappointment lasted just a moment before she'd perk up, because hey, it was Jane.

The trust between them was total. Well, almost total. In one of Marilyn's diary entries junior year, after she had scribbled on and on about how "I just can't figure out guys," she suddenly added an aside: "Jane, you're probably reading this. Let me tell you. I DON'T GET ALL THE GUYS!

Believe me! They don't like me more than you!"

Marilyn confided in Jane about Billy, the brother she never knew, but she didn't talk much about him to the other girls. A part of her felt uncomfortable with the topic. She remembered what happened one day in elementary school. There had been a girl outside their group who knew the whole story of the car accident and the meaning of the pregnancy that followed. One day, the girl got angry at Marilyn for reasons no one can recall, and blurted out: "I wish your brother had never died, because if he were alive, then you wouldn't be here!"

Marilyn's father was the sort of man who could explain what made kids say such things and why they needed to be forgiven for it. He was pediatrician to several of the girls in Marilyn's group, and he served as a wise counselor to them. "When I was a kid, he was the smartest person I had ever met," says Jane, "just a total renaissance man."

When Karla, Jane, Jenny and Karen were newborns, making their first office visits to Dr. McCormack, he talked about how mothers often held babies as if they were delicate objects. Then they would hand their babies over to Dr. McCormack, who flopped the girls from back to front, front to back, as if they were pancakes on the griddle. "Don't worry," he said. "It's fine. They're not as fragile as you think." Some mothers were startled, but also relieved by his words. He enjoyed dispensing advice any way he could. Jenny's mother was taken with the signs he'd post in his examining rooms. "Ant poison is dangerous," read one. "Better to have ants than poisoned children." She thought of Dr. McCormack one day when she discovered Jenny's brother had eaten a cracker with ants on it.

The girls went to Dr. McCormack all through their childhoods, and they have sweet memories of checkups with him. Karen appreciated the time he told her mother that kids needn't eat all the food on their plates. Dr. McCormack was amused by the clean-plate-club fixation of parents in the 1960s. "Relax," he told Karen's mom. "Most kids end up getting the proper nutrition to stay healthy. Their bodies just know what they need. Offer them three square meals a day, but you don't have to force-feed them." When Karla went to see Dr. McCormack, her mother would marvel at how he never seemed rushed. He calmly answered every question. It was as if Karla were the only patient he'd see all day.

He also made a point of being honest. In

those days, many doctors believed that if they didn't mention or acknowledge pain, kids wouldn't feel it or focus on it. But Dr. McCormack gave it to kids straight: "This shot is going to hurt." It was refreshing to find an adult who cared enough not to sugarcoat things and talk down to children.

As a kid, Jane loved to play doctor. But unlike girls today, she never thought to give herself the role of the doctor. Instead, she'd always assign herself the part of "Dr. McCormack's nurse." She spent countless hours in her fantasy world of a pediatrician's office, saying things like, "Yes, Dr. McCormack, I'll take the baby's temperature for you."

Some of the girls understood that Dr. McCormack was more than just a neighborhood pediatrician, but except for Jane, most didn't know the full extent of his accomplishments. In the 1960s, he had invented a respirator that helped premature babies with underdeveloped lungs survive. Later, he invented a warming blanket used to transport sick infants between hospitals.

He was way ahead of his time on social issues, too. He passionately advocated the idea of bringing sex education into Iowa school districts and even into preschools. He felt that kids at the youngest ages should be given information about their bodies and their feelings for the opposite sex. "Don't teach children to feel shame over their genitalia," he'd say, "or they'll harbor that shame as they grow older." He used words that made Iowans blush, but even those who disagreed with him, and there were many, would say they respected his passion. (The Ames girls' parents tended to be pretty enlightened and never took issue with him.)

Dr. McCormack was described by others as a "people collector," because he was so engaged in learning about people, asking them to share the details of their lives. He looked for what was special in everyone, including Marilyn's friends. He'd ask for their opinions about the hostages in Iran or about feminism, and he'd look at them like their answers really mattered to him. He also was good at offering advice that made the girls think. "When you grow up and have kids of your own," he'd say, "always try to treat them a couple of years older than they are. They'll rise to the occasion." Marilyn once had a party and Diana decided to smoke a cigar. No one had told her not to inhale, and soon enough, she was wheezing and sick to her stomach. Marilyn ran up to her parents' bedroom and got her dad, who grabbed his stethoscope and helped Diana through it. Whether Marilyn's friends spent too much time in the sun or had too much to drink or had questions about menstruation — whatever — Marilyn's dad was someone to turn to, and he was there for them without being condescending or judgmental.

Maybe that's why Marilyn, of all the Ames girls, was often the most willing to confess her sins to her parents. Her father just seemed able to put things in perspective. Once, during a Christmas vacation, Marilyn's parents weren't home and Marilyn had some of the girls over. Boys came, too, and soon it was a full-fledged party, with drinking and making out and too many kids coming and going. When it was over, Marilyn cleaned up perfectly. She made sure the Christmas tree and decorations were exactly right. The place was spotless. And that's when she noticed: There was a large ugly crack in the plate-glass window of the family room.

She was horrified. She asked Jane what she should do. Should she confess to her parents that she had a party? Jane, a habitual good girl herself, argued for honesty, and Marilyn agreed. Marilyn couldn't live with herself if she didn't tell her dad right away. He was on call at the hospital emergency room, and she went to see him. "I did something very wrong," she told him, and then it all came out in one run-on confession. "I had a party, Dad, with lots of kids, I'm so sorry, and something happened, the plate-glass window in the family room is broken, really, Dad, I don't know what to say, except that I'll pay whatever I have to pay to fix it."

Her father listened to her story without saying a word. Then he shrugged. "Well, I know you learned something from this whole experience," he said. "I bet you won't do it again." He told her he'd see if their homeowners' insurance policy would cover the damage. Just before she left, he gave her a hug and told her he loved her and appreciated that she'd been honest with him.

As soon as Marilyn walked in the house and saw the window again, she burst into tears — tears of relief that this was off her chest and that her father had been so forgiving and understanding. Her older sister Sara asked why she was crying, and Marilyn pointed to the window. Sara took a closer look. "Well, what do you know?" she said. Turned out, this "crack" was actually a long strand of tinsel from the McCormacks' Christmas tree that had somehow adhered to the plate-glass window. Maybe some kid had soaked it with beer and stuck it there. Whatever had happened, there was no crack in the window at all. Marilyn called her father. She called Jane. She also called herself an idiot for confessing so quickly and unnecessarily. She could have gotten away with the whole party! And yet, a good part of her was glad she had gone to see her dad about this. She had learned something about him, about how he'd react when she disappointed him. At the same time, he had learned something about her and her conscience.

Hearing about how Dr. McCormack reacted to Marilyn's lapses left the other Ames girls envious. Somehow her dad was a mixture of square and cool — sort of like Marilyn. In their own homes, some of the girls had to go to diabolical lengths to keep their parents in the dark about their activities. More than once, they'd impersonate their own mothers on the phone, to give reassuring explanations about what they were up to. Once, Kelly wanted to go to Iowa's Lake Okoboji with Karla and two male friends. They planned to stay by themselves in a summer home owned by one of the boy's parents. Understandably, Kelly's mother wanted to know: "Will his parents be there?" Kelly told her: "Oh yeah, for sure. Just call Karla's mom. She has the details."

Kelly quickly called Karla, told her to expect the call, and hung up. Two minutes later, the phone rang at Karla's house. "Hello, this is Mrs. Derby," Karla said in her best mature-woman's voice. She proceeded to reassure Kelly's mom. "Don't worry about a thing. Kelly will be fine." Kelly's mother said she appreciated the call, and off the girls went.

The girls knew Marilyn was too much of a Goody Two-shoes to try something like that. But they also knew that part of what attracted her to the larger group was her unstated urge to be in the vicinity of thrill-seekers. She was a funny mix: careful, reserved, prudish. And yet she had a longing for adventure. She also had a father who, given his eagerness to teach sexuality, seemed to be giving her more than a few green lights.

The girls, of course, found that side of him fascinating and quirky. One day, when they were in their teens, he sat some of them down in his family room for a sex education speech. He used a pointer and diagrams on the chalkboard he kept there, and spoke so frankly that the girls blushed. They still giggle about it today. They have shorthand references for what happened that night: "Marilyn's Father's S-E-X Talk" and "The Day We Got Too Much New Information." Cathy recalls leaving Marilyn's house shaking her head and saying to the other girls, "Wow, what was that? Did that just happen? Did you hear what I heard?"

Marilyn's father was unlike most of the other girls' parents in another respect. Not only did he understand the hormonal urges of teens, he also believed in accommodating them — within reason. There was the time Marilyn was setting up for a party, this one with her parents' permission, and her dad offered a suggestion. "You need more than one couch over there by the fireplace," he said. "Pull a couple more couches over there. You can't have just one couple getting cozy."

Kelly's father, the junior-high guidance counselor, oversaw sex education presentations at school assemblies. For years, teachers had made fumbling attempts at addressing the issues. Too often, however, they spoke cryptically, confusing the kids. Proof of that would come during the question-and-answer sessions that followed the talks. Once, a seventh-grader raised his hand and asked: "When adults want to have babies, where do they go to have sex? Do they go to a doctor's office and do it under the doctor's supervision?"

Such clueless questions convinced Kelly's dad that students needed more explicit information. He decided that Dr. McCormack was the man for the job. Dr. McCormack was happy to come to the school with his diagrams and slides. He spoke all about how sex was enjoyable, how feelings of love enhanced it, how using contraception was crucial. He delivered all the key words without flinching. "It's healthy to have sex," he'd say, and the kids paid close attention. By the end of his talks, they certainly knew they'd never have to go to a doctor's office for supervised sex.

For Marilyn, it was exciting being her father's daughter, but it wasn't always easy. For one thing, there were high expectations. Her older siblings all performed well in school. She felt she had no choice but to equal them. And she was always aware that adults she met could be the parents of her dad's patients. Being "the doctor's daughter" could feel like a burden, especially when some of the other Ames girls seemed to care more about good times than what adults thought of them.

At the same time, Marilyn was enormously proud of the impact her father was having on his patients and community. One of Dr. McCormack's patients was Jane's older brother, who in tenth grade was diagnosed with Hodgkin's disease. Dr. McCormack oversaw the boy's treatment and was a reassuring presence for Jane's worried parents. A bond developed between the two families that remained in place for decades. Maybe it was because Dr. McCormack had lost a son — and his children had lost a brother — that he gave so much of himself to this case. Jane's brother survived and is a doctor himself today, crediting Dr. McCormack as his role model.

When they were young, both Jane and Marilyn knew that part of what they loved about each other was how comfortable they felt with each other's family. They would invite one another on week-long summer vacations. They could raid each other's refrigerator without asking permission, or lounge around each other's house in their pajamas all day, or take over each other's kitchen to cook whatever concoction struck them at the moment. Marilyn's diaries are filled with detailed descriptions of meals she and Jane made together, often serving them to their families. Almost always, Marilyn ended her culinary tales with the same word and punctuation: "Yum!"

It was reassuring to both girls to know that there were people outside of their immediate families who loved them and wanted the best for them. In fact, all of the Ames girls' parents had a similar connection with at least one or two or three of the girls.

Given her attachment to Jane and her family, Marilyn was curious to learn about Judaism. Jane's father was born in Lincoln, Nebraska, and unlike most Jewish-Americans, he had roots in the United States going back to the early 1840s. Two of his great-grandfathers fought in the Civil War, one for the North and one for the South.

Jane's mother, Hanna, was not American-born. She left Nazi Germany in 1937, just shy of her second birthday, and her family settled in Lincoln, where there were about five hundred Jewish families. Hanna's family was lucky. Many other relatives, including her father's parents, were unsuccessful in their quest to obtain exit permits and visas. During the late 1930s and early 1940s, they wrote increasingly desperate letters to children and cousins who had emigrated to the United States, Palestine,

Egypt, Cuba and Argentina, seeking their assistance in surmounting the bureaucratic hurdles. More than a dozen of these relatives never escaped and died in concentration camps. Some fifteen hundred of their letters remained boxed up at Jane's grandmother's house, their pleas too painful to talk about. (In more recent years, Jane's parents began translating the letters and presenting the family's story in schools, helping to explain the Holocaust.)

Jane's parents knew each other as toddlers in Lincoln and began dating in high school. They married in 1957 and moved to Ames in 1962, when Jane's dad was hired at Iowa State. There were only about twelve Jewish families in town then, which was a challenge. On the East or West Coasts of the United States, Jews could drop their kids off at well-staffed Hebrew schools. They could nod off during services in giant synagogues, letting the rabbis and cantors lead their services. But in Ames, Jews had to roll up their sleeves and get involved — reading the Torah, crafting sermons, taking turns teaching the community's few kids at Sunday school, keeping Judaism alive. "If we're going to be Jewish in Ames, we have to do it all ourselves," Jane's father would explain to Marilyn. "There's no magical religious specialist to do it for us. But that's good. Because it forces us to figure out why we're here and what we believe. In Ames, we know who we are, because in a way, we've chosen to be Jews."

In the 1960s, some Ames residents had never even met a Jew before, and a few would say objectionable things. A town leader once announced at a public hearing that he had gotten a great price from a supplier. "I was able to Jew him down," he said proudly, and couldn't understand why a Jewish woman in attendance found his remarks offensive. Mostly, though, the Christians in town were welcoming and accommodating, and Jane rarely felt self-conscious about being Jewish. One big reason for this was that the other Ames girls seemed unfazed by her religion. Especially when they were young, it hardly even registered with them.

For years, the tiny Jewish congregation in Ames held services in the lounge of a Baptist church. Later, as the Jewish population grew to sixty families, they moved into a former bowling alley. Jane didn't have a bat mitzvah. Instead, she was confirmed at age fifteen, with the Ames girls at the ceremony. The confirmation was a reminder to them that Jane was different, and they were curious and respectful; for some of the girls, so accustomed to church, it was as if they were given entrée into a secret society.

Dr. McCormack was a spiritual man whose faith was based on the wonder of life and the daily practice of the Golden Rule, rather than the precepts of organized religion. He appreciated differences in people's beliefs, and would tell Jane and her parents that he admired the Jewish people because so many of them valued education and had stable families.

Marilyn liked to ask Jane questions about Judaism. She followed along closely when she was invited to Passover seders at Jane's house, and she thought of Jane when she stepped into the world beyond Ames and saw hostility toward Jews. When Marilyn was sixteen, she went alone to Europe for a summer tour, and made a stop at the Anne Frank house in Amsterdam. Stepping through the bookcases to the Frank family hideaway, she began crying, unable to get Jane out of her head. That night in her journal, she described how enraged she felt. She had the first homicidal urges of her life. If anyone ever comes for Jane and her family, she vowed, "I will kill them first!"

For Jane and Marilyn, being exposed to

each other's family offered not only lessons in cultural differences, but also in how families overcome obstacles in their own way. Jane saw firsthand that in the decades after losing his son, Dr. McCormack was able to persevere and develop this contagious positive attitude. He came to look at life as a glorious adventure, and he threw himself into hiking, skiing, geology. One of his favorite words was "magnificent." "Did you catch the sunset tonight? It was magnificent!" "That concerto? Magnificent." "Marilyn, your friends look magnificent!"

And when Marilyn was feeling vulnerable or afraid, Jane always encouraged her to talk to her dad. So often, Dr. McCormack knew just the right words to say. A few nights before Marilyn was about to head off to college, she went into her parents' bedroom. Her dad was there alone, and she asked if he had a minute.

She'd been accepted at Hamilton College in Clinton, New York. Jane would be going to Grinnell College in Grinnell, Iowa. "I'm not sure I want to go so far away," Marilyn said flatly, and a good part of her meant it. "I don't know that I can be away from my friends or from Ames. I just don't know that I can be away from home."

She was also worried about how her

parents would cope with her absence. "Won't you be sad when I go?"

"Sad?" her dad replied. "I won't be sad. Not sad at all. In fact, I can hardly wait!"

He told her that he was thrilled when he thought about the "magnificent" adventures that awaited her. He said her friends, especially Jane, would remain in her heart, and she could write them every day if she wanted to. She could call them from the dorm phone. She could visit them. She could conjure up her happy memories of them. As for Ames, it would always be there, locked in the middle of Iowa, waiting for her. "Mom and I will be here, too," he said.

Marilyn was near tears. "But you'll be so far away from me."

"No, don't think of it that way," her dad told her. "Here's what we'll do. We're going to keep you at the end of our fishing line. And if you ever need anything, you just give a little tug and we'll reel you back in."

On the day that Jane got married in 1989, with Marilyn standing at her side, one of the most meaningful moments for her was just after she walked down the aisle, when Dr. McCormack gave her one of his heart-felt bear hugs. He was a man who hugged like he meant it, an uncommon trait for a man of his generation. And in the whir of emotion that surrounded his hug, a clear thought came into Jane's head: "I've really arrived at a good place, haven't I? I made the right choice in a man, didn't I? It must be true, because here's one of my heroes giving me all of his support, all of his approval."

When some of the other girls reached adulthood, they would remark to each other that they could never find a doctor they really liked. They figured out why. No one had Dr. McCormack's bedside manner. No one cared about them like Marilyn's father had.

After the girls started having children of their own, they'd take their kids to pediatricians. It didn't always feel right. One day Karen, now living in Philadelphia, called Marilyn. "I want a doctor for my kids who would be like your father was to me," she said. Marilyn had been having her own issues finding a good pediatrician for her children. She told Karen, "I'm searching for that, too."

By the time Marilyn had her kids — two sons and a daughter — her father was no longer practicing medicine. His retirement was a bit premature because, in the late 1980s, he began showing early signs of dementia. He quit his practice unexpectedly one day in 1989. A boy had come to his office with a minor problem — strep throat or an ear infection — and as usual, Dr. McCormack prescribed amoxicillin. A few hours later, the pharmacist called him, a bit concerned. Dr. McCormack had written the wrong dosage on the prescription, and luckily the pharmacist had caught the error.

Dr. McCormack, who had written thousands of amoxicillin scrips over the years, knew his mistake was a memory issue. "I don't ever want to hurt a child," he told Marilyn's mom when he got home that night. In that moment, he decided to retire, and he never worked as a doctor again. Eventually, he was diagnosed with Alzheimer's.

The disease came upon him gradually, but given his knowledge of medicine, he was well aware of the long, lonely good-bye that awaited him and his family. Marilyn became determined to hold on to whatever gifts his mind could still offer. He was a man who spent his life imparting perfectly stated life lessons. And so, in his final years, Marilyn would sometimes bring a tape recorder and sit with him. "Give me some of your wisdom before you can't give it to me anymore," she'd say to him, and for a while, he was able to answer her.

He'd tell her things like: "When you see your kids, remember me." Another time he told her: "Remember the things I did for you that made you happy, and do those things for your own children."

Marilyn found herself looking back at both her father's life and her own. She tracked down that doctor in California, by then an old man, who had performed her dad's vasectomy reversal. She sent him a simple friendly Christmas card, with no explanation about who she was, but he recognized her name and wrote back to her. He told her he recalled her father well, and even said that he remembered the day in April 1963 when she was born.

By the time her dad got sick, Marilyn and her husband and kids (and her two sisters) had long lived near Minneapolis. She and her siblings convinced her parents to move there so they could help care for their father.

Marilyn had made new friends in Minnesota, and they were kind and well-meaning women who would often ask how her dad was doing. But they knew him only as an old man with Alzheimer's. They had no sense of him in his years as a doctor, when he mattered to his community, when he felt free to counsel Marilyn's friends because he had cared for them all their lives — and because he cared about them.

During the years her father was fading, Marilyn usually felt fairly strong. But when she would reunite with the girls from Ames, she felt surprisingly emotional. The first sight of them would bring her to tears. In time, she figured out why. They reminded her of her dad when he was vigorous and in his prime. Whenever she talked to Jane, who became a college psychology professor in Massachusetts, they could return together in their minds to the McCormacks' summer house on Lake Minnewaska in Minnesota.

In his final years, Dr. McCormack's lucid moments became rarer and rarer. Still, there were flashes of exuberance that reminded his loved ones of who he had been. One day he was in the car, and Marilyn's mom was driving and talking to him. She was so engaging and, as always in his eyes, so beautiful. He smiled and stopped her, midsentence. Then he spoke to her wistfully but firmly: "You're a fascinating woman. But I'm married."

Dr. McCormack died in Minneapolis in June 2004. He was seventy-nine. Marilyn's new friends from Minnesota offered their condolences, gave her hugs, wished her well, and told her they'd be there for her. She appreciated that.

But the girls from Ames, their condolences were so different. It was as if they hardly had to share any words with Marilyn. "Her new friends, they didn't get it," says Jane. "They might have met Dr. McCormack in his last few years, but they didn't know the real man, the man he was. And we did. We knew him as this completely phenomenal human being. And so we knew. We knew what Marilyn had lost."

3
KARLA

Karla is cranky. For starters, it's too loud for her. The other girls are chattering away, getting caught up on each other's life and children, laughing long and hard — and loud, so loud. For Karla, this reunion at Angela's is sensory overload.

She's also not getting enough sleep. Most of the other girls are staying up late, talking and talking, dragging her into their conversations. Because the reunion will last only four days, some of them see sleep as a waste of precious time. Karla, on the other hand, needs her rest in order to function.

"Let me go to bed," she says every hour or so, starting at ten P.M. But her protestations are ignored. The others figure, and they're not all wrong, that she doesn't really want to go to sleep, either. She'd miss too much. (Besides, as Cathy jokes: "The fear of being talked about will keep you up." Jenny, who got to the reunion eighteen hours after everyone else, called ahead: "Don't talk about me until I get there.")

Karla apologizes for being cranky. Truth is, she's just being straightforwardly Karla. She needs her coffee. She needs her sleep. She needs them to quiet down.

There's another factor at work, too. Not long into the weekend, a part of her is absolutely ready to go home to see her kids. That's always been an issue for her at these reunions. In the days before cell phones, the girls remember her standing at pay phones outside bars or restaurants, calling home to her kids. Kelly would have to nudge her along: "Come on, Karla, enough! Get off already."

"We're all moms who completely love our kids," Kelly says. "But Karla, wow, she *really* loves her kids."

Karla isn't one of those mothers who spoils her children or gets overly involved in their lives. It's just that her love translates into an urge to spend total time with them. For years now, on Saturday nights, she has never felt compelled to go out for dinner and drinks with her husband and some other couple. "I'd rather spend Saturday nights with my family," she says. The other girls understand this about her, even if it makes Karla a wet blanket.

Here at Angela's, the girls discussed drawing straws to see who slept where and who'd share a bed with whom. But even before partners were chosen, Kelly agreed to sleep in the downstairs bedroom with cranky Karla. "I'm the only one brave enough to stay with you," she says. Karla smiles slightly and doesn't argue the point.

Throughout the weekend, there are flashes of the bubbly, funny Karla they knew when they were kids. But there are times, also, when she's obviously subdued or a bit disconnected.

Kelly thinks everyone is giving Karla a little more room to be cranky. "She wants quiet, we're quiet," says Kelly. "She wants to sleep, we try to let her sleep." The girls have been doing this for a few years now, a slight indulgence — actually, an act of love — that has become an unspoken agreement.

Karla dismisses this. "That's Kelly," she says. "She thinks she knows . . ."

Whatever the case, Karla is tremendously grateful to all of the girls. Her intermittent crankiness aside, she is well aware that they have been in her corner when she needed them the most. Through the hardest moments of her life, their devotion to her has been tested, and they all came through. That's why, though she'd like to go to bed, and she'd like them to shut up already, and a part of her would like to get home to be with her kids, she's here, on the porch, with them.

Like Marilyn, Karla was born into circumstances that set her apart from the other Ames girls. Marilyn was a baby who was desperately wanted; after all, her father had reversed his vasectomy to have her. In a way, Karla's arrival in the world was the mirror opposite of Marilyn's.

She was born on April 25, 1963 — just seventeen days after Marilyn and nine days after Jenny — in the same maternity ward at Mary Greeley Hospital. For the five days that followed, Karla was brought to her mother's side for every feeding. Her mother held her, nursed her and talked to her. And then, on the sixth day, her mother gave her up for adoption and disappeared from her life.

Now, as a mother herself, Karla finds it almost unfathomable that a woman could nurse and hold a child through all those feedings, and then walk away. That image of abandonment would remain with Karla, informing the woman she became. Decades later, with her own kids, she became a mother who was willing to sleep by their bedside when they were sick, to hold their hands for as long as they needed her, to skip Saturday nights out to be with them.

Growing up, the Ames girls were always intrigued by the story of Karla's birth. They didn't dwell on it, but it was there, in the back of their minds.

As teens, seven of the girls, including Karla, worked together at Boyd's Dairy Store. One day a woman came in for ice cream. She stared at Karla, almost as if she knew her. "She kept looking at me and looking at me," Karla recalls. Everyone noticed. Finally, Cathy broke the silence by saying, "Hey, maybe that's your biological mother!" There were laughs all around after the mystery woman left, though Karla's laughter was more self-conscious. The woman never showed up there again.

Karla knows little about her biological mother, except for tidbits shared by nurses on duty the day she was born. They said the woman was a doctoral student at a college out of town; she came to Ames because her sister lived there. Her pregnancy was the result of an affair with a married professor who was Catholic and had several children. On the night Karla was born, the professor came to the hospital.

Whether or not the woman was also Catholic is unclear, but the professor had asked that she not have an abortion. It was important to both of Karla's birth parents that they find adoptive parents who were college-educated. The professor had some kind of double doctorate.

The day before Karla was born, the phone rang at the home of Barbara and Dale Derby. Mrs. Derby recalls the moment with remarkable clarity, right down to the type of cookies she was baking when the call came: chocolate chip. The birth mother's doctor was on the phone. He said he had talked to a local attorney, who knew that the Derbys had been looking to adopt. The doctor explained that an available baby would be born, possibly within hours, at Mary Greeley Hospital. But this offer, out of the blue, came with a stipulation. "We can only give you ten minutes to decide," the doctor said. After that, he'd offer the baby to another couple.

Unable to have children of their own, the Derbys had just adopted a little girl the year before, from an orphanage. Did they really want another baby so soon? Mrs. Derby hung up the phone and ran outside to find her husband, who was weeding in their garden. She told him about the surprise phone call, the ten minutes to decide, the urges within her to have another child.

"Well, we'd want a boy," Mr. Derby said. "How do we know this baby will be a boy?"

"I don't care," Mrs. Derby said. "I want this child. Girl or boy, I know this is our baby."

Mr. Derby took a breath, told her that if she wanted another baby, girl or boy, then so did he, and sent her running back into the house. Perhaps seven minutes had passed. Mrs. Derby called the doctor back. Yes, she told him. Yes, they'd take the child.

She was so nervous that she could hardly hold the receiver in her hand. It was shaking against her ear. She asked if the birth mother had been getting prenatal care.

"Do you want this baby?" the doctor asked. "If you do, don't ask questions."

In terms of education, the Derbys fit the criteria requested by the biological parents. Mr. Derby, being a bridge designer, was a civil engineer. Mrs. Derby had a business degree and worked for the phone company. And because this was an adoption that wouldn't be going through an agency, it was put together without great formality, in the small-town way that things were done then. The nurse who brought Karla to the Derbys' home had no paperwork. She just handed Mrs. Derby the baby and one extra cloth diaper, then wished her well and drove off. Karla was wearing a thin little dress she'd been given at the hospital. Mrs. Derby stood there, tears running down her cheeks, holding tight to Karla and that extra diaper.

It would take a year for the adoption to be legal. So for twelve months, Mrs. Derby feared that the biological mother would return and take Karla away.

During her childhood, Karla felt comforted to know that several of the Ames girls had a connection to her adoption. There was Marilyn, whose dad, as Karla's pediatrician, helped facilitate the paperwork that permanently placed her with the Derbys. There was Jenny, who was born at Mary Greeley Hospital the week before Karla. In those days, new mothers remained hospitalized for seven days or more; "veterans" with week-old babies would be recruited to push around the juice carts and serve the newer mothers. Karla liked to imagine her biological mother and Jenny's mother crossing paths or talking — or even rooming together. But Jenny's mom has no recollection of meeting the birth mother.

Over the years, Mrs. Derby tried to locate the woman. Her full name was on Karla's birth certificate. Mrs. Derby would go to the Ames Public Library to look through old phone books and city records, trying to figure out what became of her.

Then one day about a decade ago, Mrs. Derby came across an article in a newsletter she received through work. The author had the same first and last name as the birth mother. There was a photo of the author, a full body shot of her walking. She looked so much like Karla — tall, thin, striking — and the way she was walking, her gait, was also so completely Karla. The moment Karla saw the photo, she was certain. "I know that's her," she told her mother.

The woman's article was about how cancer was prevalent in her family. She had lost her mother and a sister to breast cancer, and another sister had also been diagnosed with the disease. The article detailed the author's anguished decision to have both breasts removed as a precaution, even though she had no sign of cancer.

Understandably, Karla was upset by the article. If this woman was her birth mother, what cancer risks had Karla passed on to her three children? She went to the doctor to be tested and was told she showed no signs of cancer. Still, the uncertainties raised by the article remained with her.

Mrs. Derby felt 99 percent sure that she had found the right woman, and one night she worked up the courage to call her. The woman answered some questions, declined to answer others, and was vague about several points. She insisted she was not Karla's mother, and Mrs. Derby ended the call without confirmation that her suspicions were true. Karla, however, needed no convincing.

"We found her. That's her," Karla said. "But she never wanted me and she now wants nothing to do with me. All I'd want from her is a medical history. I feel that's what she owes me. And if she's not going to give me that, then we'll have to live with it. You're my mother. I don't need her."

Karla's relationship with the other ten Ames girls began forming in infancy. She and Jenny were babies together in the same church nursery during Sunday services. They'd take naps in adjoining bassinets.

Karla met Diana at Fellows Elementary School. Diana was the prettiest girl in the popular group, and Karla would see her playing with her other pretty friends at recess. "Those of us in the unpopular group, we were in awe of them," Karla says. It wasn't just that the girls were pretty. It was how they carried themselves through recess, with this air of confidence, no matter if they were on the swings or playing kickball or just standing around talking.

Karla tiptoed her way into Diana's popular group in seventh grade at Central Junior High. There was a boy-girl party and, somehow, she and Jenny were invited. Karla couldn't believe her good fortune. She thought to herself, "Wow, we've finally made it!" The party turned out to be a mind-opener for them. Right there on the couches, boys and girls were making out in plain view. Hands were everywhere. Kisses were long and wet. It was so much more than Karla expected. She was too over-whelmed to participate.

Karla remained painfully shy and insecure around boys for most of her childhood. That partly was because she was flat-chested longer than the other girls were. She was taller, too, and that felt like a handicap. In the presence of boys, she didn't know what to say, didn't feel smart, couldn't always articulate herself, didn't realize she was as beautiful as she was. Kelly thought that Karla never tried too hard to make herself appealing to boys. When other girls were discovering their sexuality, Karla seemed to be holding it at bay.

She ended up going to her share of junior-high and high-school dances, but they were always affairs in which the girls got to ask the boys. She'd get up her courage, ask a boy to be her date, and by the end of the night, she'd have another formal, five-by-seven portrait — of her and a boy, all dressed up, uncomfortably holding hands — to place in her scrapbook.

When she was with the ten other Ames girls, Karla was far more self-assured. She had a sense of humor that was self-deprecating, with few inhibitions. For the girls' amusement, on demand, she could stick her entire fist in her mouth. No one in Ames — certainly no girl — had that combination of a small hand and a large mouth, and if they did, no one was as willing as Karla to prove that one fit into the other.

Karla was sometimes the goofiest, most fun-loving of the Ames girls. Before they had their driver's licenses, several of them tooled around town on those mini-motorcycles called mopeds. One Halloween, Karla swiped a large carved pumpkin from Karen's house. She put her head through the hole in the pumpkin, looked out through the carved-out eyes, and was able to mount her moped and drive it over to Cathy's house, with Karen riding in back. As she pulled up, she looked like some crazy half-human/half-pumpkin escapee from Planet

Jack-o'-Lantern. Cathy's mother saw them coming and couldn't stop laughing.

Karla was also a bit of a pop-culture princess, always eager to apply things she read about in her teen magazines, or saw on TV, to the lifestyles of Ames inhabitants.

When the movie *10* came out in 1979, Karla convinced the others that Karen, who had the longest hair, needed to get the full Bo Derek cornrow treatment. It took the girls hours to get the job done. "She looked so great," Karla recalls. "She was shaking it all around. She thought she was really hot." Soon enough, that didn't sit well with the others.

Someone had to say it: "Who the hell does she think she is? Bo Derek?"

Karen was taken aback. She was swinging her hair around mainly to give her cornrow-installation team a thrill. "When I finally saw myself in the mirror," she says, "the cornrows were so crooked. Some were big. Some were small. My hair didn't look like Bo Derek's at all." She didn't have the heart to tell the girls that, even after they decided she'd gotten too full of herself. Eventually, Karla figured out the dynamics and owned up to it. "I guess the rest of us just got jealous. Sorry."

Back in the seventies, aluminum-colored

reflective tanning blankets were advertised on TV, and Karla, who always had the best tan in the group, decided that she and the other girls needed to buy some. One spring day, Sheila, Sally and Jenny skipped school with her and they all sat in her backyard, tanning on those weird sparkly silver blankets. They looked like they were lying on flattened astronaut suits. It was a short-lived adventure, however, because Karla's father caught them and — they couldn't believe he'd be such a party pooper — turned them in to the school principal. Their aluminum tans faded, but the detention slip was proudly displayed for posterity in Karla's ever-growing scrapbook.

For Karla, scrapbooking was risky business. On the one hand, she wanted to document everything going on in her life. On the other hand, if her parents came upon the scrapbooks, they'd have evidence of things she didn't want them to know about. In the end, her urge to preserve her memories almost always won out, and so she became a scrapbook risk-taker, pasting in everything from notes passed between her and the other Ames girls (about real and humorously imagined liaisons with boys) to photos of everyone holding a beer at a party.

In one scrapbook, she had photos of the

Karen, Karla, Diana and their prom dates

girls sitting in a sea of stoned Iowans at a Ted Nugent concert. In another, she posted photos of her dad's car covered with huge clumps of mud and cornstalks. There was a story behind that one, of course. She had just gotten her license and, with Sheila riding shotgun, had accidentally driven the car into a ditch. A farmer happened by on his tractor and pulled out the car, but by the time he got it back onto the roadway, it looked like it had been swallowed up by a cornfield. Karla and Sheila hosed it off with a few hundred gallons of water from the garden hose. "My parents can never find out," Karla told Sheila. "Never. This car has to be spotless!"

Still, she couldn't resist taking before-and-after photos so she could show all the other girls proof of the adventure. And after she carefully preserved the memory in her scrapbook, she casually left it lying around her room.

Her parents never went through that scrapbook, though they weren't completely in the dark about things. Karla's mom recalls a night when several of the Ames girls' mothers decided to meet at a bar. They shared stories and compared notes, had a few drinks and some laughs. "We knew the girls were doing some things we wouldn't want them to do," says Mrs. Derby. "But we knew they were good girls inside, and they were good for each other. They'd be OK."

From the time Karla and the other Ames girls were in their early teens, they always tried to get jobs together. Each job carried its own secrets or naughty moments or lessons learned. Several summers when they were in junior high, the girls worked together detasseling corn. What sounded like a wholesome summer job was actually hot, dirty, itchy labor — the hardest work they had ever done in their lives. It was also an eye-opener for them. The older boys on the crew would gather among the farthest cornstalks to smoke pot. And their crew leader was a woman with enormous breasts who, after dark, was a champion wet T-shirt contest winner.

Later, when they were fifteen, the girls found jobs that were easier and more fun. Karla and six of the others signed on at Boyd's, the ice-cream shop famous for its big plastic cow out front. The girls often had the run of the place. Mr. and Mrs. Boyd, the owners, weren't always there, nor was the manager. So the girls often felt a rush of power — as if they controlled all the ice cream in Ames.

In the late 1970s, Channel 5 in Ames had a promotional campaign for the station, showing upbeat scenes around town. There was a catchy jingle with the station's motto: "5's the one!" For one spot, the film crew stopped by Boyd's and got shots of the girls dipping five giant scoops of ice cream onto one cone.

That was the only time they were filmed at the store. Lucky thing, too. They wouldn't have fared too well if the Boyds had ever installed hidden cameras to monitor them.

When things were slow, the girls would sit on the counter licking ice-cream cones, chatting away. And when things got busy, they could be very magnanimous. They were the guardians of the ice-cream containers, and the cuter the customer, the less likely he was to have to reach into his pocket. Two good-looking boys would walk in. Free ice cream for them. Friends and family would stop by. Cones and malts were on the house. If an entire boys baseball team came through the door, Karla and the other girls would fight off the urge to give them whatever they wanted free of charge. Once, Karen gave her siblings free ice cream, and when her dad found out, he was horrified and told her she had to return her next paycheck to Mr. and Mrs. Boyd, as repayment for all of the pilfered profits.

It hadn't exactly occurred to the girls that their generosity at the ice-cream counter wasn't fair to the Boyds. When you're young and there's ice cream available, you just feel this urge to spread it around.

Usually, enough ice cream was sold to

keep the Boyds in the black, but there were times when the girls unintentionally damaged the shop's bottom line. One night after work, Karla and Sally were asked to defrost all of the ice-cream freezers. It took a while, and then they headed to Karla's house for a sleepover. In the morning, Sally asked Karla, "Did you plug the freezers back in?"

Karla replied, "No, I thought you did."

Panicked, they called Mrs. Boyd, who met them at the shop. Sure enough, everything had melted into goop: ten gallons each of twenty-five flavors.

The girls stood there, looking at the goop, staring at their feet. Finally, Mrs. Boyd said, "Well, girls, that was an expensive mistake, wasn't it?"

She didn't make them pay for the lost inventory, and they didn't lose their jobs. But Karla and Sally shared the bond of feeling guilty and stupid and of disappointing Mrs. Boyd.

Before leaving high school in 1981, Sally filled out a Boyd's gift certificate, addressed it to herself, and pasted it into her scrapbook: "To Sally Brown: 20 extra thick malts." In the space labeled "valid for" she wrote: "50 years from date of issue."

The certificate would have been good until 2031 — when she and Karla and the others could return as senior citizens for two malts apiece — but it's now unredeemable. Boyd's, which opened its doors in 1941, closed in 1987. Mrs. Boyd died in 2004.

Midway through high school, skinny, flat-chested Karla began to fill out, and the other girls knew that her moment would soon come. They kept telling her that, and they were right. By senior year, she was dating Kurt, an Ames High football player. He might not have been the first boy to notice Karla, but he was the first to show great interest in her, and she fell for him.

Kurt was very attractive and popular with the jock crowd — the sort of fun, macho guy who seemed like a necessary ingredient at a Friday night keg party. He wasn't tall, but he had wavy brown hair, a jock's body and a chiseled face with a nice smile, despite two chipped teeth. He was always a sharp dresser, and he'd drive around town in a white 1975 Monte Carlo, a car celebrated for its long hood and state-of-the-art concealed windshield wipers.

To his friends on the football team, Kurt could be just plain cool. He had this swaggering self-confidence and a slick way with words. He was always coming up with funny catchphrases that other boys would adopt. Years before it became famous in a Budweiser commercial, he'd walk around asking other guys, "Whazupp????" They'd repeat the phrase back to him, and there'd be laughs all around. "Whazuppp?!?!!" When the beer commercials first came out, those who'd lost track of Kurt wondered if somehow he'd gone into advertising.

Male friendships are often born on athletic fields, and in Kurt's case, his bonds with other boys sometimes grew out of visceral physical confrontations. At one football practice, there was a scrimmage in which tail-back Jim Cornette was pitched the football. Steamrolling right toward him at that moment was Kurt, playing defensive back. It was an almost maniacal charge. "We knew it would be a monster wreck," Jim recalls. The two boys got within a couple of feet of each other and the coach blew the whistle. Both boys stopped. No contact was made. But for two decades after that, as their friendship grew, they'd kid each other. "I would have kicked your ass!" Kurt liked to say. And Jim would answer: "Yeah, right, I'd have flattened you and kept running!"

Jeff Sturdivant, the quarterback, was Kurt's best friend starting in junior high. They were always comparing biceps or challenging each other to foot races. Jeff knew Kurt had a temper, ever since that party in eighth grade when a girl broke up with him and he put his fist straight through a wall. But when it came to Kurt, it was all part of the package. "He was very intense, but you were just drawn to him," says Sturdivant.

A lot of boys idolized Kurt, and not just for his cockiness, his physicality and his sense of humor. They also were impressed that he had been able to woo Karla. By high school, boys were recognizing that she had grown into a beauty, and that she had this loving sweetness within her. Seeing her growing devotion to Kurt, they figured, maybe he also had something special inside of him, something he couldn't easily reveal or articulate.

There were, however, people who thought otherwise. Some girls outside the jock sphere described him as arrogant. As for the ten other Ames girls, they certainly recognized Kurt's charm and charisma, but they didn't tell Karla everything they saw or thought.

Jane, for instance, had a story she chose not to share with Karla. Even though there were few Jews in Ames, Jane never really felt blatant anti-Semitism except once, from Kurt. It happened when she was in fourth grade and a bunch of kids had gathered after school to play kickball. They were picking sides when Kurt announced to everyone, "I don't want that Jew on my team!" Jane never forgot the incident and never told Karla until they were adults.

In eleventh grade, Marilyn wrote in her journal that she felt uneasy watching Kurt lay into his younger brother "for taking some of his munchies." That same day he spilled a beer on his brother for unknown reasons; Marilyn had to take out a hair dryer to dry the boy off. Though Kurt could be great fun, a part of him seemed out of control. Marilyn chose not to articulate any of this to Karla.

Angela knew something about Kurt, too. While he was dating Karla, he wasn't always faithful. Once, even Angela made out with Kurt. They snuck into a bathroom at a party, and it happened. She didn't feel right about it, of course, but she sensed that he probably fooled around with a lot of different girls. All the Ames girls had concerns about Kurt. But at least early on, no one believed Karla would stick with him.

Kurt had other issues, too. He was often mad at someone; there was always a reason. And because he took such pride in his toughness, other boys noticed that he'd often go looking for trouble. Once, after a football game, he got onto the bus filled with players from the opposing high school and started kicking and swinging at them. It was a dangerous decision. To bystanders, it was a surreal scene, as if one crazy guy had decided to declare an unprovoked war on an entire broad-shouldered army. Luckily, he wasn't injured.

Jeff Sturdivant became a more devout Christian later in high school, and his friendship with Kurt ended. Still, even though the two boys were taking sharply different paths, he continued to admire Kurt from afar.

Boys in Ames couldn't quite explain their feelings for Kurt or their need to impress him. "For some reason, we all just cared about him," says Sturdivant, who ended up becoming an orthodontist in West Des Moines. "I guess it was because we loved him. That's what it was. Even though I never saw him again after high school, as an adult I'd sometimes feel like I was reaching out to him, still trying to get his attention in some way. That's a funny thing, but it's the truth."

As Karla became more involved with Kurt, she began spending all her time with him, which caused tension with the other Ames girls. It's an old story, of course. A girl finally gets a boyfriend and puts him first. In Karla's case, she still wanted to be with her friends, but she wanted Kurt there, too. So the Ames girls found themselves spending more time with him than they otherwise would have liked.

Kelly considered Kurt to be braver, brasher and more confrontational than almost anyone she'd ever met, and she believed that's what made him a good athlete. But she couldn't figure him out. "He'll try or do anything. He's afraid of no one," she'd say to the other girls. "Where does that come from?"

Karla had promised Kelly that after high school, they'd go together to the University of Iowa. They dreamed of establishing residency in California after that and finishing school together out there. Instead, at the last minute, without consulting the other girls, Karla decided to follow Kurt to the University of Dubuque, where he'd be playing football.

Kelly felt betrayed. She was also upset that her friend seemed to be choosing a boy over a chance for the best possible education. Just before leaving for the University of Iowa in Iowa City, Kelly went to an all-night party and, afterward, stopped in front of Karla's house. She sat in her car, scribbling a long, angry note. It was 6 A.M. when she finally placed it on Karla's doorstep. Her basic message, as she recalls it, was this: "You're giving up everything for a guy. You've bailed out on me. And you've bailed out on yourself. It's a big mistake. You're going to regret this decision."

Kelly was right. Karla would go on to marry Kurt, and they would have a daughter, Christie, born in 1990. But Kurt wasn't ready to be a parent or a loyal husband. Karla ended up leaving him when Christie was three months old.

Twenty-seven years later, at the reunion at Angela's, Karla isn't thrilled that Kelly is psychoanalyzing her crankiness. When Karla says she isn't feeling well — she has slight flu symptoms — Kelly's diagnosis is that she's homesick. "She's really conflicted about being here," Kelly insists. "She cannot bear to be away from her family. She hates it. And the minute she starts thinking about it, she wants to go home. She gets crabbier and crabbier."

"Kelly is full of it!" Karla later complains to Jane. "She says I'm sick because I'm homesick."

"Don't listen to her," Jane advises.

And yet Kelly and Karla, despite this surface friction, have opted to be room-mates. As the conversation between all the girls reaches deeper into the night, Karla can no longer keep her eyes open. She'd rather not be alone in the back bedroom. She wants her friend to join her. "Come on, Kelly," she says, taking her by the hand. "It's time to get some sleep."

4
SHEILA

On the second morning of the reunion, Jenny opens her suitcase and pulls out a shopping bag filled with old photos and letters, neatly tied in ribbons to differentiate each decade. There's one photo in particular that she can't wait to show the other girls.

She came upon it a few nights earlier in a closet at her home in Maryland, and at first, she was completely confused. It's a five-by-seven portrait of her and a handsome football player named Dan, taken at the 1980 Ames High Christmas formal. The photo was still in the flimsy brown cardboard frame provided by that night's photographer, who posed every couple in the exact same position.

Jenny had an unrequited crush on Dan for two full years. He'd never shown much interest in her, yet here he was, standing tightly against her in his white tuxedo and ruffled lime-green shirt, his hands in hers, smiling like she was his girl. "Wait a second," Jenny thought. "I never went to any dance with Dan. What is this?"

When she looked more closely at the photo, she figured it out: Dan's full body had been cut out of another formal photo and had been perfectly attached over the head and body of the boy who was Jenny's actual date at that Christmas dance. To the naked eye, it was all incredibly seamless, as good as any mouse-clicking Photoshop user could produce today. Jenny held the photo in her hands for a couple of minutes, trying to do some mental detective work. And then she remembered.

"Sheila," she said to herself, and couldn't resist smiling.

One day back in 1980, Sheila had somehow gotten her hands on the photo of Dan and his real date, sliced Dan out of the picture, snuck into Jenny's room at her house, found her Christmas formal photo, and done some fantasy editing. It wasn't anything malicious; she wasn't making fun of Jenny. As Jenny now recalls: "It was an act of love. It was just her way of saying, 'Here you go. Here's that picture of the two of you that you always wanted.'"

At the reunion, the other girls pass around the photo, laughing about Jenny's oversized

Angela and Sheila

corsage and Dan's oversized bow tie. They peek underneath to get a look at Jenny's actual date in his gray suit. And they think about sweet, scheming Sheila with those scissors in her hand.

All the girls wish Sheila was here with them. It would be so fantastic to hear her recollections of how she doctored that photo. They'd have so much to ask her: What would she remember about the early years of their friendship that the rest of them don't? What would be her take on all of their middle-aged issues?

"Remember how she laughed?" asks Cathy. "It was so great. It was never a put-on, either. When she found something funny, I mean, her laugh was just unaudited."

The girls remember her childhood smile, too. "Sheila always smiled like she had a secret," says Jenny.

In their heads, all the girls hold on to an image of Sheila, smiling away. The old photos help. But that laugh of hers, that's harder to summon up, and they long to hear it again. It's funny, they say, what you miss most about a person.

In the summer of 1979, Jenny and Karla went on vacation together to California, and Sheila sent them a letter. Almost all of it was devoted to bringing them up-to-date on her boy situation back in Iowa.

First, Sheila wrote, she went for a drive with their classmate Darwin, and though she was really excited to be with him, "we said absolutely nothing to each other." Later she went to Doug's house with Sally, Cathy and Angela. Darwin was there. "He was being weird and so was I (I was nervous)," so that ended up without much conversation, too. The next day, she talked to "Beeb, Joe and Wally," a threesome whom she described, in order and very precisely, as "new, not cute, and sweet."

The next night, Sheila went to a disco where she "tried to get rid of Steve." Once he was out of the way, she danced with Joe,

Dave, Randy and then Charlie. It was a fun night at the disco until one of the guys "got pissed at another guy" — over a girl, of course — and started pounding his fists into a wall until they were bleeding. "It was terrible," Sheila wrote, before jumping to a new topic in her next sentence: "Oh, I found someone else to be in love with. His name is Jeff, but he's only gonna be here a few more days."

Sheila apologized that she wasn't able to flesh out all the details of her adventures in this particular letter. To do that, she explained, "I'd have to write a book. Maybe I'll do that when I'm old and lonely, but now I'm young and happy, so I'll just write a chapter."

When Jenny came upon Sheila's letter in her closet, those last sentences jumped out at her because, of course, Sheila never got to live the full book. She was the Ames girl who never became a woman. When her friends think of her and speak of her, she's always age seven or fifteen or nineteen — never more than twenty-two, the age she was when she died mysteriously. In their minds, she remains the carefree, boy-crazy teen they were.

"As we get older, I find myself thinking more and more about how much she missed out on," says Angela. "What sort of man would she have married? What would she be telling us about her kids? Would she have worked? How would she look in her forties?"

The girls recall Sheila Walsh as vivacious, flirty, bubbly and busty. She had curly reddish-brown hair and got a kick out of experimenting with it; at one point she had this impossible-to-manage afro-like permanent. "Sheila was a little tiny thing, and just adorable," says Sally. "She had these big brown eyes. And her family, they were the 'Wow' family — five kids, each of them gorgeous."

The oldest child, Susan, was taller than Sheila, with long blond hair and blue eyes. She had an ethereal, graceful sort of beauty, in contrast to Sheila's attractiveness, so rooted in her perkiness. Their three younger brothers were strikingly handsome; everyone thought they belonged in clothing catalogues or in movies. In fact, years later, when Princess Diana's son Prince William hit his teen years, several of the Ames girls had the same thought: "He looks exactly like a Walsh boy." One of Sheila's brothers did end up becoming a model in adulthood.

Sheila's mom and dad were also extremely good-looking; everyone in town said so. Her mom, a former flight attendant, was a classic beauty who dressed elegantly. Her dad, the dentist, was so handsome that the girls almost blushed when he entered the room. They looked forward to the days he'd come to class and give oral-care presentations. He liked to hand out these red dissolving tablets, which would temporarily stain kids' teeth to show them where they needed to brush better. Sure, it was embarrassing for the girls when every tooth turned reddish-pink. But Sheila's dad just didn't seem judgmental about it. And his oral-care plan seemed to work. The girls agreed that the Walsh kids had the whitest teeth in Iowa; word was that none of them had ever had a cavity.

Several of the girls had Dr. Walsh as their dentist, and photos of his smiling family were all over his office. Every year there was a new family photo to add to the collection. "You sat in his chair, just looking at Sheila everywhere," says Kelly.

Sheila's dad made a good living as a dentist, and so, like Marilyn, the doctor's daughter, she grew up a bit more privileged than some of the other Ames girls. The Walsh family belonged to a country club and had a finished basement with a big sofa, a pinball machine and a foosball table. They spent summers at a spacious house on

Iowa's Lake Okoboji.

Dr. Walsh, who hadn't grown up with much, wanted his kids to work hard. And so he'd have all five of them at his office on Saturday mornings, mowing and tidying the lawn out front. The other girls would drive by with their parents, and there was Sheila, pushing a lawn mower, while her kid brothers picked up stray sticks.

One day in the mid-seventies, Sheila told the girls that something exciting was happening at her house. *Better Homes and Gardens* magazine had arrived to take photos of the Walsh family's spacious new addition, a mudroom/laundry room. Mrs. Walsh's decorator had let the magazine know about how creatively she had remodeled it. She'd taken bright green laminated dental cabinets from Dr. Walsh's office and installed them in the laundry room, a creative way to alleviate storage issues with five kids. There was a place for mittens, a place for boots. The decorator would even bring out-of-towners to come visit!

When the magazine came out, Sheila proudly waved it around and acted like a celebrity. She was so cute about it, who could be jealous? And who knew? Maybe the photos would start a national surge of dental furniture in laundry rooms.

The Ames girls found Mrs. Walsh to be more formal than most of the other mothers. There was a fancy white living room in the Walshes' house and no one was allowed to go in it. And Mrs. Walsh carried herself with a definite maturity. She wasn't the type to gossip with her daughter's friends or laugh it up with them. "Other girls' moms would come up and hug you, but Mrs. Walsh was always a little distant," Sally recalls.

Teenaged girls almost always have issues with their mothers, and Sheila and her mom had their share. Her dad, on the other hand, was more laid back, and in Sheila's mind, he was her champion. One Christmas, Jenny got her brother a puppy. She didn't want to give it to him until Christmas Day, so Sheila offered to keep the puppy at her house Christmas Eve. She asked her mother if that was OK, but her mom said no. Then her dad gave her a wink and said not to worry. He and Sheila conspired to hide the puppy somewhere in the house overnight, until Jenny came by in the morning.

In sixth grade, Sheila went to summer camp with Sally, and one night, the girls were sitting around talking about being homesick. Sheila kept saying how much she missed her father.

The girls got the sense that her mom got along better with Sheila's sister, Susan. It wasn't always easy for Sheila to live in the shadow of Susan, who was both glamorous and a quintessential good girl, always saying and doing the right things. Susan was calm, smart, popular — and Mrs. Walsh was close to her and proud of her.

"Then you had Sheila, who was more rebellious," says Jenny. The girls suspected that Sheila sometimes wondered if she disrupted the image of the perfect family. In their observations, Sheila didn't think she measured up to her family on a lot of fronts — in looks, in behavior, maybe in smarts.

Among the girls, she wasn't as centered and introspective as Marilyn was, or as book smart as Jane and Sally. But she had an ability to connect with people that the other girls found not just impressive but inspiring. Starting in grade school, several of the girls volunteered together at a local nursing home, passing out cookies or reading aloud to residents with poor eyesight.

For most of the girls, the natural impulse was to gravitate toward the youngest, healthiest residents. Not Sheila. She'd head straight for the oldest and the sickest. She'd hold hands with the most wrinkled, the most senile, the most medicated old folks she could find. Oxygen tanks didn't scare her off. She'd just sit there, smiling and chatting.

"People had hoses up their noses, and it would freak some of us out," says Cathy. "But Sheila, she was so comfortable." It was like she connected right to people's hearts.

She'd been extremely close to her own grandmother, and in fact, she could get close to anyone's grandparent. Later, in high school, Sheila got a job in an assisted-living facility, passing out and collecting food trays. Jenny's widowed grandfather lived there, and every day, even if Sheila wasn't on the schedule to service his room, she'd stop in to keep him company. "He thought she was adorable. He just loved her," says Jenny. "He'd always flirt with her, and she'd flirt with him right back."

Sheila started turning boys' heads at a very early age. When she was in first grade, Duffy Madden had a mad crush on her. His dad was one of Iowa State's football coaches. As Duffy remembers it: "Sheila's face just glowed when she smiled, and there was something in her eyes that made me stare at her all the time. I'd call her every night at dinnertime until her mother called mine and told me to knock it off."

For Christmas, Duffy stole a half-empty bottle of his mother's perfume, filled it to the top with water, and gave it to Sheila as a present. She wasn't so taken with the perfume or with him, so he tried a new tactic: feigning dislike for her. Once, at the end of the school day, he chased her out of the front door of St. Cecilia's — she was literally running away from him — and he slipped on ice at the entrance. He fell hard on his chin, as Sheila turned to giggle his way and then stepped into her mother's car. "I was more stunned and hurt by that than the six stitches I got that day," says Duffy, who was just the first in a long line of boys smitten with Sheila.

In the summertime, when Sheila was up at Lake Okoboji with her family, her letters to the other girls back in Ames chronicled her life precisely — "I have 31 mosquito bites. It's so disgusting!" — and served as a travelogue of her interactions with boys. "I danced with these three creeps who just totally grossed me out!" she wrote to Sally in junior high. "But then I danced with Joe for three songs (slow!) and I was so happy! Now I like this other guy. His name is Ted Stoner and he is soooooo neat. I get butterflies in my stomach. (He is definitely 2320123!)"

139

Even though young Ted Stoner's name made him seem like some bong-obsessed character in a seventies teen movie, Sheila's description of him resonated with the girls. After all, if he was definitely "two-three-two-oh-one-two-three," that meant Sheila considered him worthy of getting her phone number. In the Ames girls' numeric code, he added up to a dreamboat.

Sheila loved coming up with her own words. She went to horse-riding camp with Jenny the summer before ninth grade and wrote to Sally: "The guys here are really duddy, but nice." In other words, they were duds on the heart-palpitation scale, but she liked them. She called the sexier boys "naabs" (nice ass and body).

Sheila was a playful storyteller. In a long letter to Jenny when they were fifteen, she announced that she was in love with a boy named George. "I've slept with him," she wrote, hoping to get a gasp out of Jenny. "I mean, I slept with his picture under my pillow. Fooled ya, didn't I?"

Sheila wasn't afraid to take charge when it came to boys. She and Darwin Trickle were longtime friends, but in eleventh grade, they'd go out driving and talking, and both started to feel something more. One day they drove to Brookside Park in Ames, pulled into a space and sat there talking. "I was very shy," Darwin recalls. "I didn't want to be aggressive. I always tried to be a gentleman. But all of a sudden, she says to me, 'Well, if you're not going to do it, then I will!' "

She leaned over and they shared their first kiss. And then she pulled back and just smiled at him, before leaning in for more.

Young girls today can forward a come-on email or instant message from a boy to all their girlfriends. In one click, everyone can judge his ability to woo with words, or they can weigh in on the photos of him attached to his email. But back when Sheila was young, she didn't even have access to a photocopy machine at her parents' lake house, so she'd mail Jenny the actual original notes she received from boys. "No one has turned me on as much as you," scribbled a boy named Tom. "I guess it's a combination of things did it. You're super looking. You've got an excellent body!!!! And the best part is your personality!" His two-page letter was littered with compliments, but Sheila never asked for it back from Jenny; for three decades, it has remained tied in a ribbon in Jenny's stack of "Sheila letters."

For a while, the love of Sheila's short life turned out to be a classmate named Greg Sims, who was a year younger than the Ames girls. He was, of course, extremely cute — a short, stocky guy with reddish-brown hair — and his dad ran the local car wash. When Greg showed interest in Sheila, starting late in high school, she'd just melt. For a while, she signed all her letters and notes "Sheila Sims." But she knew Greg was problematic. He was the kind of guy you couldn't always count on. He'd say he'd call and then he wouldn't. He'd say he'd stop at her house to take her to the movies, and then he didn't. "If Greg doesn't call within forty-five minutes, I'm giving up on him," she'd say. But she never really did. Once, they had a fight and he told her to get out of the car. She was barefoot, and it was a long walk home.

"Sheila was the best thing that ever happened to Greg, but he ignored her," recalls one of his friends, Steele Campbell. "She was going somewhere. She was great looking, she was fun, she had a head on her shoulders. We all thought: 'What's Greg thinking?' "

Sheila confided to Karla and Jenny: "I love him so much, but he's just so frustrating." Given her relationship with Kurt, Karla could empathize. But both she and Sheila soldiered on, smiling, and waiting for their guys to get it together.

In large measure because of the wilder boys they were hanging out with, the girls found themselves taking risks and making some bad decisions.

One night during high school, Sheila, Jenny and Angela were among those in a car drinking from a bottle of vodka. They saw the police coming, so Sheila opened the car door and threw the bottle out. Bad move. The cops arrested them for being underage and having an open bottle of liquor. Jenny's dad had to come down to the police station to get them.

The girls were pretty freaked out, but most of their parents were forgiving, and tried to use the arrest as a wake-up call and a learning experience. Sheila's mom was probably the angriest. For weeks, she wouldn't let Sheila have any contact with the other girls.

"She'd just ignore me because her mother forbade her to talk to me," says Jenny. "It was sad. I'd say, 'This is stupid. Why won't you talk to me?' She'd just say, 'I'm sorry, Jenny. My mom won't let me.' "

Sheila's father had a premonition that he'd

never make it to old age. That's what Sheila told some of the girls. His own father had died young of a heart condition, and Mr. Walsh assumed the same fate awaited him.

Sheila's dad was an excellent athlete, especially at tennis, and he often played basketball with guys half his age. Still, he had a sense that his good health and athleticism wouldn't translate into longevity, and he was right. Eight months after Sheila graduated from high school, her dad was running up the basketball court and died of a heart attack. He was forty-seven.

The Ames girls saw how devastated Sheila was by his death. They noticed, too, how her mother, as a young widow, remained strong and kept the family on track. It seemed almost heroic to them. "I just remember how she held it together for those boys," says Sally. "You'd walk in the house, and she'd be helping all the boys with their homework. She became a very focused single mom."

Sheila ended up attending college at the University of Kansas and then Iowa State, and after her father died, she took a special interest in grief-related issues. Eventually, she designed a major that would train her to counsel families that had just learned that their kids were ill, often with terminal illnesses. In 1986, she got an internship doing that type of counseling at a hospital in Chicago.

At the time, she was hanging out with a gregarious man she knew from Iowa who worked for Budweiser. She called him "Bud Man" — most of the other Ames girls met him, but never knew his real name — and he was also in Chicago.

On a Saturday night in March 1986, she and Bud Man were driving home from a bar and she had to go to the bathroom. At least that's the story the Ames girls recall hearing at the time. Sheila and Bud Man allegedly stopped at a friend's apartment building to use his bathroom, and he wasn't home. What happened next remains unclear, but somehow Sheila fell from that building. No one seems to know whether she was on a roof, a ledge, a balcony or a high porch. There were conflicting reports: She had jumped over a railing. Or she tried to jump between buildings, from one balcony to another. Or she tripped on wet leaves. Was she being pursued? Was she pushed? On a Saturday night, lots of young people are drinking. Was that a factor?

She survived the fall and remained in a coma for two days. Then, for a brief moment she woke up, looked straight at a nurse and said, "Dad is coming to get me." She died soon afterward.

Mrs. Walsh donated Sheila's heart, lungs, kidney, corneas and liver to transplant patients. A Chicago TV station aired a story about how her organs had gone to seven different people, saving some of their lives. A tape of that piece was played at Sheila's house after her funeral, though the station got Sheila's last name wrong, calling her "Sheila Marsh."

Only half of the Ames girls, by then spread across the country, had enough money to fly back for Sheila's funeral. "I was in Ohio at graduate school," says Jane. "I had no car, no money. When Karen called me with the news, I felt completely paralyzed, but I couldn't think of how to get there. I remember someone saying, 'Gee, if we can't go to each other's funerals, what are we?'" (The five Ames girls who didn't make it to the memorial service have great regrets about it now. They say they had no closure. "Sometimes, I feel like Sheila never really died," says Angela.)

At first, no one suspected anything sinister had happened to Sheila. Her family described her death as a terrible accident, and few details were offered. The Ames girls, just starting adulthood, accepted the bare-bones story they were told: Sheila had fallen and hit her head.

But a week after her death, Karen got a call from one of the boys she knew in high school. He asked her, "Did you hear what really happened to Sheila?" And then he told her what he had heard: Sheila had been found in an alley. Maybe she had been attacked. Karen was livid that he'd say such a thing. She hung up on him and somehow put what he said out of her mind. For a year after Sheila's death, she sometimes stood in the shower for a long time, crying. Thinking sweet Sheila had died in such an awful way was too much for her to contemplate. And yet when she thought back about that call, she had to wonder. The boy who told her the story was very religious. He wouldn't lie about something like that, nor would he joke about it. What was the truth?

Sheila's mother moved to Kansas City, and for the next eighteen years, the Ames girls never ran into her. But then in 2005, at the funeral for Cathy's mom, they saw a familiar woman. She looked older, naturally, but she was still a great beauty. They all recognized her. It was Mrs. Walsh.

When Sally thinks back to that encounter with Sheila's mom, one moment stands out for her. It was when she first saw Mrs. Walsh across the lobby of the church. "She ran over to me and hugged me," Sally says. "I'd known her my whole life, and she had always been nice and polite to me, but that was the most warmth I had ever felt from her."

Truth is, by hugging each other, they were really embracing a sweet young woman they both loved.

At lunch after the memorial service, the girls sat with Mrs. Walsh. She asked them how their lives had turned out, about their children and husbands. The girls made sure they spoke about their good memories of Sheila. And then Kelly, always willing to pose difficult questions that needed to be asked, said to Mrs. Walsh: "We never really got the story on how Sheila died. Can you tell us what happened?"

Mrs. Walsh seemed taken aback. "I don't know if I can bring myself to talk about it," she said. She told them that, yes, there were many unanswered questions after she lost Sheila. At the time, she was feeling such grief that it was too hard for her to look into all of them. And besides, she said, it wouldn't change anything. Sheila was gone.

Sheila's obituary: Sheila Marie Walsh, 22, 1019 Murray Dr., died at Grant Hospital in Chicago, Ill., Sunday, March 16, of injuries she sustained in an accidental fall. Mass of Christian Burial will be held Wednesday, March 19, at noon at St. Cecelia's Catholic Church with burial in Ames Municipal Cemetery.

Sheila Marie Walsh was born in Ames on Aug. 8, 1963, to Robert and Sunny (Clausen) Walsh. She graduated from Ames High School in 1981. She attended the

University of Kansas, studying child life specialty, and was completing her senior year at Iowa State University through an internship at Mount Sinai Hospital in Chicago.

She was a member of St. Cecelia's Church and a member of the Chi Omega sorority.

Survivors include her mother, Sunny; a sister, Susan Walsh of Kansas City, Mo.; three brothers, Mark of Omaha, Neb., and Matt and Mike of Ames; and her grandmother, Mrs. Mark Walsh. She was preceded in death by her father in February 1982.

Her heart, lungs, kidney, cornea and liver were donated for transplants at Grant Hospital in Chicago.

Visitation will be Tuesday from 3–6 p.m. at Stevens Memorial Chapel and 7–9 p.m. at St. Cecelia's. A rosary and scripture reading is scheduled for 7:30 p.m.

A memorial fund has been established and gifts may be sent to the home, 1019 Murray Dr.

5
KELLY

Kelly is proudly liberal and often disarmingly outspoken. That's been her role in the group since childhood, and here at the reunion nothing has changed.

"I have such respect for you, Kelly," Marilyn tells her at one point, "for your heart, for your ability to write, for all your knowledge and how smart you are. But there are things you do in your life . . ."

Kelly is smiling, waiting . . .

". . . that I would never do in my life," Marilyn finishes. That's absolutely OK by Kelly. Marilyn then adds, "But I don't judge you."

Well, in truth, the girls do judge Kelly. And they do talk about her to each other. And they do worry about her. But most of all, as Karla explains it, they do love her.

Kelly has offered some details to the girls about not being completely faithful in her marriage, and about spending almost

$30,000 on her divorce, much of it for a custody study and discussions concerning parenting arrangements. Since her divorce after twenty years of marriage, Kelly has had a social life that some of the other girls consider more active than they'd engage in. "Kelly doesn't need everybody's approval," says Marilyn, who calls her, delicately, "the strongest personality" in the group.

As long as everyone can remember, Kelly has tended to be purposely argumentative and predictably unpredictable. "She goes for the shock value. She always has. And she just spills," says Diana, her closest friend, both as a kid and now. As Cathy sees it: "A lot of times, I think Kelly just likes the debate, whether she's passionate about the subject or not." Since their teen years, Cathy has advised her to consider the ways she comes off, including to men. "When a guy walks in a room, he can tell the girl who's totally going to sleep with him," Cathy tells her. "You don't want to have that energy about you."

As always, Kelly listens, smiles, and does her own thing. She thinks it can be valuable to experiment in life. (She was the only Ames girl to have her eyebrow pierced; she did it in her early thirties and has since let it close up.) She is proudly sensuous, incorrigibly flirtatious and, at the same time, a thoughtful feminist. She'll speak without a filter and ask any question that she thinks deserves an answer.

For twenty years, she has taught high-school journalism in the small town of Faribault, Minnesota, two hours north of the Iowa border and an hour south of Minneapolis. Students usually go one of two ways when it comes to her. Either they consider her the most refreshing and inspirational teacher they've ever had, or they don't know what to make of her. She encourages her young journalists to tangle with administrators over free-speech and First Amendment issues, and she leads the charge with sometimes bruising results. At times, she has barely been on speaking terms with the school principal, which is why she requests that a union rep be present when she and the principal have to interact. She has a fearless attitude, and luckily, she also has tenure.

Kelly has always had the ability to give the Ames girls an amusing jolt, and the jolt discussed at this year's reunion is "Kelly's swinging email." The email was actually a response to an email that Jenny sent out to all the girls. Jenny had attached photos of her young son. Kelly typed back that Jenny's son was a beautiful boy, and then she got chatty. She told the girls that she recently had been to a nightclub with a female friend, and they ran into a few swingers. Naturally, Kelly began asking a lot of questions about how these married couples handle their swinging sex lives. The email began: "I had my first experience with swingers, a husband and his wife. And I think she's better looking than he is!" (Kelly later told the girls she didn't actually take the couple up on their offer; she was joking about the "experience.")

In any case, she clicked "reply all" on the email, just like always, and her story headed out to the other nine Ames girls. What she didn't realize, however, was that Jenny had sent those photos in a mass email. It had gone out not just to the Ames girls, but to other friends and relatives, including Jenny's parents and in-laws. So did Kelly's swinging response.

Kelly is not easily mortified, but she was a bit embarrassed. A few months later, she ran into Jenny's mother. "She was completely gracious," Kelly says. Jenny's mom told her, "I'm glad you had a good time that night."

In truth, Kelly was mostly just intrigued by the swingers culture. Whenever she went out to nightclubs with friends, she found herself meeting more and more swingers. She even considered writing an article about the prevalence of swingers for a Twin Cities alternative magazine, but because of her divorce proceedings, she feared that writing a story might hurt her custody situation. However, she did trade a few friendly emails with that original husband-and-wife team that had approached her. "I wondered," she later said, "if it wouldn't be better to 'date' a couple rather than try to find a good man." She reflects on her feelings: She was hurting from the divorce and not able to imagine herself ever married again. "I was looking for kindness and stability. Maybe it would be nice to be with a kind, stable woman." But as she wrote in an email to the other Ames girls, when the female half of that swinging couple flashed her large breasts at Kelly in the ladies' room, Kelly was reminded of what she already knew. "She held out these gigantic things from this tattered lavender bra," Kelly recalls, "and I said to myself, 'I am so way, way straight!' I looked at those things and I knew that this was not for me. A part of me was feeling like I don't want to discriminate between men and women. But after that experience, no . . ."

Of course, the swingers email that went to Jenny's loved ones was an "oops" that got away. But Kelly also writes some of the most thoughtful and literary correspondence in the group.

Email has been a great gift to the Ames girls' friendship, as it has to so many other women's friendships in recent years. As a teacher of written expression, Kelly has talked to her students about how communications between the girls have evolved. When they were kids in Ames, they passed notes in class or wrote each other long letters from summer vacation. In their twenties, they'd trade letters and phone calls, but because they were getting so busy raising their families in different parts of the country, their interactions sometimes tapered off dramatically. Then, starting in their mid-thirties, email became their foremost bonding tool. Suddenly, they could write to all the other Ames girls immediately, simultaneously and daily. Long notes, dashed-off comments, quick questions — "reply all" became their favorite computer command. How wonderful it was that they no longer had to lick stamps, stuff ten envelopes and drive to the post office. (When they first took to the Internet, some of them shared email addresses with their husbands. But, not surprisingly, they soon saw the value in having their own private addresses.)

With reply-all emails, Kelly says, "each of us can choose to be an active participant in a conversation or to simply read without commenting. The important thing is that we are all part of the conversation when the group emails go out."

At the reunion, Kelly laughs about their early forays into email, back in the mid-1990s. Marilyn, proving herself the consummate stay-at-home mother, at first told the other girls that reply-all emails would be good for sharing "innovative dinner recipes." Kelly rolled her eyes at the suggestion, as did some of the others. Kelly joked that the only food-related emails she'd be sending out would be about the drive-through restaurants she sometimes resorted to feeding her kids at.

In practice, it turned out, Kelly's emails to everyone else often became impassioned essays about the uncertainties of womanhood and motherhood. One email she sent out just before this reunion was about teaching her fifteen-year-old son to drive. He's the first of the Ames girls' kids to get a driver's permit, and she began her tale by reaching back to the moment she fell in love with him. "Quin was born almost six weeks early," she wrote, "and I held off loving him because I was afraid of losing him. It was not until two weeks later when he was home, in good health, that I felt the immensity of the miracle of my baby. I was on the couch holding him while he slept, and I wept as a vision of his life flashed before me, and I felt all the joy that had yet to be shared between us."

From that sweet memory, she moved on to her current experiences of letting him take the wheel of her car, while she sits in the passenger seat "frantically screaming, flailing my arms, warning him of danger, danger, like the robot in *Lost in Space*. 'LOOK OUT! LOOK OUT! LOOK OUT! STOP, DAMMIT!!' " She described her son as cocky and oblivious — "someday destined to explode mightily through my garage door as a result of forgetting to open it, so confident is he in his driving skills that he need not look back." She explained that she had come to realize that his death-defying driving lessons were part of a continuum. "He was reckless as a toddler, too, and we put a big padded winter hat on him until he was steady on his feet." She explained to the other girls that she struggled to strike a balance. "I do not want to be an uptight mom who wears holes in the floor mat, always needing to put brakes on her child."

Her email ended with a recollection of the time she taught her son to ride a bike when he was four years old. She took off his training wheels, and he got his bearings quickly. Begging her to let go, he sped down the driveway, pedaling away. "There were about two seconds of ecstatic joy on both our parts as he took off and maintained his balance," Kelly wrote. "But as the bike moved faster and faster, we both suddenly understood he couldn't stop." She had forgotten to tell him how to use the brakes. He crashed into the nearby woods and hit his head on a tree, which left him "knocked out like a bird thunking into a window," Kelly wrote. "I said 'I'm sorry! I'm sorry! I'm sorry!' — every mother's mantra — as I ran into the woods to retrieve him."

Reading her email in their homes across the country, the other girls couldn't help but think about their own children and the safety lessons ahead. But they also thought of Kelly's loving relationship with her kids, and how that had been damaged by her divorce. In that email, she had written about cradling her injured son when he was young: "I'm sorry! I'm sorry! I'm sorry!"

But the girls knew that her words went beyond the bike-riding lesson — right into the present.

Kelly's great-grandmother, who lived until Kelly was in junior high, found her way to the northwest part of Iowa in the 1890s. Like many who settled there, she and her family were of Dutch heritage. Most of the new residents belonged to the Dutch Reformed Church, which had stringent rules forbidding things like dancing and drinking.

Kelly's parents, Larry and Lynn, married and had Kelly when they were in their teens. In 1963, they moved to Ames so Larry could complete an undergraduate degree and a master's degree in guidance and counseling at Iowa State. They lived in former World War II military barracks that had been turned into housing for married students. That's where Kelly, not yet a year old, got her first look at Ames.

In seventh grade, while hanging out with her friends, Kelly did the math and discovered that her mom had just turned eighteen when she had her. Over the years, the other Ames girls found it somewhat exotic that Kelly had been born to such young parents. It was almost as if it fit with Kelly's nontraditional persona. Here they were, in seventh

Kelly and Diana, then

Kelly and Diana, now

grade, and while Karla, Cathy and Diana had mothers who were forty-seven, forty-eight and fifty years old, Kelly's mom hadn't turned thirty yet.

Even though they were so young, Kelly's mom and dad were considered to be among the strictest of all the girls' parents. (Sheila's parents were also young and thought to be strict.) Kelly was often getting punished for missing curfews, and she'd respond by coming up with effective plans to stay out late or not divulge exactly where she was going and what she was doing.

The other girls loved Kelly's dad as the school guidance counselor and friendly homeroom teacher, but they couldn't figure out why he was so hard on Kelly. Looking back, her dad now realizes that Kelly was mature beyond her years in certain ways, and she was also the type of teen who had little patience for rules. Maybe, he says, he could have given her a bit more room.

Kelly recalls that it was Diana who introduced her to hot curlers. "We were all influenced by Farrah Fawcett," Kelly says, "so I purchased my own set of curlers. Then one day my dad and I fought and he took away my hot curlers to punish me. I threatened to run away from home if he didn't give them back. I didn't want to be without those curlers! My anger was beyond reason, and because my parents were on their way out for the night, they decided to give me my curlers back so I wouldn't do something terribly dramatic or embarrassing while they were gone."

Knowing Kelly as long and as well as she does, Diana can now reach back into their childhoods to psychoanalyze things. Kelly was a firstborn; she has one younger brother. "I was a lastborn, so I had more freedom," Diana says. "Kelly's life was the complete opposite. She was always getting grounded, always getting into trouble."

Diana's mom was a busy working mother, a dietician, so Diana says she had more opportunities after school "to test the waters." Her parents trusted her, and she was generally a good kid. Plus, her mother and father were more lenient, probably because she was the last of four children. As a result, she feels she got her fill of wildness when she was younger. The way Diana sees it, Kelly as an adult still has things to get out of her system — including figuring out her romantic life now that her marriage has ended.

As she headed into her teens, Kelly was certainly attractive and confident, with a nice figure and an easy way of interacting with boys. So she got plenty of attention. But because Diana was her best friend, Kelly often felt like the less noticed sidekick.

There were many moments when it was hard for her to be around Diana. Known as "the knockout" of the Ames girls, voted "best body" in a school poll, a member of the Homecoming court, Diana was literally a girl who could stop traffic. As Karla tells it: "People turned heads to see her."

One day, Diana was walking down a street near Iowa State, and college boys in a passing car noticed her. They began hooting and hollering, calling to her out the window. Then boom! The boy at the wheel slammed his car into the car in front of him. Karla witnessed the whole thing and wasn't surprised. As she saw it, it was an accident waiting to happen. "Diana was just so pretty," she says.

Kelly found herself attracted to the high-school jocks and the occasional naughty guy, while Diana tended to like guys who were thin with rock-star hair — guys who were younger versions of Rod Stewart. So it helped that Diana and Kelly found themselves attracted to different types of boys. A part of Kelly also felt lucky to be hanging out with Diana, because the cute guys would want to be around them.

Like the other girls, Kelly also appreciated that Diana rarely seemed conceited and didn't flaunt her looks. Diana had a sweetness about her that, most of the time, allowed them to be OK about her attractiveness.

Still, Kelly felt a near-constant competitiveness with Diana from the earliest days of their friendship. She'd avoid school activities if Diana was involved in them. Though Kelly had studied dance for ten years, when Diana signed up for the jazz dance class in high school, Kelly dropped out of it. "I just didn't want to compete with her," she says now.

They were partners in physics class until Kelly started failing and opted to drop the class. Looking back, she now believes she failed on purpose, because she didn't want to measure herself against Diana.

Kelly never went to the senior prom because the guy she liked ended up asking Diana. Kelly didn't stop Diana from going with him; she smiled through it. But it was not an easy experience for her.

After college, Kelly and Diana spent six weeks backpacking together through Europe. Kelly, always adventurous, decided to emulate the Europeans and sunbathe topless. Diana declined. Kelly could be impulsive, a risk-taker, opening up to strangers on trains, asking them questions. Diana was often more sensible and careful. They both grew up on that trip, and some experiences left them uncomfortable. At one youth hostel, they tried to get to sleep while a couple in a bed across the room appeared to be having sex. On another day, because of a transit strike, they decided to hitchhike to where they were going. They were quickly picked up by creepy men in their thirties and were relieved that they were actually driven to their destination and allowed out of the car.

At times, the trip tested and strained their friendship. Diana was the quintessential American blond beauty, and the men of Europe definitely noticed. "Everywhere we go, your blond hair is like a magnet," Kelly told her. Diana shrugged. What did Kelly want her to do about it? In one café, a man tried to woo Diana, and Kelly listened to his patter and thought to herself, "This guy's just icky. I've had enough." She went off and sat alone at a table sipping her drink as she watched the guy fawn over her friend.

Despite their differences, Diana says "it's really a love-hate relationship between us, but much more love than hate. My closest sibling is eight years older than I am. Kelly was and is like a sister to me; we love each other and bicker like biological sisters. I have shared more things with her than anyone else. And we always laugh."

"Diana is good for Kelly and always has been," Kelly's mom says. "People with two different personalities work well together. It's like in a marriage. Opposites attract."

Of course, at the same time, Kelly and Diana feel twinned in more ways than they can count. For instance, in driver's education class the summer before they turned sixteen, Diana and Kelly were assigned the same instructor and the same car. So they had their first driver's seat views of Ames from behind the same steering wheel. "To this day," Kelly says, "I can't parallel park without thinking of Diana hanging out the window, telling me how close I am to the curb."

All her life, Kelly has liked finding causes to rally behind. With the other girls supporting her, she ran for student-council president at Central Junior High. Her campaign platform included a promise of regular "Flip-Flop Days" and "better salad dressings in the lunchroom." She delivered on both. When she was coeditor of the newspaper at Ames High, her contrarian impulses and casual rebelliousness took many forms. She wrote editorials haranguing students for not reading the paper: "One would think that Ames High contains a vast number of illiterates!" Another editorial op-ed piece she wrote celebrated school pranks as "constructive in boosting student morale."

Angela was her coeditor in chief, and for one story, they featured retirees at the local nursing home where Sheila worked. Many of them were born in the 1880s and 1890s, and they were asked to think back to their teen years and describe what they thought the future held for them. The old people spoke of how optimistic and appreciative they were: "I never thought there would be radios, television, airplanes flying all over the world." "I thought the world was a wonderful place." "During the Depression, you worked and even if you didn't have much, you enjoyed what you had. We looked ahead to a better future."

Then, the newspaper asked graduating Ames High students: "What do you think the future holds for you?" Out of twenty-seven responses, twenty-three were bleak: "The world will destroy itself." "I don't think the future looks good at all. Technology is taking over." "Everyone is going to get more and more bitter toward each other until utter chaos will break out." "I think it is going to be disastrous and I am glad I only have one life to go through it." "My guess is there will be another World War before 1990." Of all the students interviewed, Cathy was just about the only optimist, and even she was vague. "The future will be exciting," she said. "You won't know what to expect."

As coeditor, Kelly liked the idea of using the school paper to question everything, to rile people up, to print stories calling Ames "a plastic oasis in the middle of a huge cornfield called Iowa."

She had the same authority-questioning impulses in the classroom. Several of the girls were in English class together, and they were asked to select a famous hero and write an essay about him or her. A few of the girls picked presidents. Those who wanted to choose a female settled on the usual suspects, women such as Helen Keller or Amelia Earhart. But Kelly decided she didn't want to write about a man, and she didn't want to write about a dead woman. She wanted a true living heroine, and no one came to mind. So she decided to write an essay about the sad fact that she had no female heroes at all. Her teacher wasn't pleased.

The other girls figured she was Kelly being Kelly. As Cathy always told her: "You just like to be different. You just like confrontation." Everyone else could find a hero, male or female. Why couldn't Kelly? (Her theme song could have been "Iowa Stubborn" from *The Music Man* — which, coincidentally, mentions Ames in its lyrics.)

In Kelly's mind, she wasn't just being difficult. She would have liked to write about a sports hero, but most of the female athletes celebrated back in the 1970s were gymnasts or skaters, and they were girly in ways Kelly couldn't relate to. She saw no clear heroines on TV, either. Like other young women of their era, the Ames girls would speculate about who they'd be on *Gilligan's Island,* Ginger or Mary Ann — very sexy or very cute. Though Diana was more demure, she had the looks of a perfect Ginger, of course. And Sheila was pure Mary Ann. The rest of them? "I guess we're all Mary Anns," Kelly decided. Those were the women and the choices girls were seeing on TV. There was no one suggesting any of them could play the Professor on *Gilligan's Island,* and it didn't occur to them either.

Kelly wished the other girls would understand why she longed for more heroines — or more heroes who weren't just old white presidents. She wondered why there weren't more female authors or African-American scientists to learn about. Her teacher didn't understand her complaints. She took the criticism in Kelly's essay personally and gave her barely a passing grade on it.

In the generation that followed, of course, the achievements of contemporary women and minorities would be celebrated in every grade school and middle school. But in the 1970s, the choices were often very male and very white. Kelly was the first of the girls to rail against that.

■ ■ ■ ■

Like Kelly, residents of Ames also struggled to define a new kind of hero. Few blacks lived there when the girls were growing up, yet some in town felt that the racial issues inflaming the outside world needed to be addressed in Ames, too. And so there was a movement, argued about for decades, to rename Iowa State's football stadium Jack Trice Stadium.

Trice, the son of a man born into slavery, was the school's first African-American student athlete. On October 6, 1923, he played in his second varsity football game, against the University of Minnesota. On one early play, Trice's collarbone was broken but he stayed in the game. On another play, he was thrown on his back and trampled by several Minnesota players. Trice died two days later of internal bleeding, and many in Ames believed he had been targeted because of his race. More than four thousand people attended his funeral. Just before Trice was buried, a note was found in his suit pocket. He'd written it in his hotel room the night before his last game, while his teammates were at a whites-only hotel elsewhere in Minneapolis. "The honor of my race, family and self are at stake," he wrote. "Everyone is expecting me to do big things. I will! My whole body and soul are to be thrown recklessly about on the field tomorrow. Every time the ball is snapped, I will be trying to do more than my part . . ."

For decades in Ames, Trice was celebrated in some circles as a courageous man who had given his life for the community. Still, plenty of people knew nothing about him. By adulthood, Trice's story certainly appealed to Kelly's civil rights instincts. Remember, she was the girl who couldn't stop thinking about the prospect of kissing her African-American classmate in that basement make-out party.

The efforts to name the stadium after Trice began when the girls were ten years old, with some people arguing that he was too minor a figure to be honored so majestically. Others, including several of the girls' parents, said Trice's story needed to be told and retold to the children of Ames. Finally, in 1997, Cyclone Stadium was renamed Jack Trice Stadium, and a statue of Trice reading his famous note was placed at the entrance.

To Kelly, it's a victory of sorts that young people in Ames, girls and boys, are now taught the details of Trice's life, and that on football Saturdays, tens of thousands of people pass that fifteen-foot-tall statue bearing his likeness.

In that same spirit, Kelly would always tell the other girls how important she felt it was to find and celebrate feminist heroes. She does not hide the fact that she had an abortion when she was twenty years old. ("I'm not ashamed to talk about it," she says. "I feel grateful to live during a time when women have access to safe, legal abortions. I vote for candidates who defend a woman's right to have that access.") She had her abortion while attending the University of Iowa in Iowa City; the father was her boyfriend.

As Kelly and her boyfriend nervously drove up to the Emma Goldman Clinic on January 22, 1983, they saw a mob of protesters on the sidewalk out front, many of them waving angry signs and shouting anti-abortion chants to those entering the building. "Oh my God!" Kelly thought to herself. "Is this what women have to go through if we make the decision to have an abortion? We have to walk through a line of protesters? We have to be jeered and go through this gauntlet? Is this what women who get abortions have to endure?"

What she didn't know until after she arrived at the clinic was that this day in 1983 was the tenth anniversary of the *Roe v. Wade* Supreme Court decision. Without realizing it, Kelly had picked a red-letter moment to terminate her pregnancy. And she had chosen a clinic that happened to be a historic site in the struggles over abortion. That's what had led the protesters to come there.

The clinic was named after Emma Goldman, a nurse and self-described anarchist who lived from 1869 to 1940. In her nursing career, Goldman had witnessed the ways in which unplanned pregnancies devastated poor communities. As a lecturer, she challenged the social mores of her time by speaking bluntly about birth control methods. She advocated for family planning and for teaching parents how birth control could help them space out their children's births. The Iowa clinic said it was named after Goldman "in recognition of her challenging spirit." It opened just eight months after the *Roe v. Wade* decision. It was Iowa's first outpatient abortion clinic, and it also billed itself as the first women-owned health center in the Midwest.

Kelly would learn all of this later, and as a feminist, she would consider it fitting that she happened to choose that clinic on that day.

Her memories of that day are both vivid and hazy.

Once inside the clinic, she was surprised to see a familiar face — one of her college professors, also there for an abortion. The professor, a woman in her early thirties, told Kelly a story. She said that she and her husband had been trying to get pregnant and were successful. But she had recently gotten an immunization required of students and faculty at the university. She had just learned that the immunization could lead to birth defects. "It's a very tough decision," the professor said, "but I've opted to have an abortion." The woman was grateful that she had this choice available to her; a decade earlier, she'd have had to continue the risky pregnancy.

Kelly had admired this professor as a very smart woman and thought about how she must have played out this decision in her head, weighing the pros and cons. Kelly never learned whether the woman went on to have children.

As they waited for their procedures, the professor asked Kelly if she also was there because of the immunization issue. Kelly told her no, that she and her boyfriend had decided they were too young to start a family, that they wanted to finish getting their education. In fact, Kelly recalls sitting at the clinic and being worried about the procedure, but also being concerned about missing classes that day. What homework would she miss? In her head she was still a student — still a kid herself. Even though she loved babies, even though she just knew she'd be a good parent, motherhood needed to wait. And she was mature enough to know that as someone just out of her teens, she might not be mature enough to handle all the potential issues she'd face trying to raise a child.

Kelly talked to her parents about her decision. Having been very young parents themselves, they knew how hard it was. "Their feedback made a difference in how having the abortion affected me," Kelly says now. "I was OK with it, probably because it wasn't a dark secret. My parents said I shouldn't get married. They didn't want me having a child so young. They didn't want me caught in the same situation they'd found themselves in. They told me to finish college. They knew I wanted to be a career person." Kelly had weighed input from family and friends, and made a difficult decision that was right for her.

These days, when Kelly thinks about the

abortion, she is not regretful. She says she focuses on the fact that she would not have her current three children if that child had been born. "I'd have been this young mother with a child. Maybe I would have had another child a few years later. I might have been overwhelmed by it all, and that would be it. And I love my three children so much. I am so pleased to have my children. So I focus on that. The abortion made it possible for me to have the three of them."

Kelly has always been able to place her life, and describe it well, in the context of her times. She recognizes that she and the other Ames girls, as the youngest of the baby boomers, reaped the benefits of huge changes that were already under way by the time they hit their formative years. "We are a generation who, through progressive legislation, had opportunities women before us didn't have," she wrote in one email to the girls. "We are the generation that had access to birth control. My parents didn't."

Researchers say that groups of friends such as the Ames girls — those born in the last sixty years or so — often have a greater appreciation of the possibilities of friendships than their mothers and grandmothers did, and a much more powerful bond than most men. The reason: They reached maturity in the era when feminism was blooming. So they naturally assumed that they could build sisterly bonds with friends that would feel vital and important, mirroring or contributing to the changes in society. Their mothers and grandmothers all had close, loving friends, of course, but those older women didn't have the revolution of feminism to give their connections purpose and worth.

Kelly is vocal in telling the other Ames girls that women a half generation or so ahead of them "paved the way for us." The least she can do, she says, is not be ashamed to talk about having an abortion. The other girls admire her willingness to speak out, even if they can't be as forthright themselves.

Here at this reunion, Kelly doesn't talk all that much about her decision to leave her husband, or the contentious battle that resulted in her ex's house being the primary residence of her sons, ages fifteen and fourteen, and her daughter, twelve. She was unable to convince her ex to agree to shared physical custody, and the person who conducted the child study took into account the children's input; they said they wanted to remain with their father. The kids later told Kelly they made that decision for two reasons. First, they were angry with her for breaking up the family and moving out of the house. Second, they didn't want to hurt or disappoint their already distraught father by not remaining with him. At the time, Karla had tried to help Kelly retain custody by writing a letter to add to the child study file, explaining Kelly's great strengths as a mother. Kelly appreciated the gesture, but it wasn't enough to sway the decision.

Kelly tries not to burden the other girls with details of her child-custody issues. She came close to declaring bankruptcy because of divorce expenses, and spent time feeling humiliated, depressed and ashamed that she was not spending more time with her kids than the custody study allowed.

At the previous reunion, at Diana's house, Kelly spent many hours talking about the end of her marriage and the issues that followed. The girls listened and weighed in. But this time, with the marriage finally legally finished, Kelly is quieter about it. Were she even to introduce the topic, she says, "everything will come out. They know me so well. They can pull stuff from inside me, and I might not want to go there. They go deep fast."

In one recent email to the girls, Kelly

wrote that she was seeing a kind and caring man, only she didn't find certain things about him attractive. She made a joke about him, and a couple of the girls wrote back disapprovingly. "They said that joking like that showed that I had issues," Kelly says. "They were analyzing me, and maybe they were right. I was with him, but I knew I wouldn't fall in love with him because I wasn't physically attracted to him."

Kelly isn't always up for the psychoanalyzing practiced by her fellow Ames girls. These days, she has been hanging out with a female friend she hasn't known very long. "She's a woman who was never married, has no kids, and doesn't ask a lot of questions. Right now, I like that," she says.

As for the Ames girls, they've come to a realization about Kelly. At one point, when she's not around, they talk about it. "It's an interesting thing about Kelly," says Karen. "She's always been the rebel. First she was a rebel against her parents. And she still talks like she's a rebel now, acting like a young single person with wild dating stories.

"But here's the thing. Years ago, we would have expected Kelly to be the one who took off for California. We figured she'd end up working in Hollywood or writing for some big magazine. But truth is, she chose a traditional life, didn't she? She got married young. She had kids right away. She's teaching school in a small town in Minnesota. Except for Sally, she's the one, out of all of us, who remains closest to Ames. Look how close she's living to the Iowa border. Think about that."

The girls find it interesting that when they were young, Kelly was the one always battling with her parents. If the girls had to name who had the most tumultuous relationship with her parents in high school, it likely would be Kelly. But as an adult, she has become extremely close to them, especially since divorcing her husband.

"Actions speak louder than words," says Cathy. "In my case, I had to go outside my comfort zone and move far away to find myself. I don't think Kelly has taken the hard look at who she is and who she can be. She has so much to offer — and she has to realize that."

Everything Cathy is saying she has already told Kelly directly, and she confides in the others that the result has led to some cooled interactions with Kelly. They're a bit more formal around each other, more guarded. "But I'm really acting out of love for her," Cathy says. "I'd like to see her meet a man who challenges her on every level — emotionally, physically, sexually. Someone who can step up to the plate for her. But before she can meet a guy like that, she has to step up to the plate herself."

6
THE THINGS
THEY REMEMBER

Sheila's death, of course
The role cornfields played in their young lives
Their mothers' lifelong friendships
The Elks Club
Jenny's Southern accent
Karla's getting her own "teen line" phone
The day Jane was shot
Their scrapbook tributes after John Lennon's murder
The "intervention" in Cathy's basement
The antipathy of other girls, culminating in the graduation-cake incident
Ames itself

The list could go on for pages. As the girls reminisce at the reunion, rattling off all the experiences and embarrassments that bonded them when they were young, they casually articulate what researchers can now prove scientifically: that women who nurture

Marilyn, Angela, Karla, Jenny, Karen and Cathy at Ames High graduation, 1981

long-term friendships can find profound comfort recounting shared moments, good and bad. It's OK if some of those moments make them wince or leave them saddened. Whatever the memory, it's a gift to have other people who were there with them. No one needs to say it, but they all feel it: "On the entire planet, only the rest of you can remember certain things I remember."

Among the memories:

There was the boy at St. Cecilia who had the God-given dexterity to be able to pick his nose and suck his thumb at the same time. For Sally and Cathy, it wasn't always easy to pay attention to the teacher, because they were so fascinated by his one-handed performances. (Years later, when Sally was visiting her parents, she came upon an *Ames Tribune* story about an unnamed employee being fired from a Mexican restaurant because he picked his nose. There was no mention of thumb-sucking, but Sally and Cathy felt certain they could identify the perpetrator in a police lineup.)

There was the day in second grade when Cathy got sent home from St. Cecilia's for wearing culottes. All the female students were required to wear dresses, and Cathy's split skirt broke the rules. The school couldn't reach her mom, so Cathy had to walk home alone to get into an appropriate outfit. On her return, she joined Sheila and Sally at recess, where they discussed, with all their second-grade worldliness, how they interpreted the definitions of "dress," "skirt" and "culottes."

There was that evening in seventh grade when several of the girls were at Happy Joe's, an ice cream and pizza parlor. Between them, they had enough money to buy a small pizza. They needed ten more cents to buy a large pizza. Five cute college boys sat at a nearby table, and so the girls, led by Cathy and Kelly, started repeating, loudly and dramatically: "Oh, if we only had a dime . . ." "If we had just another dime, we'd be so happy. . . ." A few minutes later, the college boys finished eating, and before they headed out of the restaurant, each of them stopped at the girls' table and put a dime on it. The boys smiled and didn't say a word. Once they were gone, the girls couldn't stop giggling. There they were, seventh-graders, flirting with college boys! Plus, they could now order that large pizza.

There was the bloody pep rally at Ames High when a football player bit off the head of a live carp to get the crowd into a school-spirited frenzy. Some of the Ames girls recall turning their heads, repulsed, as blood splattered everywhere. Later, the captain of the football team swallowed a live goldfish. It got stuck in his throat and kept moving around. The boy was choking until teachers sent him to the water fountain to wash the fish into his stomach. (Kelly, taking photos for the school paper, followed the boy out of the gym and into the hallway. "It's still moving," he said as he tried to wash it down his throat. Kelly felt sorry for him and stopped snapping photos.)

There was that lunch period in the Ames High cafeteria when an all-you-can-eat, do-it-yourself salad bar opened for business, with great fanfare. The cost was 75 cents, and back then, the whole concept was exotic for a Midwestern high school. The Ames girls ate it up.

There was that cloudy, chilly October day in 1979 when the charismatic Pope John Paul II came to Iowa to celebrate a Mass. It was the largest gathering ever in Iowa; more than 300,000 people, including six of the Ames girls, spread across the acreage at a large farm. Just as the pope descended in his helicopter, Angel One, the sun came out. Hundreds of thousands of people remember the pope's visit, but only the Ames girls recall it for the story of Marilyn's blanket. Like several of the girls, Marilyn took CPR classes, and she volunteered that day at the Red Cross tent. Marilyn met a boy and sat with him, romantically, on one of the medical blankets. She saved that blanket for many years. For some reason, she couldn't part with it.

The Ames girls also recall the day in late spring of 1980 when Jane, sunbathing in her backyard, heard a loud popping sound, saw a flash of light and then felt a stabbing pain in her thigh. She screamed as blood poured from her leg. She was able to limp to her house before collapsing. Turned out that neighborhood boys, shooting their BB guns at birds in a nearby yard, had shot her accidentally. Jane was rushed to Marilyn's dad for treatment. The pellet was embedded so deeply that Dr. McCormack realized he couldn't remove it without major surgery. (He suggested leaving it be, and the pellet remains in her leg today.) That day, the other Ames girls all signed a card that said simply, "Sorry you got shot." Jane taped it in her scrapbook. A few weeks earlier, the famous "Who Shot J.R.?" episode of the TV show *Dallas* had aired. And so the Ames girls had fun inviting other kids at school to answer the question "Who Shot Jane G.?" Was it the mafia? Out-of-town enemies?

In the girls' adult lives after Ames, they've each found newer friends. But these more recent friendships are built mostly around their kids, their jobs or their current neighborhoods. The bonds are limited to the here and now, and memory hardly exists.

Because the Ames girls carry this lengthy index of the long ago, they are often forced to be more genuine in their present interactions with each other. They can't put on airs or accents. Especially accents. One afternoon at the reunion, the girls laugh at the memory of Jenny coming home from the University of South Carolina for Christmas in her freshman year. She'd been gone from Ames just four months and already had a full-blown Southern accent. "Y'all want to go to Karla's house, or y'all want to just hang out at my house?" she asked.

"Hey, Jenny, y'all want to tell us why y'all are talking like that?" Cathy replied. In Ames, Jenny wore jeans and looked good in flannel shirts. She came back from South Carolina and wore taffeta to a formal dinner party at her house. And so the other girls were relentless in their eye-rolling over this alien Southern belle. That Christmas, they met up with some boys who'd known Jenny in high school and joked that maybe she'd had an accident and hit her head: "Did something happen to Jenny? Her voice sounds kind of odd."

Jenny's defense was that a Southern accent can inhabit any human being who ventures down South for even a few months. The girls didn't buy it. As Cathy sums it up: "She was so busted!"

Here at the reunion, the girls joke that if one of them tries to describe herself for this book as somebody she's not, they will offer up a friendly chorus of *"Bullshit!"* under their breath until the offender reverts back to who she really is.

Turns out, they never have to gang up on anybody, because when they're together, the girls almost have to be their most authentic selves. After all, the other nine girls know exactly who they started as (and the child inside them), which, in certain ways, is who they really are.

Cathy thinks that's the crux of their friendship. Or at least that link to girlhood is what she finds most appealing about their relationships. "You can tell people where you're from and who you were, which is who you are. But no one really knows you unless they were there. With the other girls, there's an understanding you don't have to explain."

Cathy is now living a life unlike any of the others. For one, she's long been in Los Angeles, where her career as a makeup artist has flourished, and she is friendly with well-known people such as actress Joan Allen. Second, she never married and never had children. So when the Ames girls trade waves of emails about their kids' attention-deficit issues or the monotony of a long marriage, it doesn't resonate for her.

At the reunion, the others often relate to each other mother to mother. They talk about being their husbands' wives. Sure, Cathy wants to know about their families, but after a while, she wants more. As she explains it: "When Karen shows up, to me she's Karen, not Katie's mom. I want to know what's going on with her, not necessarily how her family is doing. I know she's a mother and a wife, but I also know who she is as a person besides that."

Who the girls are, of course, always goes back to Ames.

Cathy's mom was a Mary Kay and Avon rep in town, a fact Cathy dropped right into the first paragraph of her online bio. For seventeen years, she was represented by the Cloutier Agency, and has now moved to Aim Artists. Both are prestigious agencies that handle many of the most sought-after hairstylists and makeup artists in the entertainment and fashion industries. Some of the bios on agency Web sites can be a bit pretentious, hammering home career highlights and celebrity endorsements. But Cathy's bio begins simply: "As a kid growing up in Iowa, I loved playing with my mom's makeup stash. . . ."

The bio serves as an introduction to new clients, and it reveals this about Cathy: Seven words into introducing herself, she wants people to know she's from Iowa.

Cathy's L.A. friends are fascinated that she has friends from Ames. They'll say to her: "It's amazing you choose to spend so much time with people you knew when you were young. What do you still have in common with them?"

When Cathy considers the question, the answer she has for herself is this: "What keeps me going back to them? What is it I don't want to sever? I think it's this: We root each other to the core of who we are, rather than what defines us as adults — by careers or spouses or kids. There's a young girl in each of us who is still full of life. When we're together, I try to remember that."

The Ames girls haven't tracked all the scientific studies about friendship, the ones showing that having a close group of friends helps people sleep better, improve their immune systems, boost their self-esteem, stave off dementia, and actually live longer. The Ames girls just feel the benefits in their guts.

The research, though, is clear about the positive implications of friendships in women's lives. There was, for instance, a fourteen-year project at Flinders University in Australia that tracked fifteen hundred women as they aged. The study found that close friendships — even more than close family ties — help prolong women's lives. Many women in the study had meaningful relationships with children or other relatives; that didn't appear to improve their survival rates. But those with the most friends outlived those with the least friends by 22 percent. In fact, researchers say a woman who wants to be healthier and more psychologically fit in her old age is better off having one close friend than half-a-dozen grandchildren.

All sorts of studies make similar points.

Duke University researchers looked at hundreds of unmarried patients with coronary heart disease and found that, of those with close friends, 85 percent lived at least five years. That was double the survival rate of those lacking in friends. A Stanford University psychiatric study found patients with advanced stages of breast cancer were more likely to survive if they had a network of people with whom they could share their feelings.

Friends such as the Ames girls, who've traveled the timeline together, tend to have more empathy for each other's ailments. They knew one another when they were younger and stronger, and they've watched their bodies change. Gerontologists say longtime friends are often more understanding about health issues than family members are. Friends are more apt to acknowledge each other's ailments without dwelling on them the way a parent or spouse might. A friend might offer a litany of health issues, especially as she ages, but then she might say: "Let's forget about the pain we're feeling today and have fun." The Ames girls do their share of talking about aches, pains and the aging process — and, especially, about issues related to how their parents are aging — but then they move onward to the next conversation. And given how much they laugh, and how laughter is good for anyone's health, they figure their time together is completely therapeutic.

"There's this comfort zone," says Marilyn. "It's good for my mental health to know there's a group of people I can turn to at any moment in my life, and they'll be my safety net."

The friendship between the Ames girls fits a common profile on other fronts, too.

Now that the girls have reached their forties together, they're almost certain to remain enmeshed for the rest of their lives. By the time women are middle-aged, most have picked the people and built the friendships that will sustain them. That was the conclusion of a study that began in 1978 at Virginia Tech, when 110 women over age fifty were first asked to name their closest friends. Fourteen years later, when these women were ages sixty-five to eighty-nine, they were asked the same question, and 75 percent of them listed the exact same names. For almost all of them, their major friendships remained precisely in place. Similarly, a Harris Interactive survey conducted in 2004 found that a healthy 39 percent of women between ages twenty-five and fifty-five said they met their current best friends in childhood or high school. Women — and the Ames girls are proof of this — are likely to connect early and then hold tight to each other. This is despite our transient society or, in some cases, even because of it.

Jane thinks that the distance between all of the Ames girls actually serves to make them closer in certain ways. "Because we live in our own communities and have our own separate lives," she says, "we become very safe and understanding ears for one another. We don't have to worry about baring our souls — concerning ourselves or the lives of our family members — and then running into each other's kids or husbands on the soccer fields or at school. And we have a pretty decent sample size for opinions and advice: nine other women weighing in about adult issues, with more than twenty kids' worth of experience when it comes to children's issues."

Jane thinks the fact that they are all so different is helpful. "It's not like we're competing," she says. "It's not like I'm a makeup artist in L.A. and I have more famous clients than Cathy does. We're all doing our own thing."

As Kelly explains it, it doesn't matter that the others aren't plugged into her day-to-day life: "Because I have no actual sisters, it is my friends from Ames who've exposed me to every facet of womanhood. I feel I'm defined by our decades-long friendship. Despite being separated by miles, despite being married, despite having children, there is a compartment in my life reserved for them. These women are the only people who truly know me."

Male relationships follow a different pattern. Men tend to build friendships until about age thirty, but there's often a steady falloff after that. Among the reasons: Male friendships are more likely to be hurt by geographical moves, lifestyle changes or differences in career trajectories. And many men turn to wives, girlfriends, sisters or platonic female friends to share emotional issues, assuming male friends will be of little help.

The Ames girls see this in their husbands. Few of their husbands have long-standing groups of close friends, with decades of history together, whom they confide in and turn to week after week. Sure, their husbands have pals, former fraternity brothers, friendly colleagues. But men's friendships tend to be based more on activities than emotions. They connect through sports, work, poker, politics. (In a study conducted by the Australian government, 57 percent of men said they are bonded to friends through "recreational activities." That compared to just 26 percent of women who defined their friendships in those terms.) The Ames girls insist that they can and will remain friends right up until the end of their lives, in part because they won't need much physical energy to maintain their bonds. All they'll have to do is talk about their feelings, their memories, their current lives. They won't have to play racquetball or walk eighteen holes on a golf course.

"It's not like we're couch potatoes," says Marilyn, "but we could sit for hours talking, and we'd be totally happy doing that. If there was a recreational activity, we might be too busy talking to even pay attention."

Bottom line: Women talk. Men do things together. Researchers explain it this way: Women's friendships are face to face, while men's friendships are side by side. In research labs, women have even proven themselves better than men at maintaining eye contact. Women's bonds are explicit. Men's feelings for each other might be strong, but their feelings are more implicit.

The Ames girls declare their love for each other effortlessly and all the time. Some of their husbands, like a lot of men, don't ever talk about loving feelings for their male friends. (Some researchers say Freud is partially to blame because he delved into undertones of homosexuality in close male relationships. Ever since Freud raised the issue more than a century ago, many heterosexual men have resisted expressing affection for each other or getting too deeply involved in each other's personal lives.) Men find it easier to dump unwanted or marginal friends, while women are far more apt to obsess about troubles with friends. "Men place less emphasis on friendship, and so friends are easier for them to discard," says Rebecca Adams, a sociologist who does friendship research at the University of North Carolina at Greensboro.

Meanwhile, like millions of other women, the Ames girls learned early on, even in grade school, that the way to keep female friendships alive was to listen and talk, in that order. This formula remained in place through every decade of their relationship, though some decades have been easier than others.

The Ames girls found that the early adult years — their twenties and thirties — required them to work harder to stay connected. That's a familiar story for women everywhere, because those are the years when women are starting their careers, getting married, having babies. They're busy.

Again, the research is consistent on this. More than two hundred girls and women were interviewed by Sandy Sheehy for a five-year study that culminated in her book *Connecting: The Enduring Power of Female Friendship.* Of the women, 85 percent said they had trouble maintaining friendships between ages twenty-five and forty. "Then all of a sudden, around age forty, an equal percentage reported an uptick in friendship activity," Ms. Sheehy explains. "It's like all of a sudden a light goes on and they say, 'I need women in my life.' "

In studies before the 1990s, researchers attributed this uptick to women's lockstep march through the life cycle. After a couple of decades spent finding a mate, building a marriage and raising kids, women finally had time for themselves because their kids were more self-sufficient. In previous generations, at age forty, the average woman already had sent her oldest child off to college or into the workforce, while her youngest child likely was in high school.

These days, at age forty, a woman might be busy having her first child or starting her second marriage. (Indeed, when the Ames girls hit forty, none of them had children older than age thirteen. Angela's daughter was three years old, and Jenny still hadn't had her first child.) Yet in this new century, even women busy with careers and child-rearing duties become more friendship-focused entering their forties. "We've begun to understand that it has to do with a life stage," says Ms. Sheehy. She identifies patterns that the Ames girls fit very neatly. In their early forties, she says, "Women are asking, 'Where do I want to go with my life?' Female friends show us a mirror of ourselves. Even lesbians say they see a need for non-sexual relationships with women at about age forty."

For middle-aged women, trying to figure out who they are, one path to self-reflection comes from getting in touch with who they were. That's part of the thrill at Ames girls' gatherings. Karen says the friends she has made in adulthood — the other mothers in her neighborhood in suburban Philadelphia

— "know me and like me for who I am now." But that's all they know; it's not a complete picture. "My friends from Ames knew me before I became a mom and a wife," Karen says. "They really know the original me — and that's the person they like." When she's with them, she thinks about the "original me." Who was that girl? How was she different or similar to the woman she has become?

Money tends to be less of a stumbling block for friendships as women get older. Middle-aged women often have more discretionary income to travel to see friends from their past. These days, the cost of a plane ticket or tank of gas is rarely an issue when the Ames girls make plans to reunite. That's in contrast to the financial decisions that kept half of them from Sheila's funeral when they were in their early twenties.

Why, in middle age, do so many women decide that good friendships are worth this price of admission? Partly because they sense that, no matter what it costs to keep these bonds intact, there are positive ramifications in other areas of their lives, including their relationships with their husbands.

Women with strong friendships often have closer marriages, according to research at the University of Wisconsin-Milwaukee.

One explanation is that women who are good at intimacy with friends are good at intimacy with husbands. But researchers also say that women with close friends don't burden their husbands with all of their emotional needs. That 2004 Harris survey found that 64 percent of women between ages twenty-five and fifty-five confess things to their friends that they wouldn't tell their husbands.

The Ames girls' husbands want the best for them, of course, but like a lot of men, they tend to show their love and concern by being solution-oriented. They want to be fixers. When a woman tells her husband that she's having issues with her mother, the husband is apt to recommend strategies: "Here's what you ought to do. . . ." She'll mention it again, and he'll say, "I already gave you my advice. As I told you, here's what you ought to do. . . ."

But a female friend is more apt to say, "I have troubles with my mother, too. And no matter what your mother says, I think you're terrific." Or a female friend might say: "Maybe your mom is thinking about what you were like in high school, when your judgment wasn't always perfect. But I think you have excellent judgment now."

The Ames girls strive to be careful in how

they advise each other. "They all know my history, every twist and turn I have taken," says Kelly. "They also have a sense of where I am going. They don't pass harsh judgments. They simply accept." Like Marilyn, Kelly uses the word "safe." "Gathering with them involves landing in a safe place," she says.

The Ames girls say they let each other vent, then strive to tell each other that they are competent. They aim to "fix" problems by validating each other's feelings, by encouraging. It's a process their husbands might find frustrating, but it's a typically female way of handling things. Because the girls can talk to each other, their husbands don't feel as much of a burden or responsibility to listen to their issues or complaints for the umpteenth time.

Marilyn says she discusses everything of major importance with her husband. However, because he's busy at work all day, "he's not always available to have lengthy discussions right away," she says. "But I can easily get on the Internet and send a message to the other girls to get their ideas about an issue." She calls herself a fact-gatherer, who then refines all the input from the others so her husband "doesn't have to hear my stream-of-consciousness thoughts. By the time I talk to him, he can just get a summary of how I'm thinking. Or sometimes, what may seem like an issue resolves itself before I even get a chance to discuss it with him."

This talking, hashing out and confiding between women actually leads to physical reactions, according to Penn State University researchers. They found that there's a chemical called oxytocin released in women's bodies when they are doing what researchers call "tending or befriending." Oxytocin helps ease women's stress. It calms them. When men are stressed, they produce testosterone, which tends to reduce the effect of oxytocin. (Meanwhile, a Harvard Medical School study found that for women without close friends to talk to, the sense of isolation can be as damaging as smoking, overeating or drinking too much alcohol.)

In the end, though, even if you set aside all the health studies, the research into emotional well-being and the observations about men versus women, there's a simple way to understand what connects women such as the Ames girls.

The Roper Organization has conducted a poll asking people what in their lives says the most about who they are. About a quarter of respondents said "my home." Others cited their jobs, their clothes, their hobbies, their favorite music, their automobiles. But the most frequent top answer, given by a full 39 percent of respondents, was not a tangible "thing." When people really want to define themselves, they look beyond how they decorate their houses or what they do for a living or what songs are on their iPods. In the poll, the number one answer was "I am most defined by my friendships."

For the Ames girls, of course, their friendships encompass who they are, who they were, how they viewed themselves long ago and how they see themselves now. And on all of these fronts, so much reveals itself through the prism of Ames, Iowa.

Ames was actually a town that, early on, formally recognized the value of friendship, especially among girls. During World War I, Ames High chartered an afterschool chapter of the YWCA's Girl Reserves, dedicated in part to improving relationships between female students. Annual dues were 35 cents then, and members recited a pledge:

As a Girl Reserve I will try to face life squarely. I will try to be . . . Gracious in manner . . . Impartial in judgment . . . Ready for service . . . Loyal to friends . . . Earnest in purpose . . . Seeing the beautiful . . . Eager for knowledge . . . Reverent to God . . . Victorious over self . . . Ever dependable . . . Sincere at all times. . . ."

The group hosted lectures on topics such as "Popularity vs. Success," "What Are You Laughing About?" and "Gossip vs. Conversation." Evidently, even then, there was an awareness of mean-girl tendencies.

By the 1970s, Girl Reserves at Ames High had morphed into a Big Sister/Little Sister program, without the sober pledge and pointed lectures. As incoming students, the Ames girls appreciated being assigned to an older girl whose job it was to look after them and care about them. They also got a kick out of the ceremonial aspects of the program. The Big Sister's identity remained secret for months; she'd send the Little Sister small presents and encouraging notes. It was a special moment when everyone gathered for "Discovery Night," and the younger girls learned who their big sister was.

From the earliest days, Ames High educators stressed the value in nurturing friendships. About sixty years before the girls got there, the principal was Albert Caldwell, a man who had survived the sinking of the *Titanic* along with his wife and infant son. In speeches, he talked of how he and other survivors were bonded by their shared experiences that night. The take-away message was that the strongest friendships are often forged from adversity.

After being rescued, Caldwell's wife, Sylvia, had told reporters that when she boarded the *Titanic,* she asked a deckhand if the ship was really unsinkable. "Yes, lady," she quoted him as saying. "God himself could not sink this ship!" It became a famous line, though some people suspected that Mrs. Caldwell was a publicity-seeker who'd made it up. She later published a book, *The Women of the Titanic,* about the "fortitude and bravery" of this band of women who had heard the dying screams of their sons, husbands and brothers — and soldiered on without them. Surviving the *Titanic* created lifelong relationships among some of the women. And though they found solace in their friendships with each other, their marriages didn't always survive. The Caldwells got divorced in 1930.

Ames was known as a "high-IQ town," and

for good reason. Many of the Ames girls' classmates were the offspring of professors at Iowa State or engineers at the Iowa Highway Commission or scientists at the U.S. Department of Energy's Ames Laboratory. The parents who worked at Ames Lab could seem like the most mysterious people in town; everyone knew they had quietly helped develop the atom bomb by producing high-purity uranium for the Manhattan Project.

Given the brainpower all over town, some adult friendships revolved around highbrow cocktail parties with visiting scholars. Marilyn's parents, Dr. and Mrs. McCormack, were benefactors of the Central Iowa Symphony, so their friends were classical music lovers. Jenny's mom, always active in politics and volunteer work, traveled in the civic-minded crowd. Because Sheila's dad was a dentist, he and Sheila's mom socialized with other young professionals.

But the adult friendships in town mostly took shape in the same frameworks found elsewhere in Middle America. For some of the Ames girls' grandparents and parents, friendships were born and nurtured through eating, dancing and Friday night happy hour at the Elks Club.

Several of the Ames girls' mothers kept in

close touch with longtime friends. Jenny's mom, who graduated from Iowa State in 1959, would get together regularly with the nineteen other girls from her sorority pledge class. (The reunions continue today, with seventeen of the women still alive and attending.) And every Tuesday afternoon, for decades, Cathy's mom would gather with three other women for what they called the Tuesday Club.

The Tuesday Club was so crucial to Cathy's mom that family vacations would be scheduled so she wouldn't miss a Tuesday in Ames. Cathy liked when the club gathered at her house, because that meant Tuesday night dinners would end with the cakes and pies her mom had baked that the club members didn't finish.

The club also offered Cathy a window into womanhood and motherhood. When she was young, she'd sit outside the kitchen, listening to the women of the Tuesday Club discuss their husbands and their kids, their resentments and their dreams. Sometimes, they'd actually take a moment and pray for their children. It was the purest form of group therapy. "Stay close to your girlfriends," Cathy's mom would tell her. "Men come and go, but you can have girlfriends forever."

Across America in the 1970s, women's coffee klatches such as the ones hosted by Cathy's mom were in transition. Without even realizing it, these women were involved in a change in the culture. In talking about their own issues as mothers, wives and members of the community, they were tiptoeing into the still-being-defined women's consciousness movement. They could see that their concerns were similar to the concerns discussed by women elsewhere. Women in Ames (and beyond) were all connected to the same fabric.

Meanwhile, as the parents and the kids in Ames socialized in separate spheres — the young and old each not really knowing exactly what the other was up to — there were always efforts underway to build a better sense of community between them. By the 1970s, the city had instituted its Blue Star child-safety program. Families would volunteer to place a blue star in their windows, letting children know it was a safe haven if they were ever in trouble.

Sally, Jenny, Jane and Cathy all grew up in homes with blue stars in their windows. When Sally sold Girl Scout cookies, she went only to homes of people she knew — and strangers' homes if they had blue stars. It was fine as a precaution. But Ames was

211

actually a pretty safe town — years would go by without a murder — so there weren't many frantic kids banging on the doors of blue-star homes saying bad guys were chasing them. Jane's mother never had any blue-star traffic at all, except for a boy who'd routinely knock on the door because he was locked out of his house when his mother was cleaning.

In 2001, the Ames Blue Star program closed down, in part due to liability issues: What if a Blue Star volunteer turned out to be a pedophile? And how could residents reconcile their advice to kids — "Stay away from strangers" — with telling them to go to a stranger's door if there was a blue star in the window?

The Blue Star program was a sweet idea in theory. But it was doomed by the currents of a changing culture.

Iowa has 2.9 million residents, and each year, the state produces about 2.1 billion bushels of corn. That translates to 41,048 pounds of corn harvested for each man, woman, and child in the state. The overwhelming presence and importance of corn in Iowa can not be overstated.

Though none of the Ames girls came from farm families, cornfields played a key role in their lives. In those fields, they learned about love and sex, about the hardest kind of work — and about death, too.

Marilyn's older brother, of course, died at that intersection of four cornfields. That car accident occurred because the corn in September 1960 had grown to nine feet tall, obstructing the view. So Marilyn knew how a cornfield could quietly become a killer.

Karla, Cathy, Sally, Jane, Karen, Kelly and Diana became overly familiar with cornfields starting at about age thirteen, when they got their first summer jobs detasseling corn. Crew members were supposed to be fourteen, but some of the girls lied about their ages and were hired.

Iowa is the top state for corn production because there's usually plenty of rain, the soil is deep and rich, and farmers have grown adept at raising livestock whose waste offers nutrients that best fertilize cornfields. More than half a century ago, corn was said to be "knee-high by the Fourth of July." But by the time the girls got their jobs, modern hybrid corn seed and better weed control meant the corn was shoulder-high in early July. And by August, when detasseling was under way, the corn was already at its maximum height of up to twelve feet tall.

For Iowa kids, detasseling is a character-building rite of passage. The job of a detasseler is to prevent corn from pollinating itself. Kids are hired by the thousands each summer to walk through the fields removing the tassel, which is the pollen-producing top of the corn plant. This allows pollen from a different variety of corn, grown elsewhere in the field, to blow over and pollinate the detasseled corn. The resulting crop is healthier, with higher yields and better-tasting sweet corn.

In theory, detasseling is a romantic notion. Pollen dust would blow across hundreds of acres, with the corn plants attempting their own form of sexual activity. The rows of stalks without tassels were referred to as the "female" rows and the ones with tassels were the "males."

As the girls quickly learned, however, there was little romance in the work. It was mind-numbing, repetitive and wearying. They'd have to wake up at 5 A.M., before the fields got too hot, and they'd get picked up by an old school bus chartered by seed corn companies. They'd spend the next eight hours walking through half-mile-long rows of corn, yanking off tassels. By the end of each day, they had detasseled thousands of plants and walked almost ten miles.

In the morning it was often chilly, and

they had to contend with dew that soaked their clothes and mud that climbed up their ankles. By afternoon, they felt like fainting from the heat and insect bites, and they were itchy from brushing against the leaves. They tried to guard against corn rash by wearing bandanas and long-sleeved shirts and pants, but it always got too hot later in the day, so they'd take off layers of clothing. The girls liked getting a tan, but the resulting corn rash felt like a bad sunburn covering their entire bodies. There were rumors that detasselers could also end up getting "corn fever" from the heat and repetitive exertion, rendering them insane. That was apocryphal, or at least they never came upon such a victim.

"The working conditions suck!" Diana wrote in a note to Kelly one night after detasseling. "It's so wet, you'd die! There are ponds knee-deep in the middle of the fields! I feel like we're in rice paddies during the Vietnam War — trudge, trudge, trudge. Half my crew goes barefoot, but I did it for one round yesterday and cut the hell out of my feet."

Despite the conditions, the girls did have their share of laughs. For a while, some of them had that buxom crew chief in her early twenties who was a celebrated wet T-shirt contest winner. The girls got a kick out of how the boys on the crew enjoyed watching the chief sweat through the day.

The girls had fun rating the cutest boys in the field, but too much of the time, detasseling was an isolating job. Because each girl had her own row and the corn was so high between them, they couldn't really see each other or talk to each other. They'd come upon each other only when they got to the end of a row. Yes, the boys were there, too, but the girls were often too dead-tired and dirty to interact much with them. (Later, when Sally met her husband, they had in common the childhood experience of detasseling. He had some good stories, too. Once, he was too slow finishing up his last row of the day and the bus left without him. In those days before cell phones, there was no way to call his mom, and there are no phone booths in cornfields. So he started walking back toward civilization and, eventually, miles up the road, someone he knew happened to drive by and pick him up.)

One day well after she arrived in Los Angeles as a makeup artist, Cathy was working with model Cindy Crawford and they got to talking. They realized they were from neighboring states, Iowa and Illinois. Turned out that Cindy, who grew up in DeKalb, Illinois, had been a detasseler at age sixteen. A photographer from the local paper took her photo working in a cornfield, and modeling scouts saw it. She never had to detassel again. By the next summer, she was a model.

Cathy couldn't help but tell Cindy about her own detasseling experiences with the Ames girls. "She and I had this whole detasseling moment," she says. "We bonded over that." And, of course, she later told the Ames girls about her interaction. After all, women who detasseled as girls feel they're part of the same battle-weary sorority, and it was fun to realize Cindy Crawford was a member.

Sally, the only one of the girls living in Iowa today — she lives in Spirit Lake, 180 miles northwest of Ames — passes by cornfields all the time. Sometimes, she thinks of the other girls and those long days detasseling. "Out in those cornfields," says Sally, "that's where we learned there was honor in a hard day's work."

Work wasn't all that they learned in the cornfields, of course. For the girls today, a stalk of corn also can bring back memories of flirting or making out or crying over a boy too drunk to notice them. All through high school, even in the winter, they went to giant keggers deep in the cornfields surrounding Ames. One of their friends, Jeff Mann, was the son of a teacher, so he had an old mimeograph machine in his basement. He'd run off maps and pass them out to hundreds of kids, pinpointing the exact spot in the specific cornfield where the beer was (and the cops weren't).

Before Iowa's drinking age went from age eighteen to age nineteen in 1978, party organizers were even allowed to give the location of cornfield keggers on the Ames High morning announcements, since many of the seniors could drink legally. (The drinking age was raised further, to twenty-one, in 1986, but underage drinking never let up. Like other college towns, Ames had to contend with high-school kids who grew up fast, modeling the university students.)

Sometimes, on kegger nights, the girls would get horribly lost driving around in the dark on gravel roads, corn all around, and then suddenly, they'd see fifty taillights off in the distance, a glowing beacon signifying "The party is this way!" When they pulled up, Jeff Mann or other organizers would be there, charging everyone $5 for an all-you-can-drink plastic cup. A keg back then cost $30 and dispensed about 165 beers. Four or five kegs could last the night, and with five bucks from each of two hundred revelers, Mann could make $850 in profit. One year, the Ames High yearbook had a photo of a smiling cornfield-keg host holding a huge fan of $5 bills.

Some of the girls started attending the cornfield keggers when they were fifteen years old. Kelly's mom even drove her to her first cornfield party, nine miles out of town, and wondered why a guy was at the edge of the field, collecting money from everyone. "We all have to help pay for the band and the pig roast," Kelly told her mother. "There's a band back there. And a big pig, too." Her mother was quizzical, but accepted the explanation and drove away. The boy who promised to drive the girls home ended up too drunk to drive, so fifteen-year-old Karla, who had no license, took the wheel. It was pitch-dark, far from civilization, on the bumpiest dirt roads, but she got the girls in the car safely back to Ames.

The keggers were a blast. Some boy would bring a boom box, with Ted Nugent or Bruce Springsteen blasting out of the speakers. Or the kids would stand around singing all the bombastic lyrics to songs on Meat Loaf's *Bat Out of Hell* album.

As they became more accustomed to those keggers, the Ames girls brought their predictable personalities. Sheila, so often the life of any party, could walk into a cornfield and, like a character from *Cheers,* elicit shouts of "Sheila!" Everyone knew her name and was glad to see her.

Meanwhile, Marilyn, the doctor's daughter, attended these parties warily, hoping not to get in trouble. She feared embarrassing her family, as if a headline — "Doctor's Underage Daughter Caught Drinking Deep in Cornfields" — might be splashed across the next day's *Ames Tribune.* Her clearest memory of a cornfield kegger was the time the cops came and she ran for her life deep into the field, the crunching and cracking of stalks at her feet. She stood hiding behind the corn, waiting for the coast to clear, her heart pounding.

Now as adults, when the girls spoon servings of corn onto their children's dinner plates, these are the sorts of memories that some of them think about.

7
THE INTERVENTION

Lately, when the Ames girls trade emails and phone calls about their daughters' social situations, they're often aghast at how girls today treat each other. Day after day, their daughters have to contend with stereotypical mean girls who are adept at belittling them, or pointing out their flaws, or telling them "you don't belong."

A couple of the Ames girls have daughters who hover at the edges of their social group, yearning to be more accepted. It can be heartbreaking for a mother to watch, especially these mothers, who feel blessed to have had ten close friends in their childhoods. Some of their children have struggled to make a meaningful connection with just one or two other girls, and even then there's a risk that the other girls will turn on them.

Here at the reunion, one of the Ames girls describes an incident that upset her twelve-year-old daughter. Her daughter had left her cell phone somewhere, and another girl got hold of it and decided to make some mischief by sending a text message to a certain boy: "I love you. How far will you go with me?" The text messaging became more explicit from there.

The Ames girl's daughter — she doesn't want to be identified — was distraught that her friend was pretending to be her. She considered this girl a close confidant, and more than the embarrassment and humiliation she felt, she was upset that the trust between them had been violated. She and the girl remained friendly, but it was a tough lesson about the realities of social interactions today.

Researchers worry about this current generation of girls. Studies suggest that the average girl today is likely to grow up to be a lifelong dieter, to have a distorted body image, and to be emotionally scarred by cliques. Some communities are now hosting girls' empowerment workshops, where session leaders try to boost girls' self-esteem. One facilitator who gives such workshops to families in the Midwest, Kimber Bishop-Yanke, leaves parents wincing as she delivers the bad news: "We have a lot of girls walking around saying mean things to themselves: 'I'm fat, I'm ugly, I'm stupid.'"

She tells parents to notice body language: "When a girl doesn't feel confident, you can watch her body shrink." At her workshops, she offers a host of warning signs: Many girls get heavier before they shoot up in height, so comments from parents or mean-spirited peers about their weight can be traumatizing. There is also great peer pressure in today's sexualized culture: If girls' bodies haven't yet developed, they may be shunned by their cliques. That's why parents such as the Ames girls are being told that it's crucial to monitor influences in girls' lives — to know not just their friends, but their friends' parents.

A 2008 study titled "A National Report on the State of Self-Esteem" labeled girls' low self-esteem "a national crisis." In part because of bullying and the troubling way girls sometimes interact, 70 percent of girls feel they don't measure up to others. In the study, conducted by StrategyOne, an applied research firm, 75 percent of girls with low self-esteem engaged in harmful activities, such as disordered eating, cutting themselves or being mean to other girls.

Just before the reunion at Angela's, the Ames girls traded emails about the mean-girl factor in their kids' lives. Several of them commented, in essence: "We were never like that."

When Jenny read those email exchanges, she felt she had to say something. "Oh yes, we were certainly like that," she typed back. She reminded them: In their heart of hearts, they know they had their mean streaks, too. Jenny was referring mostly to a 1980 incident that, using modern-day parlance, they now call "the intervention." By definition, that's when a group of people get together to help a mutual friend straighten out her life. But that's not really what happened that night in 1980, and the girls know it.

For years, they've mostly resisted mentioning that incident to each other, because some of them feel too embarrassed and guilty. Even here at the reunion, despite the deep reminiscing going on, there's a reluctance to discuss it until Sally gives the OK.

"It's fine," says Sally. "I've never forgotten what happened, but I've forgiven all of it."

Now a popular fifth-grade teacher in Spencer, Iowa, Sally is funny and laid back, and she carries herself with great self-confidence. She has a good marriage and an easy relationship with her two daughters, twelve and fourteen. People describe her as very together and levelheaded.

When she was young, however, Sally

certainly was not the coolest of the Ames girls. In high school, she was part of the group in large measure because Cathy wanted her to be. Cathy's friendship with Sally — dating back to first grade with Sheila at St. Cecilia — was rooted in loyalty, history and the comfort of familiarity. Cathy also just loved spending time with Sally. Except for Sheila, the other Ames girls didn't have those same bonds with Sally. They knew she was very smart and sweet, with a big heart and a sure sense of humor. But they also found her to be too quiet, too shy, too much of a tag-along, and too clueless around boys. Unlike Marilyn, a square who was comfortable seeing herself as a slight outsider in the group, Sally didn't have a clear sense of how she fit in, or even how she wanted to fit in.

Given the ambivalent feelings a few of the girls had for Sally, Cathy felt a responsibility to look after her welfare in the group. When all the Ames girls went to a movie, she sat next to Sally. If they were all heading out for fast food, she'd ride there with Sally. If plans were being made for a Saturday night, she'd remind everyone, "Don't forget to pick up Sally." At least once, a few of them promised to pick up Sally and never showed up to get her. To this day, her

Sally and Cathy, then and now

mother still remembers Sally waiting by the door for that promised ride.

Sally could be fun and likeable, but she also resisted growing up as fast as some of the others, and they were irritated by that. During high school, there was a Halloween costume party, and most of the girls chose to dress in flattering, even provocative, ways. Sally came dressed as a nun, which led to a bit of eye-rolling by some of the other girls.

Then came the school-sponsored East Coast Trip in eleventh grade, which most of the girls signed up for. This was a sightseeing tour of New York, Philadelphia and Washington, and from the time the bus left Iowa, Sally sensed that she was being left out.

When all the students went together to see *Annie*, some of the girls weren't especially friendly to her. She had trouble connecting with Sheila and Karen. She roomed with Jenny, but Jenny was a bit cool at times. Karla, Diana and Kelly were sometimes off on their own. (The three of them got a restaurant to serve them wine and bought themselves a *Playgirl* magazine. The school had advised all the students to bring raincoats, and so all three bought matching trench coats and walked around New York like teenaged spies. One highlight: ringing the doorbell to get into a "naughty lingerie" shop.)

As all the other girls buddied up, Sally felt alone. In New York one night, some of the girls made plans to go to a restaurant, and Sally overheard someone saying, "Why does Sally have to come with us?" To her face, someone else said, "Oh, you're coming, too?" That night at dinner, Sally was ordering her meal, and one of the girls — who it was, she can't recall — actually interrupted her and said, "We don't care what you want!" There was a bit of snickering around the table.

Sally saw clearly that she was being excluded, but she couldn't figure out why. She fell asleep saying to herself, "I wonder what

I did to them. Why don't they want to be with me?" She took the hint, though. For the rest of the trip, she palled around mostly with a girl from outside the group, as she counted the hours until the bus would return her to Iowa.

Cathy, her closest friend, hadn't been on that East Coast adventure. And when everyone returned, a few of the girls took Cathy aside and complained that Sally wasn't fitting in.

Cathy talked to her mother about the problem. "I should have gone on the East Coast trip," she said. "If I had been there with Sally, none of this would have happened. Now they're ganging up on her and I don't know what to do." The girls saw her as Sally's keeper and held her responsible. At the same time, she felt completely protective of Sally, her oldest and sweetest friend.

Her mother listened and then weighed in. "If the girls have a problem with Sally, rather than being mean to her behind her back, they ought to get together to discuss things maturely. Invite them over to our house. You can all hash things out here." It was well-meaning advice. Cathy's mother assumed the girls would talk, hug and move on.

A slumber party was planned, and the

girls arrived at Cathy's house with their sleeping bags. They first made small talk with Cathy's mom, then headed down to the basement, where they sat in a circle on the carpeted floor. Some of the girls were busy elsewhere and didn't make it over that night. Still, enough of them showed up to make a full circle.

Cathy was going to serve as a sort of moderator, but she had only to introduce the issue and the other girls immediately started running with it. At first, there were nitpicking comments. The girls said they were bugged by the way Sally dressed, talked and ate. They talked about her lack of skills at Friday night parties. "You just kind of stand there," someone said. "You don't participate in the party."

Another of the girls chimed in with "You've got to be more fun. Participate more! Talk to the boys. You're like a wall-flower. And when one of us stands up to go to the next room, you don't have to stand up and follow us. You're too much of a tag-along."

It went on like that for a while, with the girls telling Sally everything they found wrong with her. And there seemed no clear sense that the piling on would ever end, since no one had anywhere to go. This was, after all, a sleepover.

Cathy sat next to Sally through all of it, as if proximity could protect her friend from some of the verbal pummeling. Cathy knew this "intervention" was not what her mother had anticipated, but she couldn't find the words, or maybe the courage, to defend her friend forcefully enough. Even though Cathy wasn't agreeing with the other girls, just by being in the room she felt like a co-conspirator.

As the girls listed her alleged shortcomings, Sally felt stunned. She thought to herself, "I still don't get it. What did I do?" But she couldn't muster up those words to deliver them. She just sat there, feeling her heart beating in her chest, barely defending herself. And then, finally, someone said it: "We're not sure you should be hanging out with us anymore. You're too different from us."

Sally looked over at Cathy, who had tears welling up in her eyes. Everyone was silent, looking down in their laps, until Sally finally spoke. "OK. . . . OK. . . . If that's how you feel . . . OK."

For Sally, there would be no slumber party. In her head she was thinking, "Well, screw all of you!" But she couldn't bring herself to say that. She gathered up her stuff, said good-bye, and quietly left. Only after she was out the door did she allow herself to cry.

When she got to her house, Sally went into her mother's bedroom. By then, she was really bawling. She felt devastated. After hearing the whole story, her mother told her: "You know, they aren't necessarily the nicest group of girls." Her mom encouraged Sally to strengthen her relationships with other, less catty girls at school. "You're a great person. You have other girls in your life. They'll be nicer friends for you."

Sally's mother didn't consider getting on the phone with other parents to complain about what their daughters had said and done. That might be how such matters play out these days, when parents seem so overprotective, but back then parents tended to be more hands-off. Besides, Sally's mother knew any meddling by her wouldn't make the other girls embrace Sally. If they didn't want her daughter in their clique, then good riddance.

Looking back decades later, Sally says the intervention was truly a defining moment for her, devastating and painful, but at the same time liberating and life-changing. "Some of what was said had been true," she says. "I wasn't always comfortable around the guys they were hanging out with. Some of them even scared me a little.

"After feeling beat up by my friends and going home and telling my mom, she said exactly what I needed to hear. She did not go to the other moms to try to fix everything. Instead, she reminded me that I was a smart, funny, kind person who had a lot to offer and I had plenty of other friends.

"This was a great lesson in parenting for me. It is not our job, as parents, to go to coaches, teachers and other parents and try to make everything run smoothly for our kids. A lot of parents try talking to the teacher to get something special for their children. They talk to coaches to get their kids more playing time. They're trying to make everything just right for their kids. They want a perfect world for them. But I've come to see that our job is to help our kids become people who are capable and believe in themselves enough to deal with the world. Our job is to help our kids function in the world. And that's why my mother's response was such an 'aha!' moment for me. I watched her do that."

In the days after the intervention, Sally says she felt the need to take an honest look at who she was. That soul-searching process turned out to be a gift she gave to herself. "It was a moment of self-definition for me, and it was good because it made me more assertive," she says. "I realized that although I sometimes made mistakes, I was pretty happy with the person I had become and didn't feel the need to change for anyone. It was wonderful and comfortable and a huge relief to come to that realization. It helped me gain confidence."

Just sixteen years old, Sally was able to look maturely at some underlying reasons for the other girls' behavior. She thought through why some of the other girls had turned on her and decided that perhaps they envied her relationship with Cathy, because they wanted to be closer to Cathy themselves. She concluded: "There's nothing wrong with me. I'm not going to question myself. I'm going to try to be resilient. I have other friends, and I can fit in with a lot of people, and that's what I'm going to do."

As an adult, she looks back with appreciation. "The intervention allowed me to get to know a lot of other girls I never would have spent time with if that had not happened. And I was able to go off to college with a pretty good sense of who I was."

■ ■ ■ ■

There are some old photos being passed around here at the reunion that do not include Sally. They are physical reminders of the period when she was out of the group.

By the time high school was over, however, the girls all found themselves concluding that they wanted Sally around. She had remained close with Cathy, of course, and she inched her way back toward the others after they invited her along to parties or got together with her to do homework. She'd also see Karla, Karen, Cathy and Jenny on the days she worked at Boyd's, scooping ice cream, so that kept them connected.

Some of the photos the girls brought to the reunion show the other ten girls sitting together at the Ames High graduation, or embracing each other after the ceremony, all smiles. Sally isn't in any of these photos. The girls did invite Sally to sit with them at the ceremony. She considered joining them — it would have felt good to be with them — but in the end she chose to sit with her other friends that day. "Maybe I went with my other friends because I felt they had always been loyal to me," Sally says now.

"Maybe it was payback for the intervention."

Because the girls could never bring themselves to discuss what happened that night at Cathy's, it remained an unresolved regret. Even after Jenny was in her forties, it weighed on her that she thought she had never adequately apologized to Sally. So she sent her an email asking for forgiveness. "What we did was rude and cruel and petty and high-schoolish," she wrote. "I feel really horrible about it." She said she liked to think that they were not mean girls back then, but she acknowledged that what they'd done that night was mean and awful.

"Your apology is accepted," Sally wrote back. "I haven't forgotten about it. But I forgave you all a long time ago. It was a painful time for me, but I learned a lot from that. And I think it has made me a better mother and a better teacher."

(Recently, Jenny was surprised to come upon notes of apology that she had written to Sally back in high school. She hadn't remembered these attempts to say how sorry she was after the intervention, and was glad to discover that her younger self had recognized her mistakes and taken the initiative.)

Now that the girls have begun talking

about the intervention as adults, Sally says, "I've received some beautiful apologies from some of the others, too. They are nice, but not necessary. All of us behaved badly or said things we shouldn't have at one time or another, but we all seem to be forgiving people. That's probably one reason our friendship has survived for so many years."

Looking back, the girls want to believe that they weren't as hard-hearted as it seemed. They really did have Sally's interests at heart, they say, and in their own clueless teenaged way, they were just trying to offer Sally tips for overcoming her shyness and being cooler around boys. "I'd like to think that if anyone else had said these things about Sally, that we would have gone to her defense in a heartbeat," says Karen. It was like the dynamics within a family; family members can criticize one another, but no one else can.

Cathy says the incident was character-building for some of the girls. "In my case, it helped me learn that I have to let people take care of themselves." Now, as an adult living in California, Cathy has noticed that she continues to follow a pattern in which she becomes a protector and supporter of certain friends. "I used to always have a friend who I'd bring along with me, and there were people who didn't warm up to her right away. I would have to convince them how great she was." She says the Ames girls remained that group of eleven after high school because of Sally's maturity: "We're all still together because of the kind of person Sally is. She was able to see what happened for what it was: stupid-girl nitpicking."

Sally has clear memories of who said what in Cathy's basement — "when people say nasty things to you, you always remember," she says — but she's now grateful for it on other fronts, too.

Memories of the incident have led her to strive to instill self-confidence in her two daughters. She's proud that both of them aren't clingy with their friends. Meanwhile, as a teacher, she is hyperaware of mean-girl tendencies. In her fifth-grade classes over the years, there have been "cool" cliques — girls who pay more attention to how they dress or girls who have a more sophisticated sense of how to flirt with the boys. These groups have sometimes excluded other girls in the class, who are a bit slower socially. Sally sometimes thinks it's just that the slower groups aren't yet ready to be pre-teens; they want to be children for a while longer.

Sally once saw a girl get booted from a clique in the wake of an argument. Sally was impressed with how the ostracized girl responded: She had enough self-awareness and self-esteem not to fall apart over what happened. And eventually, she found her way back into the group. Sally was proud of her. "She reminded me of me."

Back in Ames, Sally's mother knows that the Ames girls are all middle-aged women now, and she appreciates that they have supported and loved Sally for decades. But she has never forgotten that night Sally came home from Cathy's house in tears, and how her heart ached for her daughter. "I think the girls now recognize that what they did, well, they shouldn't have done it. That's all. They shouldn't have done it."

There was another episode in the girls' pre-adult lives that offered insights into how they carried themselves, and how others perceived them. It was the infamous graduation-cake incident.

The night they graduated from high school, the girls gathered for a sleepover party at Cathy's house. Her mom had ordered a cake from the local supermarket's bakery, and the frosting on it was supposed to read "Congratulations S Sisters!" The

"S," of course, was an inside joke, because kids in school called them "The Shit Sisters."

Cathy's dad picked up the cake, brought it home, opened the box, and no one could believe what was inside. Someone at the supermarket bakery had written "SHIT SISTERS SUCK!" in large letters on the cake. Even worse, all over the cake were giant gobs of brown frosting. With its base of white icing, the cake resembled a snow-covered field after a pack of dogs had stopped by to leave their droppings everywhere. There were pretty flowers made of pink and green icing all over the cake, but each flower was topped with a gross brown glob. It was a cake you wouldn't want to eat.

The girls were more amused than upset — Karla immediately took a photo of the cake for her scrapbook — but Cathy's father was livid. The girls had never seen him so mad. This purposely disfigured expletive cake just set him off. "Let's go, girls!" he said, and Karla, Kelly, Cathy and a few of the others piled into his Ford LTD and sped with him back to the supermarket. He confronted the store manager, who was stunned and apologetic. The manager vowed to mount a full investigation of his entire bakery staff. If there were fingerprints on the brown frosting container, he'd find them.

The girls knew, of course, that some people didn't like their little clique. Several times, Jenny's car wouldn't start because other kids had put sugar in her gas tank. Some of the girls' houses got egged by male classmates angry at them for dating those boys from nearby Marshalltown. And once "Shit Sisters" was spray-painted on the steps leading into Cathy's house.

But who at that supermarket would want to ruin their cake?

Suspicion immediately fell on deli employee Nancy Derks, a fellow graduating Ames High senior. Nancy, who hung out with the female jocks at the school, considered the "Shits" as a group to be prissy, looks-focused, boy-teasing conformists. At the same time, however, she was neutral about most of the girls individually. In fact, she admired some of them. Now living on a farm in Stanhope, Iowa, and working in marketing at a meat-processing plant, she hasn't seen any of the girls since high school. But she says she had no issues with Marilyn ("She was really smart and had her own mind") or Sheila ("very bubbly") or Sally ("I remember her as Cathy's sidekick, and she was nice"). She was friends with Kelly in junior high and recalls her as a good athlete. In fact, she was OK with most of the girls. It was just that as a clique, they completely annoyed her.

At the supermarket, the deli section was adjacent to the bakery section, and Nancy had a friend from Ames High who worked in the bakery. This girl also was no fan of the S Sisters, and when she arrived at work on the afternoon of graduation, she saw that the cake had been baked and frosted earlier in the day. She called Nancy over from the deli section. From the moment they saw that cake, they knew they had to defile it. "It was just too tempting," Nancy now says. They took out the frosting and turned "Congratulations S Sisters" into "SHIT SISTERS SUCK." Once that was accomplished, adding the brown globs seemed like adding appropriate punctuation points.

After they were finished ruining the cake, they stapled shut the lid to the box a couple dozen times, so whoever came to pick it up wouldn't bother to open it at the store. Sure enough, it remained unopened until Cathy's dad got the box home.

Nancy and her friend were long gone from the supermarket by the time Cathy's dad and the girls showed up to complain. But the manager soon figured out that Nancy and her friend were likely suspects and he called them in. He told them that if they didn't confess, he'd hire a handwriting analyst to determine who wrote "SHIT SISTER SUCK!" in frosting. He worried that Cathy's father could sue for defamation of character. He told Nancy he had called the cops, and that she needed to go down to the police station to confess before things got even worse for her.

Nancy did as she was told, and the police officer seemed intrigued by the whole escapade. It was the first cake caper of his career, and he said he appreciated that she had owned up to it. "Could you really have done a handwriting analysis on the frosting?" she asked him.

"No," he said. "You wrote in block letters. So we couldn't have analyzed it. That's why we're glad you confessed."

Nancy was charged with criminal mischief, had to pay a $50 fine, and was fired from her job at the supermarket, which she had held for three years. The manager fired her over the phone. Her friend, however, was fired in person, and the manager yelled so loudly that every shopper in the store heard him. (That helped news of the defiled cake to spread around Ames.)

When Sally's mother learned about the defaced cake, she assumed the Ames girls had been unkind to the culprits. Given what had happened to Sally that night in Cathy's basement, she thought to herself: "People wouldn't just write something like that on a cake unless they'd been hurt in some way."

But actually, Nancy Derks says, the girls hadn't been mean to her or to anyone else she knew. It was just that some girls at Ames High were put off by their friendship, by the sometimes haughty way they carried themselves, by the way they interacted — by their whole mini-sorority-like sisterhood. In truth, of course, some girls just envied the bonds between them.

Through the years, Nancy has told friends the story about the cake, the frosting/handwriting analysis threat, and her confession to the police. People find it amusing. She has no regrets about her decision to find that brown frosting and squish it into globs on that graduation cake. "I'd do it again," she says.

Almost thirty years later, the girls can now look at the photo of that graduation cake in Karla's scrapbook and see it as a kind of badge of honor — proof that they didn't go unnoticed in Ames. But they also know that the "Shit Sisters" cake photo is a reminder of how others sometimes perceived them and how they weren't always their best selves, whether to the wider world or to each other.

8
FBB AND
OTHER SECRETS

FBB.

What was FBB, anyway?

Here at the North Carolina reunion, Jenny has brought letters from Sheila and Karla, written decades ago, and FBB is scrawled on more than a few of them.

"Fabulous Best Buddies. That's what it meant," says Jenny.

"You're so polished now," Karla says. "Maybe that's what we'd like it to be. That's not what it was."

FBB?

"It was farts, burps and boobs," says Karla.

Of course. It was like a secret code for the Sisterhood of Unladylike Behavior. If the girls were in only each other's company, with no boys around, it was no big deal to release the F, to summon up the first B, and to obsess about the second B.

When some of the girls reached their

Karen, Karla, Angela, Diana and Marilyn

twenties, FBB became their shorthand reference. Scribbled in the margin of a letter, it was a nod to the good old days when immaturity was one of the bonds of their friendship — when fabulous best buddies could enjoy their bodily functions without blushing. In their memories, FBB suggested that very little was off-limits between them.

Looking back, though, the girls realize something about all this. It's true that they weren't especially embarrassed to be caught passing gas. It's true that they felt comfortable talking openly to each other about their full bladders, the hair on their legs or the size of their breasts. But when it came to their hearts, especially their broken hearts, it could be far harder for them to open up. There were boys and then men who hurt them in ways they couldn't always bring themselves to articulate to the other girls. There were times when they felt humiliated or ashamed and kept it to themselves. Their silence stood as a reminder that there are uncertain parameters in even the closest friendships.

FBB suggested a certain kind of intimacy. But not everything was out in the open.

All of the girls knew boys (and then men) who disappointed them or behaved badly. But talking about these experiences with each other often made them too uncomfortable. Sometimes, a guy who acted in ungentlemanly ways with one of them would be just fine with the others. Given their insecurities and the uncertainties surrounding some of their romantic interactions, it was hard to completely calibrate a guy on the male behavior scale. Maybe he was OK. Maybe he wasn't.

Marilyn endured two incidents in high school that, for years, she never fully discussed with any of the girls besides Jane, her closest confidant.

One incident in Marilyn's sexual education occurred on New Year's Eve 1980. All the girls were at a party, and after midnight, a handsome college guy offered to drive Marilyn home. She knew him from his days at Ames High; he'd graduated two years earlier and was enrolled at Iowa State.

After they got in the car, he said he didn't want to drive her home just yet. "Let's just go to my fraternity house for a little while," he said. Marilyn knew it was getting late and her parents would be waiting for her, but she agreed to go. After all, a college fraternity house is an exciting place for a high school girl, especially on New Year's Eve.

Marilyn and the boy ended up in a room together, and he began kissing her. That was fine by her, she was kissing him right back, but then he reached into her pants.

"No," she said. "I don't want to do this."

"Yes you do," he said. "You know you do."

"Absolutely not," she told him. "That's not who I am." He persisted for a moment until she said, "I want to go home. Please take me home."

He just shook his head in mock disgust and walked away from her. He had no intention of driving her home after she'd pushed him away like that.

It was a cold winter night. Marilyn got her coat, left the frat house and, with tears streaming down her face, began walking the two miles to her house. It was almost too frigid to walk, and Jane's house was closer, so she stopped there and knocked on the door.

"Marilyn, what are you doing here?" Jane's mother asked. "Where's Jane? What happened?"

Jane was still at the original party, and Marilyn, her voice quivering, told Jane's mother the whole story. "How did I get myself in that situation?" she asked. "What did I do wrong?"

Jane's mom did her best to be understanding as she drove Marilyn home. Marilyn later told the whole story to Jane, but was too embarrassed to tell the others. Yes, they knew this guy, and he might have later put the same pressure on them. But Marilyn blamed herself for what happened. Had she led him on? Was she too naïve? It wouldn't be easy for her to discuss these things with anyone besides Jane.

A more serious incident happened after the homecoming dance that year. Marilyn had been drinking and ended up in the backseat of a boy's car. She was making out with him and then, because of all the liquor she had consumed, she passed out.

She wasn't sure how long she was out of

it, but when she woke up, the boy's pants were undone, she felt disheveled, and she had a clear and spooky sense that something had happened against her will. She was instantly panicked. "What are you doing?" she asked the boy, almost shrieking, feeling both the alcohol and a huge wave of terror.

"I don't know," he answered.

"You don't know? What do you mean you don't know?" she said.

"I don't know."

He wasn't going to tell her what had transpired. She left the car, found her way home, and spent the night groggy and petrified that she had lost her virginity. In all her dreams, she'd never expected this would be the way it would happen. The next morning, she talked to her sister. "I think I was raped."

Her sister told her that she could have a sexually transmitted disease or she could be pregnant, and so she'd better tell their father. Marilyn found the courage to call Dr. McCormack at his office. He could sense in her voice that something was very wrong and told her to come see him.

He had patients in various examining rooms, but he took Marilyn aside and listened to her. "I think I might have had sex last night," she told him.

He was calm; that was always his way. His words were measured. He asked her to explain what she meant by that.

She told him the story. "Dad, I saw blood."

Dr. McCormack, of course, was the biggest sex-education proponent in Ames. He knew sexual issues had to be dealt with directly and honestly. And so he got right to the point. "Yes, the fact that there was blood could be an issue. When the hymen is broken, sometimes there's blood."

Her dad was straightforward. "We don't know how sexually active this boy might be, so venereal disease could be an issue." He gave her a shot of penicillin. At the time, penicillin was considered the best treatment for gonorrhea and syphilis; now there are resistant strains of gonorrhea, so other antibiotics are used.

Dr. McCormack also gave Marilyn a gentle lecture about how she should try not to put herself in a position that could lead to this sort of trouble. He decided not to call the boy or his parents. He knew there were often gray areas of sexual behavior and that his efforts were best spent making Marilyn aware of them.

When Dr. McCormack got home from work that night, he took Marilyn aside again. Four years earlier, in 1975, the Food and Drug Administration had ruled that postcoital contraceptives — morning-after pills — would be permitted for cases of rape or incest. Dr. McCormack had decided to give the pills to Marilyn.

There were five little red pills. She took them, and they made her sick. She spent the next day throwing up.

It was not easy for Marilyn to talk to the other girls about exactly what had happened. She mentioned it in broad strokes: She drank too much, a boy took liberties, she learned a lesson, etc.

Marilyn told Jane the boy's name. Kelly found out much later. "He was probably confused about what he could and couldn't do with a girl," Kelly said when she heard the story, giving the boy the benefit of the doubt. "He thought what he was doing was OK." Kelly had had her own encounters with this very guy, and though he had been frisky, she thought to herself, "He's not a bad guy." Word was that the boy was well endowed, and so Kelly tried to reassure Marilyn that he hadn't penetrated her. "If he tried anything, you'd have known," Kelly said. "A guy that big, you definitely would have known."

But, truth was, Marilyn had to live with

the fact that she would never know. The boy would never say. And she would never be able to remember what happened while she was passed out in the backseat of that car.

The unshared secrets carried by the Ames girls could last for years. That very boy, the one from the backseat of the car, would happen upon Kelly a year or so after college. Kelly was back in Ames for Thanksgiving — she was soon to be married — and she was drinking at a bar with Diana. The guy was there with them, drinking, reminiscing about high school, as they all kicked peanuts around the barroom floor.

Kelly drove Diana home, and after she dropped her off, this guy was still in the car with her. They started making out, then went further. A few weeks later, she got married. She wouldn't tell any of the other girls about this impulsive fling until much later, after her marriage had failed. At the time, she didn't even think to discuss with them what this event might have signified regarding her feelings for her husband-to-be. (Also, she hadn't known Marilyn's story at the time. If she had, she doesn't think it would have mattered much to her anyway. She'd also have assumed it fit in the gray area of sexual encounters. She believed that the boy was basically a decent person.)

Despite how close they were, that's the way it seemed to go. Marilyn couldn't reveal that she likely had been date-raped. And Kelly, who viewed love and sex differently than the other girls, felt it best to keep her own set of secrets.

9
DEFINING LOVE

Kelly is on a roll. "I think we're meant to love many times in our lives, in many different ways, and probably more than a few different men," she says to some of the other girls sitting on the porch at the North Carolina reunion. "We're supposed to have a young love. And then maybe another love, like a middle-aged love. And then perhaps we have an old love. That might be the way we should all be going through life. But our society doesn't really allow for that."

Karla has heard it all before. "You've been saying that all your life," she says to Kelly. "And I think you've got it wrong. I think we're meant to truly love one person, to have a life partner."

Karla says she has a soul mate, someone who was chosen for her, perhaps divinely. Certainly, he was meant for her. "I just didn't find him right away," she says.

Kelly shrugs. "There are many levels of

Diana, Kelly, Karen, Cathy

love, that's all I'm saying. There's the way we love our children; maybe that's the strongest love. And there's the way we love men, which is different and not necessarily forever."

In the summer of 1990, Angela and Karen got married a few days apart. Karen's wedding was in Ames, and Angela's was two hundred miles away, in Kansas City. So the Ames girls planned to come home for Karen's wedding, then take a road trip together down to Kansas City for Angela's. (Karen was marrying a sharp guy she'd met at Iowa State; he'd gotten a job as a software developer for the Department of Energy in Chicago. Angela had been working as a bartender at Chi Chi's, and met her husband through his stepmom, a waitress there.)

Karla, then living in Arizona, brought her five-month-old daughter, Christie, to Karen's wedding, and the other girls fell in love immediately. Christie was like a little doll in a pink dress, sitting at the reception with them, a thin white headband with pink ruffles around her head, an angelic smile on her face. The girls passed her back and forth, like doting aunts. It was as if Christie belonged to all of them.

The other girls saw that Karla was completely entranced by motherhood. Christie was a perfect little baby, and Karla felt so comfortable holding her and showing her off. The girls watched her snuggle with her baby, partly envying her and partly wondering about the ways in which loving feelings would swell inside them when their time came to be mothers.

Earlier, Karen had told Karla that she wanted to honor their friendship by having her do an inspirational reading during the wedding ceremony. Karla declined, saying her presence on the altar wouldn't feel right. She and Kurt were in the process of getting divorced; she had filed just weeks after Christie's birth. "It would be hypocritical for me to do a reading about the sanctity of marriage," she told Karen.

A few days after Karen's wedding, Karla left Christie with her parents in Ames and drove down to Angela's wedding in Kansas City with Kelly and Diana. It was the first time Karla had been away from Christie for more than a few hours, and it was hard for her to say good-bye. Still, it was a necessary trip, being with the girls again, because it was on that car ride that she told the others about a wonderful man she had met.

Karla had been working in property management, and one day a man walked into her office. His name was Bruce, and he arrived with his brother to sign a new apartment lease. Bruce was six-foot-five and strikingly handsome. He had a mustache, this perfect smile, and the bluest eyes Karla had ever seen. He told Karla a little about himself. He had grown up on a wheat farm in Montana and got his degree in business marketing at the University of Idaho. He was in Arizona working in construction with his brother.

He had a Tom-Selleck-in-the-eighties look about him, but with a mullet haircut. (Given the times, that haircut looked just right on him.) Karla had immediate feelings for him. Bruce couldn't help but notice Karla, too, and thought she was beautiful and vivacious.

Bruce carried himself with a gentleness that Karla found striking. He was "kind" — that's the word that came into Karla's head. It was a form of kindness she hadn't experienced from a man before. For his part, Bruce told Karla that she had this passion within her — "gusto," he called it — and that impressed him. They felt natural together. Eventually, a friendship turned into romance.

Karla told the girls that Bruce had moved back to Idaho, where he had gone to college. They were staying in close touch, and the realization was hitting both of them that they wanted to spend their lives together, raising Christie.

At the reception after the ceremony, Cathy, Diana, Kelly and Karla sat at the same table, and the discussion turned to love and friendship. "In the end, who is more important in your life, your girlfriends or your men?" Kelly wondered. "I say friendships last a lifetime. The hell with men."

Karla listened to her and then answered quietly. "I want to be completely devoted to a man and to have a man completely devoted to me. That's what I dream of."

The other girls were taken with her optimism. She still had this utopian ideal.

"You can't count on men," Kelly said. "I believe that if we had an ideal society, we'd fall in love a few times."

This wasn't exactly appropriate talk for a wedding reception. And in any case, Karla remained firm. "There's a soul mate for everyone," she said. "I believe that." In her heart, she was sensing that Bruce would be hers.

Later that night, as Angela headed off for her honeymoon, the other girls went bar-hopping. Karla went along, but seemed disconnected. Kelly noticed. "Come on, Karla," she said. "We're here to party. Snap out of it."

Karla was kind of quiet, and as they drove around looking for the next stop, she spoke up. "I'm sorry," she said. "But you've got to get me to a pay phone." They obliged her and waited in the car while Karla leaned against the wall of a convenience store, the pay phone pressed against her ear, checking up on Christie. She just wouldn't get off the phone. It was getting annoying. She had to ask her mother for every detail about Christie's day.

When Karla returned to the car, she had an announcement. "I've got to go back to Ames."

"What happened? Is everything OK?" Diana asked.

"Yeah, yeah, fine," said Karla. "I just miss Christie too much. I want to go back."

The other girls were still feeling young, still in a partying mode. And here was Karla, completely baby-focused. She seemed terribly conflicted.

"OK," said Kelly. "We'll drive back tomorrow. But for now, you're with us, so let's go find a bar."

Karla agreed, and the girls went off to find another nightspot. They got back to their hotel well after midnight, talked for a while, and then fell asleep — but not for long. Karla woke up at 5 A.M., all churned up, and nudged Kelly awake. "We've got to get going," she said. "I want to leave now. I need to get back to Christie."

Kelly would have loved to sleep longer, of course. She hoped to have a leisurely breakfast in Kansas City. Maybe lunch, too.

"We have to say good-bye to the other girls," Kelly said.

"We'll leave them a note," Karla answered. "Come on. Let's go."

Leaving at 5 A.M. was a crazy idea, but

Kelly was so impressed by Karla's urges regarding motherhood that she groggily agreed to accommodate her. They got dressed and loaded up Kelly's little red Honda Prelude, and as the sun rose over Kansas City, they headed back to Ames.

Christie was a happy baby, and Karla loved watching her interact with Bruce when they visited each other. He'd spread out all six-foot-five of his body on a blanket on the floor, and he'd hang out there, talking to her and kidding around with her. He was just great at making her laugh, and she made him laugh, too. "Oh my God," Karla would think to herself. "He absolutely loves her."

"We're pretty good little buddies," Bruce liked to say, holding Christie in his arms.

When Karla's divorce was final in the fall of 1990, she strapped ten-month-old Christie in her car seat, left Arizona and drove to see Bruce in Idaho. She talked to Christie on the entire road trip, and Christie babbled back at her, as if she understood everything.

Karla's father died that December at age sixty-eight, and seeing her mother lose the love of her life made Karla realize that real love needs to be honored and embraced. By February, Karla was ready. She and Bruce decided to get married. Their wedding ceremony was at a bed-and-breakfast in Coeur d'Alene, Idaho. They had a three-person honeymoon weekend of skiing in Sandpoint, Idaho, with one-year-old Christie happily wearing her first pair of skis.

After marrying Bruce, Karla told the other Ames girls that it was hard to say who was more content, her or little Christie. Both of them were completely in love with Bruce and in love with Idaho. (Karla's ex-husband, Kurt, eventually signed away all parental rights to Christie, and Bruce formally adopted her.)

Karla liked to describe Christie as always smiling, always thinking, always paying close attention to adult conversations. Christie, even at that young age, carried herself with a kind of maturity that was unfamiliar to Karla. When some of the other Ames girls came to visit and met Christie, they were struck by how well mannered and mature she seemed. They'd joke that she couldn't be Karla's child.

Meanwhile, Bruce's career had begun taking off, and he was making a good living, working his way up the management ranks at a computer-network hardware manufacturer. "I don't fully understand all that his company does," Karla told the other Ames girls when they'd ask. "Next time you see him you can feel free to ask him, but you still might not be able to figure it all out."

One night, Karla was on the phone with Kelly and told her: "Christie and I are both deliriously happy. In the last few years, I could never have imagined being as happy as we are." She talked about the little ski boat she and Bruce had bought, and how they were going boating every weekend. She talked about their German shepherd, Luke, who had become Christie's companion and playmate. And she explained how Bruce was so easy to live with and to love. "There's a calmness in my life now that I just appreciate so much," she said.

One day, when Christie was just under two years old, Karla's idyllic life in Idaho took a terrifying turn.

Karla and Christie had gone to Bruce's parents' house on Lake Coeur d'Alene to pick raspberries in their sprawling garden. At one point, while Karla's back was turned, Christie opened the gate and walked off.

Karla called her name, but there was no answer. Where could she be? How far could a twenty-two-month-old go in that short a time? Was it possible someone took her?

Karla felt a panic unlike anything she'd

felt before. From her in-laws' house, she could run in two directions — up into the mountains or down toward the lake. She figured that Christie could survive longer alone in the mountains than if, God forbid, she had wandered into the lake. And so Karla sprinted through an open field down to the lake, screaming, "Christie! Christie!"

There was no response. Karla knew every second mattered.

Karla kept running and came to a two-lane road. There in the distance, she saw their dog Luke walking on the shoulder of the road. A pickup truck was on the side of the road next to the dog. And then Karla saw a woman holding Christie in her arms. Karla ran to them and hugged Christie with all her might, wiping away tears.

"We were driving along, and we saw the dog and your little girl," the woman said. Her husband was still behind the wheel in the pickup. "Anyway, your dog kept pushing your little girl into the ditch on the side of the road so she wouldn't wander into traffic. We saw what was going on and we stopped to help. You're very lucky. Your dog here saved your little girl's life. That dog is a hero."

The woman said she would have brought Christie inside the pickup, but Luke just kept barking. He knew she was a stranger, and he was being protective of Christie. The woman felt as if Luke was telling her: "Don't put this little girl in your vehicle. Keep her out here, where I can see her."

Karla thanked the woman and her husband, held Christie tighter, and reached out to hug Luke, too.

Later, she would tell the other Ames girls about what happened — about the panic she felt in those awful moments before she found Christie unharmed, and about the relief she felt holding Christie in her tightest embrace. Karla was ahead of the girls on so many fronts — from marriage to motherhood. And in experiences both awful and wonderful, she was a reminder to the rest of them about the most visceral feelings of love that a woman could have.

10
"If Not for You"

In the living room at Angela's, the girls are reviewing the boys they had in common back in Ames during their teen years. The photos they're sharing are bringing back memories.

There was sweet Darwin Trickle, of course, who at different times dated Diana, Cathy, Angela and Sheila. As a celebrated jock, he was the guy at school who could pretty much have any girl he wanted. But he never took advantage of that. The girls remember him as a gentleman who wasn't especially full of himself.

There was Jeff Mann, the cornfield keg organizer, who shared his first kiss with Marilyn in sixth grade, had one short moment with Sally at a party in high school and later dated Karen. He was a nice guy, a football player, who one day accidentally cut off his big toe while mowing a neighbor's lawn. On the football field, Jeff became known as "The Nine-Toed Wonder," a moniker preserved forever in the sports-page clippings pasted in Karla's scrapbooks.

"He had to go to the hospital and he never finished mowing the lawn, so his neighbor only paid him for half the job," Karen says. "Jeff wasn't too happy about that."

"Well, he could have finished mowing while they were waiting for the toe truck," Cathy says. It's a joke as old as the injury, but everyone still laughs. (Kelly recalls Jeff from their days together in a youth group at their Presbyterian church. Marilyn was also in the group. "Jeff was one of the few guys who could tell me to behave — and I would," Kelly says.)

The girls keep naming names — laughing, talking, recalling.

"Remember who took me to the prom?" Cathy asks. Not everyone does, but a few of the girls pull up the memory and then break into smiles. Cathy went to the prom with a boy who had a crush on her starting in junior high. He asked Cathy to be his prom date in October of their senior year — a full seven months in advance. For a high-school kid, that's a lifetime away. "I told my mom it was way too early," Cathy says. "Who asks a girl to the prom in October? What if I fell in love with someone else in all those months?" But her well-meaning mom insisted she accept the invitation, and so she did.

Once the girls' conversation turns to their lives after they left Ames, the male names they have in common dry up. In their college years and in their twenties, they were scattered. So they didn't have the same kind of immediate shorthand they had as kids. Sure, they phoned often, wrote letters, visited each other. But they were mostly on their own, with too many miles between them.

When Marilyn went off to Hamilton College in Clinton, New York, a part of her liked living in an environment where she wasn't always being identified as Dr. McCormack's daughter. She could just be Marilyn, even if she wasn't sure just who Marilyn was. At the same time, she desperately missed her family, her dad's daily wisdom, and especially the familiar connections she had with the other girls. Even though she had often felt like a slight outsider when the eleven of them prowled around Ames together, she now appreciated them more than ever. In a way, they were a lifeline for her.

Her college roommate was a girl who

loved rainbows so much that she had a rainbow mug, coat, sweater, suspenders . . . everything! An arc of rainbows covered her side of the room. The girl had an upbeat rainbow personality — she was the type who'd happily say, "Have a nice day!" She and Marilyn got along; still, Marilyn never could match the easy and loving rapport she felt with, say, Jane. She'd sit in her dorm room, surrounded by all those rainbows, and she'd try to imagine the humorous comments that Jane and the other Ames girls would likely make about the décor if they ever visited.

Sometimes, Marilyn found herself feeling strangely emotional at unexpected moments. Freshman year, she was invited to someone's house for Thanksgiving, and as soon as she arrived in the living room, she felt tears welling up in her eyes. She walked into the kitchen, and again she was choked up. What was going on? Why was she losing it? And then she realized: The home had the exact floor plan as Jane's house in Ames. She missed Jane.

She wrote a lot of letters to Jane, who had stayed in Iowa to attend Grinnell College. Marilyn's letters were often addressed to "my absolute bestest friend," and some of them were wide-eyed travelogues about the thrills of freshman-year independence. She began one letter: "I'm having a good time, a yabba-dabba-do time!" But Marilyn would also honestly assess her college experience with a bluntness she couldn't bring herself to share with any of her fellow students at Hamilton. "I want to fall in love," she wrote in one letter to Jane. "I'm physically lonely."

She told Jane about her yearnings for a real friend on campus. "Oh God, Jane, I'm depressed," she wrote. "I need a close friend here, someone who knows what I'm doing and, more important, cares about what I'm doing. Every once in a while, I just feel bummed that nobody loves me here. I have a photo of you and me together above my desk. If not for you, Babe, I'd be an absolute basket case."

Her birthday went unacknowledged by her college friends and acquaintances. In another letter to Jane, she said the day was bearable because of the cards and phone calls she received. "I heard from Karla, Diana, Jenny, and of course, you remembered. I knew you'd remember."

In those years, as the Ames girls started spreading around the country for college and then jobs, Marilyn wasn't the only one articulating a sense of longing and disconnection. It was impossible to re-create the comfortable lifelong friendships they had with each other in Ames. They missed their friendships terribly, and often questioned themselves. Diana, working as an entry-level accountant in Chicago, shared an apartment with two roommates. "I've been really bummed out, just going through a down period," she wrote to Kelly. "My two roommates have been making dinner together almost every night. I know that when three people live together, two of them will naturally get along better. Still, I've cried over this. And I haven't made any friends at work, either. I wanted to call you and ask why you are my friend, and why you think other people don't want to be." Another letter from Diana to Kelly began: "I get so sentimental about us sometimes. . . ."

From the University of South Carolina, Jenny told the other girls how she decorated her half of her dorm room. "It's so 'me,' " she wrote. "You know, I've got all kinds of Shit Sisters pictures around. It's excellent!" In saying "me" she meant, by extension, "them."

Karen, at Iowa State, lamented in letters to the others that the phone company was no longer allowing long-distance calls from the sorority house where she lived. In those days before cell phones, making long-distance calls wasn't always easy for college students. The girls without regular access to phones often felt isolated, which is why letters became their lifelines.

Karen liked most of her sorority sisters, but she was struck by the phoniness and the prejudices of some of them. At one sorority meeting, the discussion turned to whether a certain girl should be invited to pledge. A few older sisters from back east announced that the girl was Jewish, insinuating that that could be a problem. Karen immediately thought of easy-going Jane — "Why in the world would being Jewish have anything to do with anything?" she said to herself — and she realized that what she loved about the Ames girls was how accepting they were.

In those first years apart, the girls would cling to the things that kept them connected. A simple birthday present would be appreciated as if it were a way to be in each other's presence.

One summer Jane went to Portugal and brought Marilyn back a sweater. Even though it wasn't yet cold, Marilyn started wearing the sweater in September, and she sent Jane a long letter with all the details: "I must have received at least 15 compliments today on the sweater you gave me. The sweater was perfect for walking from class to class, though it's not cold enough to wear inside. So many people said, 'You look warm' or 'Did someone make that for you?' I told them, 'My best buddy from home bought it for me in Portugal.' " Marilyn just kept going on and on about that sweater. "If it's chilly outside, I'll just put it over my outfit. If it's really cold outside, I'll wear it as my outfit." It's possible that no sweater ever has been described more exuberantly. Eventually, Marilyn sewed up her sweater commentary with a simple declaration: "I love you."

Marilyn could reveal to Jane her dorkiest efforts to fit in at college. She had gone off to school with her dog-eared copy of *The Official Preppy Handbook,* the 1980 best seller, and was earnestly dressing and conducting herself based on what she'd read in the book. Jane sent back letters reassuring Marilyn that she was wonderful just the way she was, even if she was carrying a few extra pounds or wasn't dressing up to the standards set by the preppies on her campus.

As Marilyn yearned for love, a girl living on her floor — a senior — was having sex five to eight times a day. "It's a problem," Marilyn wrote to Jane. "She's quite a moaner! But at least she's graduating early.

I'm glad about that." Rather than knock on her door asking her to quiet down, Marilyn found it easier to endure the moaning and just spill everything to Jane.

While Marilyn was at Hamilton, her older sister, Sara, was working on her master's degree in psychology back at Iowa State. For her thesis, Sara had mounted a research project tracking loneliness. As the data accumulated, Sara was able to accurately predict where study participants would be on a scientifically calibrated loneliness scale. Not surprisingly, both males and females with close female friends were far less likely to be lonely. (Even when females spent time with male close friends, but little or no time with female close friends, their loneliness scores were high. Women need other women.)

As Marilyn's sister explained to her: Men who've confided only in a spouse or girlfriend can feel lost after a breakup or divorce, because they've lost their only confidant. But for women with close female friends, the end of a romantic relationship is more bearable because they haven't lost their entire support system. That's also why retirement is easier for women. Men too often define themselves by their job, while women have a social network that provides a gauge for their self-esteem in their retirement years.

Marilyn found Sara's findings reassuring. Even if she was at times struggling socially on campus, even if her romantic life wasn't what she wanted, because of her bonds with the other Ames girls, she'd be OK.

When she was in high school, Marilyn was always making lists. That's why the other Ames girls had once given her *The Book of Lists* as a birthday present. Now, in college, she compiled a long list of attributes she sought in a man and mailed it to Jane. She told Jane that she wanted to find a guy like her father. Her perfect-man laundry list included:

He'll love his own family, and eventually, he'll love mine too. He'll be educated. He'll love the outdoors. He'll appreciate the arts. He'll have a good heart. He'll want to cuddle with me. He won't feel the need to belittle me. He won't be afraid to plan for a future with me. He'll have a great sense of humor. And he won't chew with his mouth open.

"I'm too picky, aren't I?" she asked Jane.

276

"Well, if you're looking for someone like your father, that could be an impossible standard," Jane told her.

Marilyn's reply: "I know. I'll probably never get married because my expectations are so high."

At one point during college, Marilyn fell in love. He wasn't necessarily the man of her dreams, but she appreciated that he helped her feel good about herself. He was so attentive and chivalrous that she felt loved. As she told Jane: "He carries my tray to the trash cans at dinner. He opens doors for me. He writes notes and puts them in my mailbox, saying that 'a beautiful woman should always have mail in her box.'"

Later, there was another guy who didn't smile much, which bothered Marilyn, but he had a way of giving advice that reminded Marilyn of her dad. She was intrigued by him, even if she didn't feel anything for him romantically. She confided in him that she wasn't fitting in socially with certain girls at Hamilton. He told her she shouldn't expect to re-create the lifelong, close friendships she already had back in Ames.

"He says there are some people in your life that you will learn from, and then they will go their own way and you won't need them in your life anymore," Marilyn explained in a letter to Jane.

Back in Ames, Marilyn and Jane had always loved cooking and eating together. Marilyn's high-school diaries were filled with descriptions of meals shared and enjoyed. There were also plenty of descriptions of pounds added — of looking in the mirror and not being pleased with the image there. Knowing Marilyn so well, Jane filled her letters to Marilyn with encouragement and reassurances.

"I might be happier if I didn't put myself down all the time," Marilyn said to Jane in one phone call.

"You're great just the way you are," Jane replied. "You really are."

In the letters between them, Jane and Marilyn traded detailed plans for what they'd do together once they were home from college for the summer. They vowed to play the Hall and Oates song "Kiss on My List" again and again (because that's what they did when it was first released in the spring of 1981, their senior year of high school). They also planned to sit in front of the fireplace at Marilyn's house, sipping hot chocolate mixed with peppermint schnapps. Then they wanted to go over to Jane's house and, as Marilyn put it, "boogie to the Carpenters!"

Just before leaving college for the summer, Marilyn was in the computer center at Hamilton. Computers back then were these giant machines and were still being operated with thin rectangular cardboard keypunch cards. Marilyn was in the lab waiting for a fellow student. She had nothing to do, so she decided to play around and put together a computerized message for Jane. When she was finished, she stacked up all the keypunch cards and mailed them in a long manila envelope to Jane.

Days later, when Jane fed the cards into the computer at her school — with all those punched-out numbers — the message that came up was: "Isn't this groovy? I am so excited to see you in two weeks!!!! We will have a wonderful time!!!!! I. . . . . . LOVE. . . . . . YOU!!!!!!!"

Their friendship had entered the computer age.

After graduating from Hamilton, Marilyn knew she wouldn't fully enter adulthood if she settled back in Ames. She had spent her childhood bumping into people all over town who told her how great a doctor her dad was or how they had always admired her mom. Once, home from college on break, Marilyn went to a photo store to get film developed. When it came time to pay, she was $3 short. The woman behind the counter saw her name on the order blank, asked if she was Dr. McCormack's daughter, and then said, "Don't you worry about the bill, honey. If you're Dr. McCormack's daughter, the three dollars are on me."

A large part of Marilyn loved such Ames encounters. It made her feel special and lucky to be a product of her family. But, just as in college, she needed to establish her own identity. Besides, Ames was a college town and a family town. It was no place for a single woman in her twenties.

She ended up in St. Paul, mostly because her older sisters were already there and it wasn't a long drive back to Ames. It was a decision that felt safe to her. She landed a job teaching a ballroom dancing class for beginners at Arthur Murray Dance Studios, a natural fit for her outgoing warmth and ability to connect with people.

At times, she felt inferior to some of the other Ames girls, who were taking more academic and professional paths. Jane was studying for her Ph.D. in psychology. Diana was working as an accountant. Jenny had gotten involved in politics. Sally and Karen were teaching. Angela was building a public relations career.

Marilyn later got a job selling Mary Kay cosmetics.

When she was deciding whether to take the Mary Kay job, she worried about what her friends would think. The company's director said, "Do you generally rely on your friends' opinions to make a decision?"

"Yes, I guess I do," Marilyn admitted.

"Is that how you want to make decisions in the future?"

"No, I really don't," Marilyn said.

"Then, now would be a good time to start believing in your own strengths."

The director's words tapped a source of confidence in Marilyn that gave her direction in jobs and relationships. Her energy, thoughtfulness and ability to read people eventually led to jobs in insurance, ophthalmology and the publishing business.

For a while, Marilyn struggled romantically. She tried a couple of dating services. "Everyone I like doesn't like me. They don't call me back," she confided in Jane. She dated one guy a few times and then casually asked him, "What are you doing for Thanksgiving?" He actually took a step backward. "Whoa!" he said. "Back off."

Some men did show an interest in her. "But so far," she told Jane, "the guys who like me, well, they're not for me."

She and Jane — and the other Ames girls, too — would sometimes talk about how it was hard to find men who possessed the qualities they were looking for. "Why is it that I can find those attributes in plenty of women?" Jane would ask. "Why do so few men seem to have them?" She had decided that there seemed to be more interesting women in the world than interesting men. "There are definitely great guys out there," she'd say, "but not a lot of them. So a lot of really neat women who'd be great wives are not going to end up meeting someone special."

The inability to find impressive men who'd also make them swoon could be disheartening for all the girls. Marilyn briefly dated a man in Minnesota. He was obese, without social graces, and without much personality, but he was confident. He said to her, "I'm everything you're looking for!" As soon as the words left his mouth, Marilyn thought to herself: "You're not what I'm looking for at all." But she smiled and said nothing.

Eventually, most of the other Ames girls started meeting their future husbands, and Marilyn felt stuck in place. Diana was set to marry a strikingly handsome businessman; her equal in the looks department, the other girls decided. When Marilyn met him she was happy for Diana, but envious, too. Here was this guy who looked like a prince and had a complete romantic streak. He once gave Diana a Louis Vuitton purse, and when she opened it, there was a string of pearls inside. That was an incident the Ames girls couldn't stop talking about for months. Marilyn felt like the perennial bridesmaid, wondering if her time would ever come.

Jane, meanwhile, after being Marilyn's confidant in the "it's so hard to find a good guy" conversations, finally met a very special man. Problem was, he wasn't Jewish. So she put him out of her head as a prospect.

At the time, September 1985, Jane was in graduate school at Ohio University in Athens, Ohio, majoring in experimental psychology. The guy — his name was Justin — was a Ph.D. candidate in clinical psychology, and she first saw him while standing in line at orientation to get her ID card. He was wearing a blue-striped shirt and khaki pants, and Jane immediately thought, "Wow, this is a nice-looking guy."

"The thing is, he's Catholic," she later told Marilyn. "That's fine. We can just be friends."

Jane and Justin got close pretty fast, having long talks over regular lunches and evening phone conversations. Jane was impressed by what a great listener Justin could be. He was so emotionally intuitive. At least to her, it felt platonic.

But early in October, in a surprise four-hour conversation over the phone, Justin confessed to Jane that he felt far more than a friendship with her. It took Jane a few more weeks to admit to Justin that yes, perhaps she had feelings for him, too. But even at that point, the two of them had never had a romantic moment. They had never touched each other. They'd never kissed.

Jane went back to Ames for Christmas break and told the whole story to Karen and her mom. "I think this could be it," she told them. "He's the greatest guy I've ever met, but I'm scared. I don't know if I can marry a guy who isn't Jewish."

Karen's mom listened to all she had to say and then responded simply: "Honey, you have to go with your heart. If you do that, and your heart says this is the man, then you can work out the religious issues."

When Jane talked to Marilyn by phone, Marilyn offered the same advice. "You've got to go for it. Period."

After New Year's, Jane flew into Columbus, Ohio, on the same day Justin flew in

Jane and Marilyn at Jane's wedding

from his home in Rhode Island. He was standing waiting for her at her gate when her plane arrived. It was a seventy-mile drive to Athens in a rental car, and as Jane later explained to Marilyn, they both felt a heightened sense of things. "We were talking and talking. The whole conversation was just, 'Oh my God, will this even work?' "

Justin drove Jane to her apartment and parked the car, and she invited him in. It didn't take long before they shared their first kiss.

By the time Jane got married in 1989, with

Marilyn by her side, the other Ames girls had decided that Justin reminded them of a Kennedy. He was this bright guy with a New England accent and this terrific smile. "I feel like I'm talking to JFK when I'm with him," Karla liked to say. "He just has this East Coast charisma."

Justin and Jane would eventually settle in New England as academics — Justin at Brown and Miriam Hospital, Jane at Stonehill — and the girls were unanimous in deciding: There might not be enough quality guys out there, but Jane had found one.

A year later, in the fall of 1990, Marilyn's time finally came. She had joined the Jaycees board as a way to do volunteer work and to meet new people. At a Jaycees social event, she met an attractive fellow board member named Chris Johnson. He was on his way to a career as a business consultant, and he just seemed at ease with himself. The conversation had an effortless feel about it.

Marilyn threw the bait in the water first, casually saying, "I don't have anything going on this weekend."

Chris got the message. "Me, either."

He'd later say it was love at first sight. He was taken with Marilyn's eyes and with her straight-forward personality. He'd been in relationships that felt tedious, because there was such game-playing. But Marilyn just seemed so natural and honest, with a gee-whiz sense of life.

For their first date, they went on a picnic together at Lake of the Isles in Minneapolis. Marilyn packed a lunch for both of them, and they walked around the lake together. Eventually, they stopped to buy ice cream, and later, they went to Chris's condo to listen to the Broadway original cast album of *Phantom of the Opera.*

On the second date, Marilyn got bold. She asked Chris, "So how many children do you want to have?"

He answered: "As many as I can put through college."

Marilyn smiled at that. She thought it was a perfectly reasonable answer. Maybe he'd end up a billionaire and they'd have 750 kids.

Chris was a practicing Lutheran, and he told her that his faith guided his life. As he and Marilyn got more seriously involved, he encouraged her to find her way closer to her own faith. Her dad had been a questioning Christian, and that had influenced Marilyn over the years. As Chris got to know Dr. McCormack, he suspected that the 1960 auto accident had been a turning point for him. "Having lost a child in a tragedy like that, he couldn't help but curse God," Chris told Marilyn. "And your dad was a doctor, unable to find a way to save his son. That had to add to the pain. Anyway, that's my hypothesis on his feelings about God." Chris helped Marilyn better understand her father, and at the same time, he held her hand as she came to embrace a life more centered around faith.

Within a year, Marilyn was on the phone with Jane. "I've got a question," she said. "Would you be my matron of honor?"

Jane thought of the thousands of hours she and Marilyn had spent talking about love, wondering about the possibility of marriage, doubting whether they (or any of the girls) would find their ultimate soul mate.

"Would I be your matron of honor?" Jane asked, and paused before answering.

If you've spent your entire life knowing you were the most qualified person in the world for a certain job, and then the offer finally comes, well, it's beyond meaningful.

"You know what?" Jane said. "I just happen to be free that day. I'll be there."

11
THE BONDS
OF POP CULTURE

The girls have piled into two cars, and they're headed to a restaurant in downtown Raleigh for the reunion's only night out. In Angela's car, Cathy is answering questions and the mood is giddy.

As is often the case when they get together, the girls have been pumping Cathy for the latest trends from California. Over the years, Cathy has told them about enema-loving Hollywood stars who, while in her makeup chair, would gush to her about the therapeutic value of colonics. At other times, Cathy has told the girls about the good karma and positive energy to be found in crystals. And once, when Karla, Kelly and Diana visited Cathy in L.A., Cathy was in a soy phase. (Karla kept saying, "Look, I'm from the Midwest. I want dairy. I want cheese and a glass of milk. All you have in this refrigerator is soy!")

Now, here in Angela's car, no one can stop

laughing as Cathy reports on yet another trend she's been hearing about on the West Coast: "the Aussie makeover." Cathy has no personal interest in this, so-called down under cosmetic procedure. But she has learned the details about vaginal Aussie makeover specialists call "asymmetrical" issues brought on by age and childbirth.

From there, the discussion turns to anal bleaching, a new cosmetic procedure to bleach the pigmentation of the most private circle of skin on a person's body.

As the girls laugh and cringe about this, Angela comes up with a marketing plan. "A company could offer a service where they bleach a gerbil," she says, "and then they send the gerbil right up there. They could call it 'The Herbal Gerbil.' " Everyone roars at that.

Eventually, the conversation morphs into a discussion about body image, dieting and the new horizons of healthful eating. "Mark my words," Cathy says. "In two years, you'll all be cooking with coconut oil."

"Or bleaching with it!" Angela says.

The girls always have been each other's pop-culture monitor and barometer. They've spent their lives trading stories of fads worth emulating, singers worth appreciating and their own celebrity sightings.

In elementary school and junior high, Sally and Cathy shared crushes on teen idol David Cassidy. Sally was also partial to Bobby Sherman. Diana, meanwhile, had a "Donny Osmond Kissing Poster," which was very useful when the other girls visited and had an urge to kiss Donny Osmond.

The girls watched *The Partridge Family, The Cosby Show, M*A*S*H,* and, in reruns, *Gilligan's Island.* In their preteen years, they thrilled to the PG sexuality of *Love American Style.* Each week, the show offered a few unrelated episodes about love, romance and sexual urges, and it seemed so risqué at the time. The girls didn't really notice that parts of the show were politically incorrect — the leering men, the women as playthings. It just seemed like a cool vision of adulthood, with the same large brass bed playing a role in so many of the episodes.

In those days of just a handful of channels, the girls often would watch programming with their parents. Cathy liked to come home from school in the afternoon and sit on the couch with her mom to watch Merv Griffin. Her friends also watched talk shows with their parents: Dinah Shore's *Dinah's Place* or *The Mike Douglas Show.* It was so unlike TV viewing today. The Ames girls' children are more apt to be on the computer in the afternoon, or they have all sorts of youth-focused channels to choose from — the Disney Channel, MTV, Nickelodeon, the Cartoon Network — with programming designed specifically for them. As kids, many of the Ames girls liked watching stars from their parents' and grandparents' eras; it was kind of cool when Jimmy Stewart or Cary Grant showed up on Merv or Dinah or Mike, offering a window into this older world. These shows helped young and old get to know each other's icons.

For those living in Iowa, the forces of pop culture emanating from the East and West Coasts could seem very far away. But sometimes there would be reminders that Iowa, too, was on the map. On *Star Trek,* the character of Captain James T. Kirk proudly hailed from Iowa. There was even a line in the 1986 movie *Star Trek IV* in which a woman from twentieth-century Earth comes upon Kirk and asks him if he's from outer space. "No, I'm from Iowa," he tells her. "I only work in outer space."

Nice line. For Iowans, it offered a reminder that even the sky wasn't the limit.

Though TV and movie stars rarely or never made it to Ames, musicians did. They passed through on concert tours or, at the least, came as close as Des Moines. And whether they came to town or not, the Ames girls' connections to their favorite singers and groups were often as close as their bedside tables. Cathy considered it a big deal that Sally had a record player in her room. They'd sit in her room in the afternoons, playing records by the Osmond Brothers and the Jackson 5. Then, as they got older, their tastes ran to groups such as Styx and Journey. Over at Jane's house, she and Marilyn were often listening to Fleetwood Mac: "Don't stop thinking about tomorrow . . ." Diana and Kelly obsessed over a certain Andy Gibb video.

Sheila, Cathy and Sally attended their first concert, a performance by Bread, with Sheila's dad as chaperone. Later, when the girls started driving, they'd head south to Des Moines for shows by Foreigner, Little River Band and, at the Iowa Jam outdoor rock concert, Ted Nugent.

Several of the girls stood in long lines to get Bruce Springsteen tickets when he came to Ames in 1981. (Bruce's posters and backstage passes actually featured an illustration of a large ear of corn; he knew where he was performing.) At one point toward the end of the concert, Bruce pulled the young daughter of one of the Ames High teachers, Mr. Daddow, out of the audience to join him onstage! As Mr. Daddow's daughter danced along with Bruce, and some of the Ames girls danced in the audience, it was an absolute vicarious thrill, as if Bruce had invited all of them on stage.

The girls sometimes rewrote lyrics to their favorite songs. As senior prom approached, Marilyn wrote in her diary about how she and her friends had recast the words to the Carpenters' song "Close to You": "Why do tears suddenly appear / Every time, prom is near? / Just like me, girls long to be, at the prom . . ."

By high school, most of the girls agreed that though Rick Springfield was cute, Rod Stewart was just about the sexiest thing going. There was something about the gravel in his voice, his unbuttoned shirts and that sly smile of his. As the girls got older, and so did he, they still felt that Mod Rod had a certain magnetism. As Cathy puts it one night at the reunion: "Now he's ugly sexy." Her words make perfect sense to everyone else. There's just something about an ugly sexy guy that's even more viscerally tantalizing than a handsome sexy guy.

On countless other pop-culture fronts, the girls have spent decades keeping each other

Diana, Jane and Rod Stewart, then

Diana, Jane and Rod Stewart, now

informed — and amused. They taught each other the dance moves to accompany the soundtrack to *Saturday Night Fever.* Later in the seventies, Karen was the first one to get baggy jeans, pleated in the front, and then they all wore them. In 1981, Diana turned everyone on to the mushy soundtrack for the movie *Endless Love,* which she played again and again each night as she tried to fall asleep in her freshman dorm room.

The girls helped each other catalogue the various stunts associated with watching *The Rocky Horror Picture Show.* Many years later, at an adult reunion, they went as a group to see the new *Sex and the City* movie; the girls who were fans of the TV show helpfully explained all the idiosyncrasies of the characters to the girls who didn't watch it much.

When Jane went to Spain for a semester in 1984, the girls mailed her letters with helpful news reports from the States. It was very selective reporting. For instance, Diana prepared what she titled "An Update on America." Her reporting for Jane focused solely on the quirkiest news: an out-of-control Pepsi commercial, a disconcerting muffin recall, and the details of an attractive but unknown "fox."

First, the Pepsi debacle: This was a pyrotechnic accident that occurred during the filming of a TV commercial for the soft drink. The victim? Michael Jackson, then twenty-five years old. "His hair caught on fire!" Diana wrote. "I really thought he was gone!" She then reassured Jane by saying that the singed singer went on to win eight Grammy awards. (Diana's point: They put out the flame on his head, but Michael Jackson was still red hot.) She also decided Jane needed to know the lyrics to "Eat It," the new Weird Al Yankovic parody of "Beat It," and so she typed them out for her: "Don't you know that other kids are starving in Japan / So eat it, just eat it . . ."

Regarding the muffin recall: "There's this big government scam on this chemical called EDB [ethylene dibromide]," Diana wrote. "It gets rid of bugs or something, but it causes cancer. Anyway, it's in stuff like Duncan Hines blueberry muffin mix, so it has been pulled off grocery shelves. We were all quite interested in this development considering we have consumed massive quantities of muffins this year." (Jane was left with the impression that if the other Ames girls didn't die from the EDB, they'd explode from overdosing on muffins.)

As for the unknown fox: "There's a new movie out called *Footloose*," Diana wrote.

"It's like *Flashdance,* but with a guy. The guy dancer is some unknown fox who does gymnastics, too." (For the record, the unknown fox in question was Kevin Bacon.)

The girls also loved sharing reports of their own celebrity encounters.

Marilyn worked one summer in food service at Snow Mountain Ranch in Winter Park, Colorado. One night, a guest at the hotel looked very familiar and everyone in the kitchen started buzzing. It was Ann B. Davis, who played Alice the housekeeper on *The Brady Bunch.*

In letters to the other Ames girls, Marilyn described how she approached the actress: "After dinner, I went up to her and said, 'Miss Davis, I decided that I would regret it if I didn't come up to see you, so I've decided to introduce myself.' She said, 'Well, what's your name?' And I said, 'Marilyn,' and she gave me a hug saying, 'Glad to meet you, Marilyn!' "

Marilyn wanted proof of the encounter to show the other girls, so she got her camera and Ann B. Davis posed with her for a picture. 'She's a great woman," Marilyn wrote to Jane three days later. "Unfortunately, the picture was #24 on a roll of 24." The photo didn't come out, which was very disappointing. Would everyone really believe her? (Of course, Marilyn was always so earnest and honest that none of the Ames girls doubted her Ann B. Davis interaction. Who'd make that up anyway?)

Karen had an "almost" celebrity encounter that was intriguing to the other girls, even though she never actually saw the celebrity in question. In her early twenties, Karen worked as a dental assistant in Ames. One Sunday afternoon, the dentist she worked for, Donald Good, got an unexpected call. Billy Joel, in town for a concert, had chipped a tooth. A crowd of 14,800 was slated to gather within hours at the Hilton Coliseum in Ames to see the show, and Dr. Good was asked to meet Joel at his office to try to repair the damaged tooth before show time.

Though the dentist thought about calling in Karen and other office staffers for help, once he looked at the tooth, he decided he could treat the singer without assistance. Karen wasn't happy about that, of course. But she did have a story to tell the other girls, because Billy Joel ended up giving Dr. Good choice seats to the show and then thanking him from the stage. The singer told the audience about his chipped tooth and the dentist who made it possible for him to perform that night. Just before singing

"Only the Good Die Young," Joel dedicated the song to Dr. Good.

Some of the Ames girls thought the dedication was a bit ghoulish, given that Dr. Good, at age forty-three, was still young enough to actually die young. Even so, Karen found it all terrific. She enjoyed contemplating the idea that Billy Joel had been sitting in the very chair in the very office where she worked, and that the dental instruments she sterilized had actually been in his mouth. It was a pretty close brush with a major celebrity, all things considered.

For her part, Angela had cool stories to share, too. One day in 1991 she went to see the movie *Thelma and Louise.* There was an actor in the movie who looked exactly like this pleasant-but-not-especially attractive journalism major she knew from her days at the University of Missouri. She had been the social chair of her sorority, Chi Omega, and this guy had been social chair of his fraternity, Sigma Chi. They had planned joint parties together. He was nice enough, Angela always thought, though as she later told the girls, "he was kind of smallish, and not the sort of guy who stood out in any way."

Because she thought this actor in *Thelma and Louise* looked like him, Angela stuck around to watch the credits at the end, just to see if she was right. Sure enough, the actor was Brad from Sigma Chi. "Wow," Angela thought to herself. "Brad has gotten better looking since college."

When she first told this story to the other girls, it didn't make a great impression on them. OK, Angela knew some guy who got some minor role in a movie. But soon enough, as Brad Pitt's career took off, Angela's connections to him seemed pretty impressive. She even had an old calendar with his phone number scribbled on it; she had it so she could call him with questions about who'd buy the beer kegs or what time a party should start. (Angela also crossed paths during college with Sheryl Crow, who belonged to Kappa Alpha Theta. Sheryl was in a local Top 40 band Cashmere that played a lot of fraternity parties. Angela always thought Sheryl was very talented, but, as she later told the other Ames girls, "very plain-looking. She got better looking after college, too. Just like Brad.")

Brad. Sheryl. Among the Ames girls, Angela probably comes in second in the ability-to-name-drop sweepstakes. But no one, of course, can top Cathy.

Working as a makeup artist, Cathy has had hundreds of celebrity interactions and helped Victoria Principal develop a cosmetics line. Some celebrities get very chatty in the makeup chair, confiding in Cathy about their affairs or their deepest secrets. Cathy knows when it's not appropriate to reveal things, even to the Ames girls.

Over the years, she has resisted sharing too many stories with them, even though they were always eager for details. In L.A., she and her fellow makeup artists make the sound of a dish dropping to the ground every time any of them name-drop, just to keep each other in check. So Cathy didn't want to seem like she was bragging to the Ames girls. Still, sometimes she relented and revealed the behind-the-scenes machinations.

She told the Ames girls about the time Martha Stewart's aides — her "people" — demanded that Cathy get new makeup brushes before working on Martha's face for a Kmart commercial. "I was thinking, 'What? My kit is immaculately clean and I've used these brushes on everyone else. I'm not buying all new stuff,' " Cathy said. On the day of filming in Arizona — it was a scene in which Martha was hanging towels across the Grand Canyon — Cathy smiled at the handlers and never told them whether she had or hadn't bought new brushes. Martha arrived and was very pleasant; she never questioned the brushes. "Sometimes, the people around the celebrity are the ones who are most difficult," Cathy said. "Maybe Martha didn't really care."

It's easy to get jaded in her line of work, but once in a while Cathy has encounters that make her feel like a teenaged girl again. Those are the stories she most enjoys telling her Ames friends.

She thrilled them with her description of the night in 1997 when she was called to Sting's house to style his wife Trudie's hair. She and Trudie were in the large master bedroom, and in walked Sting, wearing a silk bathrobe and holding a cup of tea.

"Baby, you need a haircut," Trudie said to him, then turned and said, "Cathy, would you mind cutting my husband's hair, too?"

So Sting sat down and Cathy began trimming. From then on, things felt kind of dreamlike. "He actually started singing 'Roxanne'!" she later told the other girls. "It was totally surreal. He was talking about his kids, and I told him I was from a big family from Iowa, and that I liked his music, and then he just started singing . . . 'ROXanne!!' " (The song had come out in 1978, their sophomore year at Ames High, and most of the Ames girls had absolutely loved

303

it. Sting almost rivaled their hero, Rod Stewart.)

Sting's hair was already a kind of buzz cut, and Cathy worried that she'd accidentally knick him while he was hitting the high notes in "Roxanne." He survived the haircut unscathed.

After the haircut and the impromptu performance, Sting went to the sink and brushed his teeth, still chatting away — or was he still singing? — as he brushed. Just then, his two-year-old son walked in, and Trudie asked if Cathy could give him a haircut, too. So the boy sat on Sting's lap while Cathy cut his hair.

A few minutes later, the door to the bedroom opened and in walked Madonna. Yes, Madonna! Turned out, Sting and Trudie were hosting a fund-raiser dinner party, and Madonna was invited.

She didn't start singing "Material Girl," but she did say to Cathy, "What are you, a barber?"

Trudie explained that Cathy was actually a makeup artist sent by the agency to do her hair.

Cathy never mentioned to Madonna that her mother had the same name. "I had Sting in the chair, his kid on his lap, scissors in my hand, 'Roxanne' in my ears, and Madonna is standing there. So no, at that moment, I wasn't thinking about my mother."

Karla actually credits the conception of her third child to Cathy's glamorous career and her celebrity encounters. It happened in October 1992.

At the time, Cathy was traveling the world on Michael Jackson's eighteen-month-long Dangerous Tour. One night, from her hotel room in Bucharest, Cathy placed a call to Karla, who was still living in Idaho. Christie was then almost three years old. And Karla and Bruce had also welcomed a son, Ben, ten months earlier.

It was late afternoon at Karla's house, and she was sitting in a rocking chair in the nursery. Little Christie was on the floor, playing with their dog. Ben was on Karla's lap.

Like any mother with two young kids, Karla was feeling a bit overwhelmed. It had been a long day, so Karla decided to have a glass of wine while she waited for Bruce to come home from work. She sipped the wine, rocked Ben, kept an eye on Christie and talked to Cathy.

They had a long conversation, and at first Karla was just enthralled with all of Cathy's stories. Cathy had been hired to apply makeup only on the background singers and dancers, not on Michael Jackson himself. But as Cathy explained, one day Michael's makeup artist had to return to the States unexpectedly.

"So there was a knock on the door of the makeup room," Cathy told Karla, "and Michael's assistant said to me, 'Cathy, Michael is ready for you now.' I was being summoned to his dressing room.

"So I go walking in with a tray of my stuff, and as usual, he already has on makeup. But for the stage, he'd always enhance it.

"Anyway, Michael looks up at me and smiles, and he signals to me to put down the makeup tray. And we both knew that he didn't need me. He was pretty good at putting on his own makeup every day. So I just said to him, 'You know, Mike, if you need anything, I'm right next door.' And I walked out.' "

Karla ate it all up. Cathy told her about the private jet she and the others on tour were flying around on. "I've never even had a passport before, and now I'm seeing the whole world — Oslo, Dublin, Berlin, Barcelona . . . ," she said. She also told Karla that during a rehearsal she had gotten to dance on stage with Michael, just fooling around, and he seemed to enjoy their interaction.

For one show, Cathy filled in for the person whose job it was to hand Michael water and a towel on stage toward the end of the show. "He always throws the towel into the audience," Cathy said. "Every night. And no matter what country we're in, people go insane!"

Cathy was just explaining her life with a true sense of wonder. She wasn't bragging. And Karla was completely proud of her. But as the conversation continued, Karla started feeling surprisingly envious. "Here I am," Karla thought, "a stay-at-home mom sitting in a rocking chair in a nursery, and there's Cathy. She's living this incredible life while my life is just here in this house."

She couldn't exactly tell Cathy how she was feeling. So she kept listening and asking questions.

She heard the front door opening. "Bruce just got in," Karla told Cathy. "I've got to go. Stay safe. I love you."

Just then Bruce entered the room, looking awfully handsome to her. Given the combination of the wine, the conversation about Cathy's exciting life, and the swirl of emotions, Karla was feeling passionate. She and Bruce had no intention of having another child just yet. After all, Ben was only ten months old.

But that's the night her third child, Jackie, was conceived.

The other Ames girls know the story of that passionate night in Idaho — how Cathy (and Michael Jackson) unwittingly helped bring a new life into the world — and it comes up in conversation at the North Carolina reunion. "We were all younger then," Sally says, "and what Cathy was doing was completely impressive to us. It was just a big wow."

"A lot bigger than any of our wows," Marilyn says.

They all say they were excited for Cathy, and slightly envious, too.

Now, of course, Cathy speaks openly of how she often envies the other girls. They all have been married. They all have children. "My life took a different turn," she says.

Cathy had moved to California with a boyfriend from Iowa. They were together nine years. She had thought they probably would get married, but for a variety of reasons, it didn't happen. They broke up when Cathy was thirty years old and they've remained close friends. She has dated ever since, but hasn't found a man she wanted to marry.

Cathy says her marital status does not separate her from the other girls. "I could choose to be the outsider because I'm not married and don't have kids," she says. "If I just wanted to focus on one part of my life, I could certainly alienate myself." She enjoys hearing the domestic details of the other girls' lives, and tries to understand what that's like for them.

Each year at Christmas, she writes a tongue-in-cheek poem and sends it to the other girls. In 2001 it began: "I hope your holiday season is full of joy / I'm still single . . . there isn't a boy / So I don't have a picture of me to send / Unless it's of me, and another gay friend / Don't get me wrong, I'm happy as can be / I still feel sure I'll one day be a 'we' . . ." In another letter to all the girls she wrote: "My love life? Well, I love life. That's about all to report."

Every so often, the other girls find some geographically undesirable Midwesterner to suggest to her. She almost always passes, but appreciates the efforts.

In the end, Cathy, living in glamorous Beverly Hills, offers the girls a perspective that took decades to completely get their arms around.

When Karla thinks back to that day in Idaho, she says, "Life felt so ordinary —

home with Christie and Ben, changing the umpteenth diaper. And here was Cathy; her life was so special. She was hanging out with celebrities and flying all over the world with Michael Jackson."

For those at home with kids, it was easier to take their lives for granted.

12
THEIR FIRST CHILD

From the moment she received it in a Christmas card, Jane has loved a certain black-and-white sepia-toned photo of Karla and her family. It was taken in a studio near their home — they had moved to Edina, Minnesota — in the fall of 2001. Karla, Bruce and their three children are sitting on the floor, their arms nonchalantly on each other's shoulders or knees. They seem so comfortable pressed together, all of them barefoot, in jeans and casual shirts.

Karla looks like an absolute beauty. If the photo were in a clothing catalogue, she'd be the idealized vision of the modern wife and mother. Her legs are tucked sideways as she leans into Bruce, who is cradling the family dog between his arms.

Eight-year-old Jackie, a perky smile on her face, pokes her head between Bruce and Karla. Ben, age nine, is petting the dog with his left hand, and resting his head on

311

Merry
Christmas
Love,
Bruce,
Karla,
Christie,
Ben,
Jackie

Bruce's shoulder. And then there's Christie, age eleven, who is just beaming in her sleeveless shirt, her hand nestled at the edge of Karla's hair. Christie is just starting to lose her little-girl looks. In her pretty face, it's easy to see the teenager to come.

Mom, Dad, the three kids, the dog. "This is what people think about when they picture the all-American family," Jane thought to herself the first time she looked at it.

Here in North Carolina, Jane is telling some of the other girls how she decided to use that photo in a psychological study she recently conducted at Stonehill College. The research project, which involved 140 participants, investigated the effects of family values on sexual prejudice and homo-phobia. Karla's family was used to get participants thinking about a traditional family structure.

When Jane asked Karla for permission to use the family photo, Karla was very touched. She tells the other girls she feels honored that Jane would want to use her family in her work. "I really love that photo, too," Karla says softly.

It was a snapshot in time, an image of her family at a serene and very happy moment.

The Ames girls find a lot of admirable traits in each other's children. They've loved watching all twenty-one of the kids grow, and seeing all the personalities develop. When the girls hang out together as families, it's as if they're stepping into the future and back into the past all at once. Being with each other's kids sometimes gives them a feeling of being in a time machine, because when they look at all of their daughters' faces — from certain angles, or when the children grin or giggle — they can again see Kelly, Marilyn, Karen, Sally or Diana as young girls back in Ames. So many of the children's faces feel familiar to them; it's both disorienting and comforting.

The girls first had that feeling when

Karla's daughter, Christie, was born. They've always had a very special place in their hearts for Christie. Part of their affection was rooted in the fact that Christie was the first child born to any of them. But there was also something incredibly endearing about Christie herself. She had this life-loving glow about her. Some kids you can just tell are special, and Christie was one of them.

As an infant, she got passed around by the other Ames girls as almost a trial child. The girls held her in their arms, looked in her eyes, cooed to her, and thought about the mothers they hoped to be.

Once they all started having children of their own, the girls often turned to Karla to learn what Christie was up to developmentally — walking, talking, potty training, everything — so they'd have a sense of what was ahead for their own children.

From just about the moment she was born on January 9, 1990, Christie had been an easy baby with a contagious smile. She grew into a happy kid, extremely close to both Karla and Bruce. Karla loved observing how comfortable Christie felt in Bruce's strong arms.

As Christie got older, she developed this fun-loving devilish side. She'd get a kick out of manipulating kids, especially her two siblings, Ben and Jackie, who were two and three years younger. In Christie's mind, younger kids lived to serve her. And she was so pleasant and engaging that other kids always fell for whatever she was asking of them.

"You know what would be fun? If you each took turns giving me backrubs," a ten-year-old Christie would say to Jackie and her little friends. "Go ahead. Give it a try. You'll love it."

And so the younger girls would line up and do just that. And they did love it. Being in Christie's presence was a blast.

"There's a deviant side to her," Karla joked in conversations with the other Ames girls. "She's so smart and manipulative. And she never gets caught at it."

Sometimes, Karla would sit nearby and marvel at Christie's audacity.

"Hey, Ben! Hey, Jackie!" Christie would say. "Let's play servant."

Servant?

"I'll sit here and you guys will be my servants."

Karla tried to explain to the other Ames girls why Christie could be such an operator and, at the same time, be so lovable. "Maybe it's because she has the cutest, sweetest giggle. Maybe that's why she gets away with everything. We all just love that giggle."

Christie had Ben and Jackie fetch things and do her bidding. "OK, servants," she'd say. "After you get me a glass of water, go over there and get me all the Barbies with blond hair."

Given Christie's Barbie collection, the blondes alone were a whole army. But her little servants complied.

Christie loved playing with Barbies, even as a preteen, well after her friends had outgrown them. She had bins of Barbies. She had the Barbie moving van and the deluxe Barbie Town. She had plenty of Kens, too, of course.

"Christie is so mature in so many ways," Karla explained one day to Kelly. "She's got a self-confidence that comes from being wise beyond her years. So her Barbies don't embarrass her."

Karla was secretly pleased that Christie was such a die-hard Barbie lover. "Kids grow up way too fast. I'm glad she's still playing with her Barbies. It's better than doing who-knows-what."

Christie may have held on to her dolls longer than most girls do, but in other ways, she was far ahead of her peers. The Ames girls found Christie to be a thoughtful observer of the world. She was the sort of kid with whom you could have a very adult conversation. She listened intently to what adults were saying. She questioned. She commented. Sometimes Karla felt obliged to tell her to go away; maybe other adults didn't want her horning in on their conversations.

When the Ames girls' families got together, Christie reveled in being mature. She would look after the younger kids like a doting mother hen. She'd enter a room where the adults had gathered, and the other children would tag along behind her. She was like a Pied Piper, rising from the basement with her own entourage.

Christie had taken babysitting courses at age eleven and had become a very popular neighborhood sitter. Parents liked that she was sweet, confident and responsible. Younger girls loved her because she'd go right to the floor with them to play Barbies until bedtime. And she loved turning household objects into playthings. She'd pretend that laundry baskets were boats; she'd have her servants push her around in them. Sometimes she'd push them, too.

Especially when she was young, some of the Ames girls and their kids thought Chris-

317

tie looked just like the Olsen twins from *Full House.* Christie was completely flattered by that. Karla loved watching her get excited about things. She loved playing soccer, but she also loved being what Karla called "a girly-girl." "She runs like a girl — arms flying," Karla said to Kelly. "When she runs for the school bus, those arms of hers are just everywhere."

Even though none of the Ames girls' children lived in Ames, Christie sensed the importance of carrying on the girls' bonds to this new generation. Once, when the girls' families were gathered together, Christie made friendship bracelets for all the kids to take back to wherever they lived. She saw what her mothers' friends from Ames meant to her, and she wanted to build her own connections with the other "Ames" kids.

"Now you're my friend!" she told the children of the other Ames girls as she handed each one of them a bracelet. "And now I'm your friend."

During the summer of 2002, Christie just wasn't feeling well, and on September 16, after several doctors visits and a lot of tests, Karla and Bruce learned why. Christie was diagnosed with acute myelogenous leukemia. It was a devastating moment for Karla and Bruce — Bruce would later call it one of the saddest days of his life — but they quickly went about figuring out their options.

The other Ames girls were alarmed and worried, of course. They called or emailed Karla, each expressing her love, her promise of prayers, her offer of help. Karla appreciated it all, but was overwhelmed with doctors' visits and decisions. She couldn't spend a lot of time on the phone. Within days, however, there was a way for the girls to channel their concern — to remain in Christie's life, and in Karla's.

Christie learned about an organization called Caring Bridge, which allows the families of ill children to post messages and updates on a Web site. Friends and loved ones can visit the site to keep track of a patient's progress and to post messages of their own.

In many cases, the parents write the entries. Christie, then twelve, wanted to write the online diary herself. Her first entry was written from her room at a children's hospital in Minneapolis on September 27, 2002, at 5:19 P.M.: "Hey, thank you everyone for caring about me. I am doing fine now. On Sunday I go to chemo again. I still have my hair!!!" The next day she wrote another short note: "My friend Meggan is here and she has Krispy Kremes!"

In those early entries, Christie certainly sounded like a kid. But over the months that followed, her voice matured as she did. Her writing became philosophical and achingly honest, revealing a courageousness that the Ames girls found remarkable.

She wrote clearly about every detail of her experience. At times, for instance, she had trouble keeping food down. "The doctor said my body is eating itself. So they decided to give me a naso-gastric tube. It goes into my nose and all the way down to the small intestines. The doctor put it there, rather than in the stomach, because it is far enough down so I can't throw up the food. It is pretty much baby formula in a bag. I am already putting the weight on. I will get up to 'fighting weight' in no time." She was concentrating on the bright side. "I really don't like the tube, but I am getting used to it. It's nice to have some of the pressure taken off of me to eat."

Some of the girls thought Christie's diary was reminiscent of Anne Frank's. Day after day, she described a world that had been terribly unfair to her, and yet Christie's sense of hope and optimism rarely wavered. Of course, unlike the diary of Anne Frank, read well after she had died, Christie's diary was read in real time by friends and loved ones. She'd post an entry, and minutes or hours later it was being read by her thirteen-year-old friends and by the Ames girls spread across the country.

As she described her friendships in the online diary, the Ames girls were transported back to their earliest days with each other. Some of them checked the Caring Bridge Web site every few hours, waiting for Christie's latest entry, hoping for good news.

In suburban Philadelphia, Karen felt she was becoming obsessed with Christie's site. She found herself reading and rereading it ten times a day. She'd come home with groceries, and before she even put them away, she would head for the computer to see if there were any postings from Christie or from other Ames girls giving Christie encouragement.

All the Ames girls thought back to their interactions with Christie over the years. Kelly found herself focused on how inquisitive Christie could be. Once, when Christie was almost two years old, she and Kelly were walking together, and Christie kept looking over her shoulder. She seemed to be very frustrated. "What's the problem?" Kelly asked. Christie had found her shadow, it turned out, and each time she tried to step away from it, there it was. "It's stuck to me," she told Kelly.

Whenever the Ames girls had gotten together, Christie had a habit of sidling up to Karla and eavesdropping on the women — trying to figure out the world of adult friendships, eager to chime in. Karla would shoo her away, sending her off to watch the other kids, which seemed appropriate at the time. But Kelly, for one, was now feeling regretful that they had been so dismissive. Her kids had begun doing the same sort of eavesdropping, and Kelly found herself hesitant to send them away. She wished she could go back in time and welcome Christie into the circle of Ames women.

Now all they could do was read Christie's diary, feeling helpless as she described her nausea, fevers and vomiting spells. The Ames girls would read the entries, teary-eyed, wondering how much more her little body could take. But Christie had a way of couching bad news with humor. In one entry she wrote: "My faith in 'everything happening for a reason' is slowly slipping. Just kidding! But I'm sure ready to be done with puking and pain." She'd give regular updates about other ill kids at the hospital, asking her readers to keep them in their hearts, too.

In their postings to Christie, the Ames girls' messages matched their personalities. Jane always found the most positive news and commented on it: "Glad to hear you had a good day, Christie. Your great attitude is so inspiring for all of us, young and old. Continue to stay strong." Jane could be playful, too: "We loved the new pictures of you with your friends! How many rules did you have to break to get all those lovely friends of yours in your hospital room?"

Cathy, usually reluctant to boast of her celebrity connections, made an exception for Christie: "I'm going to be traveling to London with Pink for ten days. Are you a fan? Would you like some 'swag'?" Another time, Cathy was working as Courteney Cox's makeup artist. She knew Christie was a huge *Friends* fan, so she had the show send her mugs, a hat, a T-shirt.

Meanwhile, Kelly took on the persona of the fun aunt, making funky suggestions. "Does your school celebrate homecoming, Christie?" she asked in one posting. "To get you in the fall spirit, your mom should TP your hospital room. Have the nurses catch her in the act and chase her down the halls. ☺" After the East Coast blackout in the summer of 2003, Kelly wrote to Christie:

323

"We had no idea that the cord we tripped over and disconnected from the wall while touring Niagara Falls would trigger the blackout. . . ."

Still, at times, Kelly's postings had a more reflective tone: "Thanks for being such a wonderful teacher through your Web site, Christie. Many people look forward to your words and we have all learned so much from you."

Christie often wrote about her feelings for Ben and Jackie, wishing they could have a more normal life, despite the abnormal effect her illness was having on the family. In the middle of everything, Jackie had a far-less-serious medical issue; she needed to have her tonsils taken out. Still, Christie didn't dismiss it as trivial. She described her kid sister's recovery and wished her well.

One day, Karla cooked homemade chicken soup for Christie, and Jackie held the container on her lap as they drove it to the hospital. While they were driving, the lid came off and the soup spilled. Jackie ended up with second-degree burns and had to be taken to the hospital's emergency room. The Ames girls couldn't imagine how Karla could cope with all of this — having two daughters on opposite ends of the same hospital.

Jane found herself thinking: "We all love our kids. But Karla loves her kids with a capital bold-faced L. She's so devoted. It seems absolutely cruel for her to be the one going through this."

The Ames girls pooled money to pay for a cleaning service to clean Karla's home and to have catered meals sent in. Karla actually was living at the hospital, in Christie's room. Even though their home was just a few minutes away, Karla didn't go back to the house for a month or six weeks at a time. She didn't want to be away from Christie. One night, because her other two children missed her, she went to the house and Bruce spent the night at the hospital. It didn't feel right.

The Ames girls sent email after email to Karla, letting her know they were thinking about her. Karla rarely responded. When they called, she wouldn't call back or she'd speak only briefly. "I have to get back to Christie," she'd say. The girls found it all very frustrating and painful. Kelly thought to herself: "We're locked out of Karla's life just when she needs us the most."

As Karla saw it, she had to cast her friends to the side. On the day Christie was diagnosed, a doctor told Karla that Christie could die. Given that, Karla wanted to be

Karla and Christie in Minneapolis

with her daughter every possible minute. The Ames girls would have to understand. For the most part, they did.

For a while, Kelly, living in Minnesota, was visiting the hospital every Wednesday, and reporting back to the other girls. "Karla is in good spirits — very positive and upbeat, which fills the room. Christie looked good and was in good spirits," she wrote in one email. "She has the power to transform the air around her."

For Kelly, those Wednesday experiences were life-changing. She saw the loving bonds between Karla and Bruce, and between the couple and their three children. Seeing their strength and closeness, especially given the awful circumstances, made Kelly reconsider her own home life, her own marriage. It was on those Wednesdays that she began to think seriously about the possibility of ending her marriage.

Kelly's hospital visits had a different effect on Karla, however. Each time Kelly stopped by, her reporter's instincts kicked in, and she'd have a barrage of questions about Christie's care or how Karla was holding up. She meant well, but Karla found it annoying. After a while, Karla began to view Kelly's visits as intrusions, and the questions as "the interrogation." Once, Kelly came with her entire family, and Karla felt churned up inside. "They're making small talk," she thought to herself, "and all I can think about is germs."

Karla had been sleeping night after night, on a pull-out bed in the hospital room, and Kelly was amazed by her commitment to be by Christie's side twenty-four hours a day. Kelly later wrote out her impressions: "How can Karla be there every night, with all the sounds, the glowing lights, the smells of that place? I would not be able to do it. God forbid if it was my kid, I would have asked my parents or friends to take a shift."

On her visits, Kelly sometimes would ask Karla to take a break, to walk with her down the hall to the visitors' lounge for a few minutes. Invariably, Karla declined to go. "I want to be with Christie," she said.

When the other Ames girls called Karla and asked if they could visit, Karla turned them down. Visitors were hard on Christie, who was often so weak, and they threatened her immune system. If friends were going to be there, Karla decided, they ought to be Christie's friends, not Karla's friends.

Diana came from Arizona to visit, but Karla asked that she just go to the house, not the hospital, and see Bruce, Ben and Jackie. Karla stayed at the hospital. Bruce seemed to be doing OK. He was able to joke around. He said the neighbors had sent over yet another care package dinner of "pity pitas." It all seemed surreal to Diana, so unlike the easy visits of the past.

Karla found herself contemplating the fact that she didn't know the whereabouts of her own biological parents. She couldn't help but wonder: What insights to Christie's illness might be revealed in their medical histories? Was the woman named on Karla's birth certificate the same woman Mrs. Derby had phoned years later? Mrs. Derby had come upon the woman because of the article she wrote about the high prevalence of cancer in her family. The cancer connection was concerning at the time. Now, given Christie's plight, it was frightening. Would this woman have medical information that could help Christie?

Karla was too overwhelmed with Christie's care to pursue any efforts to find her biological parents. But she thought about them. They had let her out of their lives on that spring day in 1963 with nothing but a cloth diaper. OK, that was the choice they made. But now Christie, their biological granddaughter, was very sick. And Karla felt that her other two children were also entitled to crucial answers about their genetic backgrounds.

Karla didn't bother Christie with any of these details about the genetic history that may have led her to that hospital room. And in any case, Christie was a realist. She believed in playing the cards she was dealt. Rather than crying over her bad hand, she wondered how she might improve it.

She decided to try cutting-edge treatments. Her antinausea medicine wasn't working, so her oncologist had her trained in the relaxation technique of guided imagery, where she used her five senses to imagine visiting "a happy place." Her family had once lived in Seattle, so for her happy place, she chose Seattle's Pike Place Market. She'd imagine herself at that market, tasting the fruit, smelling the flowers and watching all the fish being thrown around and loaded onto carts. Often, when she used guided imagery, she wouldn't throw up.

A reporter from *Newsweek* who, doing a story on alternative therapies, learned about her from the hospital and interviewed her. She was so excited by the possibility of being quoted in the magazine. In her online journal she continually reminded people to look for the story, but the news cycle kept getting in the way. First, the piece was bumped to make room for coverage of the Washington, D.C., sniper attacks. A week later, Christie wrote, "Don't go out and buy *Newsweek*. I got bumped again, because of the election." Finally, the story ran. "Two exciting pieces of news!" Christie wrote. "I'm in this week's *Newsweek* and I get to go home for Thanksgiving. It doesn't get any better than this!"

Workers at Pike Place Market in Seattle saw the *Newsweek* story, and a month later, two of them surprised Christie by flying to Minneapolis. They brought gifts for every kid on her floor at the hospital. They had real fish, fruit, T-shirts, flowers, hats. They even brought stuffed fake fish to the hospital playroom, and they threw the fish back and forth, just like they do in Seattle. Christie wrote about the thrill of seeing her "happy place" come to life right there in the hospital.

Christie's journal was also a document of what the early teen years were like, circa 2002/2003. When she was out of the hospital and got to see movies (often wearing a mask to avoid infections), she'd review them in her journal. She found that *Legally Blonde 2* wasn't as good as the original, "but I still thought it was cute." She also got a kick out of Jennifer Lopez in *Maid in Manhattan.* (The Ames girls took note, and in a parallel universe where life was still normal, sent their healthy daughters to the same movies.)

Christie's writing was conversational. She took to calling the hospital "the Ritz," as in: "My brother, Ben, and mom slept over here last night at the Ritz." Her sense of humor came through in most every entry. She called the anesthetic she'd taken before surgery "milk of amnesia." When her hair eventually grew back after chemotherapy, she described what it felt like to use shampoo again and the thrill of walking around with a head that "smells like fresh fruit."

From the time Christie was in fourth grade, she and Karla had been in a mother/daughter book club with six of Christie's friends and their moms. The club continued even after she got sick. Christie sometimes felt self-conscious, given her condition and the fact that she needed to wear a mask over her mouth and nose to avoid other people's germs. She wrote about one book-club meeting: "Of course my mom made me wear my mask." Then, as usual, Christie turned positive, with a happy face emoticon as punctuation: "I have established quite a talent, through all of this, where I'm able to eat and drink with a mask on!! ☺"

Reading Christie's journal day after day, Sally eventually came to a realization: The entries, with all the descriptions of Karla's devotion, were turning Sally into a better, more patient, more loving mother. As a fifth-grade teacher, Sally noticed something else. She was becoming a better, more patient teacher, too. The kids in her class were "the most important people in the universe," Sally would tell herself, simply because each one of them was someone's child.

By May 2003, doctors considered Christie to be in remission. She went home and eventually rejoined her soccer team, with what she called "a very cute, short short haircut." In her journal, she remarked about how far she'd come. "We were all getting lined up and ready to play, and that's when it really occurred to me: I had cancer and I had beaten it."

For the girls from Ames, that entry was a great relief. Kelly decided to mark Christie's improved health by using frequent flier miles to get a plane ticket for Karla to fly to Maryland for an Ames girls get-together. Karla at first agreed, then tried to back out. She called other Ames girls, saying she didn't want to leave Christie. But because Kelly already had the ticket, she eventually felt compelled to go.

When Kelly came to Karla's house to pick her up for the trip, Christie was home, standing on the front lawn in her soccer uniform. Her hair, short and very fine, was blowing in the breeze. It's amazing, Kelly thought, how strong she looks in that uniform. Christie told her mom to have a great time, and as Karla and Kelly drove away, Christie waved good-bye with this giant smile on her face. Maybe she'll be OK, Kelly thought.

They spent the weekend at Jenny's house

in Annapolis — Angela and Jane came, too — and they all celebrated their fortieth birthdays and the fact that Christie was in remission. Karla was weary but grateful — for her old friends and for her daughter's good news.

They talked about very serious things: Angela opened up to the other girls about her younger brother, who in 1999 died of complications from AIDS. She explained how he was on his deathbed and the family minister came by to suggest that he still had time to repent for his homosexuality. Kelly, who had a close gay relative, was empathetic. She knew well what it's like to have a gay loved one in such a conservative part of the world.

It seemed to Kelly as if Christie's illness had opened all of them up, brought them closer.

There was plenty of laughter, too, at the gathering. One night, while talking about sex, the girls laughed so hard that they all needed to use the bathroom at the same time. "I was actually crawling to the bathroom, trying to get there before Karla," Kelly wrote in an email to the girls who couldn't make it. "We were laughing so hard we could hardly function. Next time, I'm bringing my Depends!"

The weekend also had moments that hung in the air in frightening ways. At one point, Jane talked about how thrilling it was that Christie was in remission. What incredible news! Karla spoke but didn't smile. "It's all so fragile," she said. "I don't know what I'll do if I lose her." Hearing the fear in her voice left the other girls feeling collectively crushed.

As usual for these get-togethers, Karla and Kelly were roommates. They shared a queen-sized bed in Jenny's guest room, and the bond between them was strengthened. After they returned their rental car at the airport, they were heading to the terminal on a shuttle bus and Karla snuggled up next to Kelly and said, "I'm going to miss sleeping with you." The other people on the bus stared at them, taken aback by what they'd just heard, and Karla and Kelly couldn't contain their laughter.

Even after Christie was feeling better and had moved home, she kept writing in the online journal, detailing what she considered "regular kid stuff." Then came the entry on June 16, 2003: "About a week ago, my mom started to notice I had a lot of bruises, more than a regular kid. I, of course, had an explanation for it. I had fallen down on my roller blades. But I think I secretly knew it wasn't because of that. Yesterday, I was talking to my parents while reading my new 'Chicken Soup' book. I was wearing shorts, and I had a lot more bruises than earlier in the week. Then last night, when I was brushing my teeth, I noticed a black mouth sore. I told my mom and she called the doctor. The doctor said she wanted me in at 9 A.M. today for a complete blood count and a bone marrow test. I knew this all a little too well. After they got my blood back, the doctor told us my platelets were low and my white count was very high. I have relapsed."

Scheduled for surgery the next day and then a new round of chemotherapy, she typed the entry from her hospital room: "One of my good friends, Jessie, came down to the hospital today. After tears and silence, we were 13-year-old girls again. We read magazines, played games, and did what we do best, talk and laugh. Thanks, Jessie, for coming down. You are a great friend."

As Christie got sicker, confined to the hospital, she wrote about getting "fidgety" in her room. She longed to breathe fresh air, to walk her dog. "The walls are closing in around me," she wrote. It was another echo of Anne Frank, who was unable to leave the secret annex where she was hiding.

Christie's relapse weighed heavily on the Ames girls, especially Kelly, who decided that she couldn't handle visiting Christie anymore at the hospital. Overwhelmed by what she came to call "the sadness of it all," she stopped calling or emailing Karla, too. "We're used to Christie being a girl with this frail, luminous beauty, and now her body has just swelled," Kelly told the other girls. "It's hard for me to see her." She was terribly upset with herself: How could she break off contact at a time like this? "But I was literally unable to find words to tell Karla it would be OK," Kelly later explained. "I didn't think it would be OK, and I couldn't face Karla — or Christie — and pretend."

Christie, meanwhile, remained upbeat. After a seven-week hospital stay in the fall of 2003, she got to go home for a while. She typed out her entry on the home computer and ended it by writing: "Well, got to go. My parents are making something in the kitchen that smells pretty good. Ahh! A home-cooked meal at home, where a kid should be. Life is good, and you just need to take it day by day. Be thankful to see the sun rise and set each day. Thank you for your love and support."

On December 31, 2003, back in the hospital, she wrote that she had much to be grateful for. Her family had come to be with her. They ate popcorn, shared a bottle of sparkling cider, and toasted the new year.

Her fourteenth birthday was January 9, and she described it as "a great day" even though she had a temperature of 100.7 and a two-hour nose-bleed. Three days later, she still had a fever. She wrote of having a scan on her lungs and a scope up her nose. On January 14, she wrote of being "tired and weak." She ended the entry, "Thanks for checking in on me. Love, Christie."

From then on, Karla and Bruce took over posting updates. They explained that Christie had developed fungus in her lungs, a very serious condition. She was on oxygen to help her breathe. "The doctors are very concerned with Christie's current condition, and have told us not to give up hope. However, they have prepared us for the worst. We ask again for your thoughts and prayers."

By February 1, Christie had been heavily sedated for days. "She's unable to give us any response," Bruce wrote. "We still talk to her, read to her and play her favorite music. We've got a nice window to watch the snowstorm from."

On February 12, Karla wrote that Christie was awake, but perhaps due to the morphine, she seemed "scared, confused and very agitated. She screams a lot of the time. She doesn't know her name, age or the rest of our family. She talks a lot of nonsense, which is very hard for us, because we were so excited to 'have her back.' "

On February 16, doctors found blood clots in her bladder and urine. The painful procedure to irrigate her bladder didn't go well. "She screamed in agony for about 36 hours," Karla wrote. "It was excruciating to watch."

At 11:47 A.M. on Friday, February 20, Karla posted this entry: "Christie has taken a critical turn for the worse. She has multisystem failure. Bruce, Ben, Jackie and I are all here with her. Please pray for answers and comfort for her."

At 8:07 P.M. that night, all Karla could bring herself to type onto the Web site was this: "Christie Rae Blackwood, 1/9/1990–2/20/2004."

At her home in Northfield, Minnesota, Kelly saw the online posting and touched the words on her computer screen. It was an impulse, she later thought, to wipe the words away.

In Massachusetts, Jane had been monitoring the site all day. When that final posting went up, she mouthed the words "oh my God," and was soon calling the other Ames girls. She, too, described her response as an instinctual act, as if she were a bird calling out to other birds that they all needed to return to their nest. The girls began calling their bosses to say they wouldn't be coming to work the next day. They tracked down baby-sitters for their kids. They called their husbands. And one by one, they made plans to head for airports. They were going to Minneapolis to be with Karla.

Angela was the only one who didn't think she could make it. But when an email finally came in that she, too, would be there, Kelly again found herself touching the computer screen. (As she later put it: "It was like I was feeling the power of my friendship with these women.") Through tears, she allowed herself to smile. "We're all going to be here," she thought. Because Marilyn had a big house and lived just a half hour from Karla, she invited all the girls to stay with her.

Later that night, someone wrote on the Web site that families in Christie's neighborhood in Minnesota had lit candles in the

Blackwoods' yard. They also turned on lights in their homes, as a way to honor Christie. Thousands of miles away, in different corners of the country, the Ames girls turned on lights in their homes, too.

Of course, it was the least they could do. And some were already feeling guilty for not having done more while Christie was alive: Why hadn't they flown to Minneapolis more, sent more money, asked Christie how they might make her happy, told Karla they loved her? The responsibilities of friendship are not easily defined, especially in traumatic times. How much is too much? How little is too little? They had trouble talking about these guilt feelings in the days after Christie's death. But the feelings were there, unspoken, in all of their heads.

All of the Ames girls arrived within hours of each other on the day before the memorial service. Jenny, flying in from Maryland, was the last to land at the airport. At age forty-one, she was pregnant with her first child, and the sight of her was such a thrill for the other girls that, for a brief moment, it overshadowed their grief.

All the girls, except Karla, of course, camped out at Marilyn's house the night before the funeral. It was a tremendously sad evening, and yet, like always, the girls reminisced and found themselves giggling. "I feel guilty laughing," Jenny said, and that was a trigger for all of them, so they'd get teary again. That's how it went all night.

The conversation turned to how sex-toy parties were being run like Tupperware parties in some of their neighborhoods. One of the girls — they've sworn not to say who it was — talked about using a silver bullet during sex. It was all surreal. Talking about sex toys. Grieving for Karla. Crying, then laughing, then crying, then laughing.

It was perhaps the most intense bonding they'd ever done, and Jane said aloud what all of them were thinking: "I wish we could call Karla. I wish she could just come over. She'd want to be here with us."

Christie's church memorial service was attended by 750 friends, relatives, classmates and medical staffers. Karla, of course, sat with her family. But the other Ames girls filled a pew. It occurred to Kelly, as they sat there in shades of gray and black, that it was not unlike their school years, when they'd all sit in the same row for assemblies.

Dozens of Christie's middle-school classmates entered the church together, and because the pews were already filled, they sat three across in the aisles. Almost all of the Ames girls began crying at the sight of Christie's girlfriends, all of whom had decided to dress in pink as a way of honoring her. The Ames girls were reminded, of course, of their middle-school years together. They knew how profound the loss would be for Christie's friends.

At one point, though, Kelly found herself feeling almost elated. She looked over at Jenny, pregnant and healthy, about to become a mother. Yes, they had lost Christie, and that was awful. But there was new life coming into their lives, too. "I was feeling joy in that moment," Kelly later said.

After the service, everyone went back to Karla's house. There were more than a hundred people there, and though the Ames girls mingled for a while, they naturally gravitated toward each other. One by one, they ended up in the master bedroom, until all ten, including Karla, were sitting on the large king-sized bed.

Someone closed the door, and there they were. They could hear the muffled noise from all the people in the kitchen and living room, but it was as if no one else existed. They noticed that they were touching each other. Everyone had a hand on a shoulder, an arm, a hand. It was a physical connection they hadn't planned, but it felt natural and inevitable.

Someone asked Karla if she wanted to talk about the last moments of Christie's life, and it was comforting for her to share those details with all of them. Jane stroked Karla's arm as she spoke about Christie's final hours — and then about her final minutes.

Karla used so many complicated medical terms as she spoke. Her eighteen months at Christie's bedside had left her sounding like a med-school graduate. Kelly marveled at her command of the details. "I've never heard Karla sound so articulate," she thought. "I'm so proud of her."

The girls found a few reasons to smile and even to laugh. They reminisced a little, too, about the eleven girls they were, when Sheila was a part of them.

Gathering together on that king-sized bed happened spontaneously. But in that moment, all ten of them later realized, they saw clearly that true friendship means a willingness to share both joy and complete despair.

As Kelly later described it: Outside that door, grief was waiting to envelop Karla. But in that bedroom, for that half hour, a profound sisterly love was holding it all at bay.

13
TEARS IN
THE LADIES' ROOM

Over dessert one night at the reunion, Jane asks if she can stand up and say a few words. Her daughter, Hanna, has just celebrated her bat mitzvah. For her "mitzvah project" — her effort to do a good deed — she chose to raise money for Caring Bridge, the Web site where Christie had posted her journal.

When Christie was diagnosed, Hanna was only eight years old, but she had immersed herself in Christie's Web postings. Now Hanna is thirteen. "She's the same age as Christie was when she was sick," Jane tells the other girls. "So Hanna feels even more moved by what Christie went through."

Hanna raised $420 for Caring Bridge, and wrote an essay about how Christie's journey helped her put her life in perspective. "My challenges seem like ants compared to Christie's challenge, which was a monster," Hanna wrote. "She has inspired me to never run away from my dreams. From now on, I will not take each day for granted. Christie's spirit lives on inside of me. I will never forget her."

When Jane finishes reading, she looks up and her eyes meet Karla's. Both of them smile weakly at each other. Around the table, some of the other girls have tears in their eyes.

The room is silent for a moment, and then Kelly talks. "Christie had this short life," she says, "but there was this force about her. You see it in her photos. She literally glowed in her years here."

A few of the other girls weigh in with compliments, too, and Karla tells them she appreciates their words. She says she's buoyed when people tell her how they've been touched by Christie. "Her oncologist called her the most balanced and focused person she had ever known, child or adult," Karla says.

She knows how the other girls ache for her. She knows that her loss has left them all doubly grateful that their children are alive and healthy. "Please thank Hanna for me," Karla tells Jane. "Christie would be proud of her."

On the evening of Christie's memorial

service, after everyone had gathered at Karla's house in Edina, the time eventually came for the Ames girls to leave. They had to drive back to Marilyn's house, thirty minutes away, to get their suitcases. The following morning, they would head for the airport to return to their own lives.

Karla watched them gather up their coats and felt an urge that she didn't articulate. "I want to go with them," she thought. "I don't want them to leave without me."

It would be such a relief if she could squeeze with them into a crowded car and just drive away, as she did on so many nights when they were young — crammed together, giggling and chattering and nudging each other. Of course, she didn't tell them, "Please take me with you." She remained strong. She hugged each one of them good-bye, longer and tighter than she ever had, and then she returned to the kitchen, where some of her newer friends from Edina were gathered.

The weeks and months that followed were extremely difficult for Karla. The girls would call her house and invariably get her answering machine. That was because Karla often just let the phone ring. Her life had become very narrow. She was getting up in the morning, making breakfast for Ben and

Jackie, packing their lunches, getting them on the bus, and then vegetating for much of the day, often in bed.

For months, her biggest goal was to shower and get dressed before the kids got home from school so there would be some semblance of a normal home life. "That's all I could do," she later confided to Kelly. "I don't mean to sound dramatic. It was just the only way I could cope, in little steps."

Bruce was a rock for Karla, a hero, but she tried not to overwhelm him with details about her emotional pain. She just tried to get through, mostly on her own.

It took about a year after Christie's death for her to begin turning back to the Ames girls, sharing with them things she had trouble telling others in her life.

She told them of how she'd fall asleep each night feeling sad and restless. At 3 or 4 A.M., she was often waking up with a start, in a cold sweat, confused, thinking she was back with Christie and needed to help her with her IV line.

Early in September 2005, she sent an email to everyone. "I'm having quite a week, grief-wise," she wrote. "The first day of school was agonizing, only putting two kids on the bus, and knowing Christie would have started high school that day. Cancer sucks. I'll sign off now, I'm such a downer this morning."

As time went on, Jane became an especially valued confidant for Karla. "I don't think I'll ever again be the happy person I was," Karla told her on the phone one night. "I accept that. I know I can't expect to be happy, not right away, not in the same way. But I just feel as if it will never happen at all."

When they were younger, Karla and Jane weren't considered a close pair within the Ames girls' universe. Jane was more serious, always twinned with Marilyn. Karla had more of a free spirit. So Jane and Karla were never an obvious twosome.

As adults, however, in the wake of Christie's death, they became more closely connected. Jane could see both the intelligence and the heart within Karla — facets of her she hadn't always paid close attention to before. And at her very lowest times, Karla found Jane to be a wise and loving source of comfort.

Both were pleased with the blossoming of their relationship, and it was noticed in the dynamics of the larger group. At their reunions after Christie died, some of the girls would mildly complain that they couldn't get time alone with Karla because Jane was always by her side.

(Jane would remain forever bonded to Marilyn, of course, rooted in how close they were in Ames. As adults, though, there were subjects they didn't talk about in great detail. Marilyn had married a man who viewed his Christian faith as the cornerstone of his life, and she had embraced that way of living, too. She had been taught that the only way to enter heaven was to believe in Jesus. Because she had close Jewish friends in Minnesota, and then Jane, of course, she was troubled by the thought that she'd get to heaven and might see people she cared about being turned away. "I would hate that," she said. "I'll want to see all my friends again after I die." She called Jane, who explained that many Jewish people believe that when they die, they die. Jane pretty much rejected the idea that there was an afterlife. Marilyn said she has great respect for the beliefs of others, but "I'm concerned by the idea that some people may be excluded.")

Meanwhile, in part because of her time spent with Jane, Karla became interested in Judaism. Christie's death had led her to question her faith, and the idea of heaven and hell. She felt Judaism might be clearer about things: You die and you return to the earth. It felt more direct and manageable to Karla.

Jane answered Karla's questions about Judaism, but never pushed. She knew that Karla's uncertainties about faith were part of the grieving process.

Karla also confided that she sometimes felt uncomfortable seeing people at church or when she was out in public. Many people in Edina were aware of Christie's story. After a child dies, word spreads. So when Karla ventured out of the house, she could feel people looking at her. She sensed they were whispering: "There's that mother who lost her daughter." She'd meet someone, introduce herself, and the other person would invariably recognize her name and say, "Oh yes, of course, you're Karla. How are you doing?"

"Here in Edina, Bruce and I will always be the couple who lost a child," she told Jane. "That's just the way it's going to be. And we make some people uncomfortable. I know we do. There will be acquaintances at the supermarket. I know they see me. But I can feel them turning their carts to go up a different aisle. They don't know what to say, so they avoid me."

As time went on, Karla was asked to be a

spokeswoman of sorts for parents who had lost children to cancer. She agreed to attend some local cancer-research benefits, but it made her uncomfortable. "All I wanted was to be a mom, at home with my husband and kids on a Saturday night with a big bag of popcorn, watching a movie," she said. "Now I feel as if everyone wants a piece of me."

Karla also spoke frankly with Jane about the emotions she felt when she'd run into Christie's old friends around town. A part of her loved seeing them blossom into teenagers — reaching age fifteen, then sixteen, then seventeen. But she also found herself feeling melancholy when she saw them.

As Bruce and Karla tried to resume their normal lives, they made a point of going on a "date" to Starbucks once a week. One day, while they were having coffee, they saw Christie's close friend Kate at the counter. Kate gave them a big hello and told them that a lot of Christie's old pals were there, too. "We're all in the back doing homework," she said. "Come say hi."

Karla saw them back there, all of them looking so mature. "They had their laptops out. They were cramming for finals," she later told Jane. "They'll be seniors soon, looking at colleges. And I couldn't stop thinking: Christie should be there. She should be there in Starbucks with those girls, buying coffee, studying for finals, talking about going to the prom, picking a college."

There were too many encounters like that, and it was hard for Karla to find a place where she could retreat from it all, somewhere she didn't feel sad or uneasy. "I've always loved my house. But I'm unhappy being in it," she said. "I've always loved my neighborhood, loved Minnesota, but it doesn't feel right being here."

Jane listened to her. "I think it's hard for you to be in a place where Christie suffered so much," she said, and her words resonated with Karla.

Christie had been cremated, and a portion of her ashes were in a garden at the church Karla's family attended. Christie's room had been left pretty much as it was when she lived there. For those reasons and hundreds of others, it would be hard to move out of Minnesota. The family didn't want to feel as if they would be leaving her behind.

Still, maybe Jane had it right. "Maybe I can never be happy again if I stay here," Karla said. "Maybe we have to think

Jane and Karla today

about going."

In the first three years after Christie's death, the Ames girls tried to calibrate the depths of Karla's grief and her progress in finding ways to smile again. Many times over the phone, they just let Karla talk.

"This woman asked me if I think about Christie in every thought," Karla said one night to Kelly. "I told her, 'No. She's not in every thought. But she is still definitely in every other thought.' That's a change from how I've been. So maybe that's progress.

For a long time, I was thinking of Christie every minute of every day."

The girls had long discussions about a gift they might get Karla that would mark their friendship and remind them that they'd always be there for her. Eventually Jenny decided to commission a *Scherenschnitte,* which is German for "scissors paper-cutting." It included the words "Friends by Chance, Sisters by Choice," along with silhouettes of ten girls holding hands, encircling a map of the United States. On the map, ten stars marked the ten cities where the girls now live. The city of Ames, just about in the center of the map, was marked by a heart. Inside the heart was another little silhouette of a girl; this represented Sheila, who grew up in Ames and is buried there. The paper-cutting turned out to be a gift for Karla that they all shared. The next time they gathered for an annual reunion, at Diana's house in Arizona, Jenny gave everyone a copy as a gift.

When they weren't physically together, the girls found email to be a great way to unobtrusively stay in touch with Karla and support her. In their chatty "reply all" emails, sometimes they would mention Christie and sometimes they wouldn't. Whether Karla answered them or not, the emails allowed Karla to know they were all thinking about her. They sent emails to mark Christie's birthday, January 9, and the day she died, February 20. Karen sent Karla flowers on her birthday, April 25. Jenny was always sending handwritten cards.

Since both Kelly and Marilyn lived in Minnesota, they were able to pin down a few lunch dates with Karla. Once, the three of them walked around a nearby lake, just talking. Karla told them of her worries about Jackie and Ben. Ben was always a bright boy, but when he had a few issues at school — focusing, turning in homework — was it laziness? Attention deficit disorder? Or was he mourning Christie and unable to focus because he was worried about how his parents were coping? "I just don't know the dynamics," Karla said.

"Ben and Jackie are so protective of you," Kelly told her. "When I see them with you, I can see them taking care of you, as if they're saying, 'Mom, don't worry. It'll be OK.' "

"Those poor kids," Karla answered. "They've got so much to handle."

"It'll get easier," Marilyn told her.

"It's got to get easier," Karla responded, "because I can't imagine living like this forever."

At one point, the conversation turned to Marilyn's dad and his memorial service in Ames after he died in 2004. Dr. McCormack was seventy-nine. "It really was a celebration of his life," Kelly said of the service. "He lived such a full life." That got Karla thinking about her own father's death in 1990.

"I used to think that my father died young," she said. "I used to think, 'Oh my God, he missed out on so much. He was just sixty-eight. His life was so short.' I don't think that way anymore. Now I think that my father lived a long time. I have this totally new perspective. The way I think now, any life that lasts longer than fourteen years, well, that feels like a full life to me."

Sheila's death was the major loss that all of the Ames girls shared in their early twenties. But as they aged, each of them experienced deaths in her own family. By their thirties and forties, they all had endured grief that would inform the rest of their lives. No one ever wanted to compare the magnitude of their various sorrows. But they came to have a shorthand sense of grief that helped them comfort and buoy each other — especially Karla.

Like Karla, Karen had insights into the

pain of losing a child.

Her first son was born in 1992, and nine months later, she found herself unexpectedly pregnant again. It was a shock to her that she became pregnant so soon, and she was less than overjoyed at the news. It was a difficult pregnancy, too. She spent much of the first trimester vomiting. In time, however, she embraced the idea of having another child. When she and her husband learned they would be having a little girl, they selected the name Emily.

Five months into the pregnancy, however, when Karen was already in maternity clothes, she had an amniocentesis that showed the baby had severe spina bifida. The baby's brain was actually growing outside of her head. (Spina bifida, which means "split spine," occurs when a baby's spinal column doesn't close completely in the womb. Scientists suspect that genetic and environmental factors conspire to cause it. Seven out of every ten thousand babies born have spina bifida; those with less serious forms of this birth defect can live a normal life.)

In Karen's case, the situation was dire, and one of the doctors who made the diagnosis got right to the point. "You have to decide whether to terminate the pregnancy or go through with it," he said. "Think about what is right for you and your family."

Her primary care physician, who happened to be pregnant herself, was furious that this doctor had phrased it that way. "Listen, Karen," her doctor said, "you do not have a choice. If you go the full nine-month term, your baby will die within minutes of being born. She will not live. You have a year-old child at home. I don't want you waiting four more months to deliver a baby who will not live. End this pregnancy now and move on with your life."

It was December 1993, and Karen was planning to return to Ames for Christmas, then fly to Hawaii with her family for vacation. She called Jane and Cathy, both of whom took the news calmly and weighed in supportively. But it was Jane who first uttered a word that Karen hadn't heard from her doctors and hadn't even contemplated. "You have to do it," Jane said. "You have to have the abortion." Karen hadn't allowed herself to think that the "procedure" being talked about was an abortion. So Jane's comment was sobering and haunting, especially since Karen was Catholic. It put everything in a new and awful light.

Karen told Jane and Cathy how guilty she felt. "I hadn't wanted to be pregnant again so soon," she said. "Maybe this was punishment for not being happy when I learned I was pregnant." Both girls reassured her that she had nothing to feel guilty about. "It's a genetic disorder," Jane said. "That's it."

Karen decided to take the vacation in Hawaii as planned and then have "the procedure" when she returned. Her week away would allow her moments to say good-bye. At night in Hawaii, her hands on her belly, she'd talk to the little girl she felt moving inside of her, offering words of love and apology.

When she returned home, she went to the hospital, where labor was induced. "I was in the maternity ward," she told Cathy, "but they didn't want me near the other moms and babies. They had me way down the hall, where I wouldn't be seen or heard."

She was in a room without any clocks, which led her to think: "They don't want me to know what time I deliver my baby."

Her husband, Kevin, stood by her side, devastated but trying to stay strong. When the tiny baby was delivered, Kevin felt it would be best if they didn't look at her. "They had her in a blanket, and they took her out of the room," Karen told Cathy. "I kept saying I wanted to see her, and Kevin said, 'No you don't.' And I said, 'Yes, I do. I do!' and then I fell asleep."

Karen understands and appreciates that her husband was acting out of love, but she still regrets not taking a look at the little girl she would have named Emily. And she wonders where the nurses took her when they carried her away. There was no burial, no funeral.

In memory of Emily, Karen has long worn a "mother and child" charm on a gold chain around her neck. It was given to her by her husband in the days after Emily was delivered. Karen rarely takes it off.

One summer back in Ames, Karen met up with some of the other girls, and Kelly watched her as she held that charm between her fingers. "I can only imagine the pain of that," Kelly thought.

Karen went on to have two more children, a son and a daughter. And after Jenny had two miscarriages of her own, Karen helped her by talking about her experience losing a child she never got to know. Jenny and Karen also found strength in the knowledge that fully half of the Ames girls had had miscarriages, and all of them later gave birth to more children.

After Christie died, however, Karen never

tried to tell Karla that she empathized. "It has to be so much worse to really know and love the child you've lost," she thought. "I can't tell Karla, 'I know how you feel.' I'm not sure any of us can know how she feels."

On the back porch of Angela's house, as some of the girls sip their morning coffee, Cathy and Angela happen to be seated on the so-called crying couch. Within fifteen minutes, there are tears.

First, Angela gets to talking about how her brother learned he was HIV-positive and about his 1999 death, offering details she has never shared before. "Growing up, he knew he was different," she says. "He once told me that in Sunday school, when he was eight or nine years old, he'd pray that he wouldn't have the feelings he had." As he got older and more comfortable about being gay, Angela's parents would talk to their minister about him. "The minister said, 'If you pray really hard, it'll go away,'" Angela says. When her brother was near death, this minister came to the hospital to suggest that he seek forgiveness for his sins. As Angela recalls it, the minister's basic message was "You can still change. You can still say you were wrong."

Angela's mom had passed away four years

earlier from breast cancer, and her dad had remarried. Angela says she is so grateful for her stepmother, who turned to the minister that day and politely asked him to stop. Deftly but respectfully, in so many words, she gave the message: "This young man feels like he's going to hell because people like you have told him this. It's time for you to leave this room." When the minister left, Angela's stepmother went over to Angela's brother, held his hand and comforted him.

"Thank God she did that," Cathy says.

Angela gets tearful at the memory, and Cathy moves closer to her, wrapping her arm around her. After Angela composes herself, she says, "My stepmother later told me that maybe her purpose in life was to help my brother die."

Angela's story triggers memories in Cathy, who offers details of her mother's last moments before she died in 2005. She was seventy-seven and had leukemia. Cathy and five of her six siblings were there at the end. Her mother was home, on a rented hospital bed with a special air mattress. She was lucid, talking to everyone until 4 A.M. She passed away later that day.

"Just after she died, my brother said a lovely prayer. It was helpful. I felt this kind of calm numbness," Cathy tells the other girls. She describes the scene in the room. "My mom had been on oxygen, and the machine was kind of loud. So we turned it off. But there was still this whirring noise in the room. It seemed to be coming from that hospital bed. So my brother-in-law kneeled down next to my dad, who was praying, and he decided to reach over and turn the switch for the air mattress on the bed. Suddenly, the air in the mattress started going out really fast with this big whoosh, and my mom's body started getting lower and lower . . ."

Cathy makes the sound of the bed deflating. ". . . and so my father turned to my brother-in-law and said, 'Why did you do that?' And my brother-in-law, you could see on his face that he was thinking, 'Oh my gosh, I don't know why I did that!' So he turned the bed back on, and my mother started rising up . . ."

Cathy is laughing now, and so are the other Ames girls. "My mom would have thought that was hysterical."

"Your mom had the best sense of humor," Karen says. All the girls remember Cathy's mom as perhaps the friendliest of the mothers. Whenever they came to Cathy's house, she wouldn't head into another room, like most mothers did. As Cathy always said,

"She loved to yuck it up with you guys." She'd sit down with the girls to get the scoop on their lives. And she loved being dolled up. She wasn't very tall, so she liked to wear shoes that gave her a few more inches. The girls remember her looking great, vacuuming her house in her high heels.

"For the funeral, my dad wanted to make sure my mother looked good," Cathy tells the girls, "because, of course, she always wanted to look her best." And so her dad asked Cathy, the well-known makeup artist, if she'd apply her mom's makeup.

Cathy tells the girls of going through her mom's things with her siblings, picking out clothing in just the right colors, and then taking her makeup kit to the mortuary. She stood over her mom's body. "I thought I would be really freaked out, but it was just an act of love. It turned out to be a gift, that I had this chance to do that."

Her mother had really full lips, so Cathy made sure to give her the right shade of lipstick. She worked on her mother's face for about fifteen minutes, and the woman in charge of doing makeup at the mortuary was very impressed. "She asked me if I wanted a job there," Cathy says.

Kelly, Sally and Karla had made it to the

funeral for Cathy's mom, which was held in Kansas City. It was a year after Christie's death, and it was not an easy journey for Karla to drive down for it.

The talk on the porch turns to the girls' recollections of that funeral.

"There was that procession, when the whole family was walking out of the sanctuary," Kelly recalls. "It was very emotional."

"I felt so weak. Kelly, you were holding me up," Karla says.

"And we were crying," Kelly says. "People thought we were crying for Cathy's mom, and we were. But it was more that that. We were crying for Karla and for Christie. We were crying for ourselves and our friendship."

It was at that funeral that they saw Sheila's mom after all those years, and asked her about Sheila's death. So that particular day was overwhelming, and unforgettable, on several fronts.

Kelly tries to describe for the other girls what happened after the service. "We ran to the bathroom, Sally, Karla and I, just like we used to do in high school. That's the refuge. And we cried. Horrible, awful crying. And I looked at Sally and said, 'You know, we've done so many important things in ladies' rooms, haven't we?' We smiled at each other. I think Karla smiled, too. And then we hugged Karla, and she cried and I cried and Sally cried. And being together like that, together in that ladies' room, it was just a nice moment for us. A nice moment at a very hard time."

14

COOPERATION
AND APPRECIATION

Seven of the girls are power walking around Angela's North Carolina neighborhood, and the conversation has turned to parenting.

"Cooperation and appreciation," says Jane. "That's my mantra."

Jane says that she keeps repeating the same words to her children. "I tell them all the time: I want them to cooperate and I want them to appreciate. Cooperation and appreciation."

All the girls are now raising their children with a higher standard of living than they knew growing up in Ames. Part of this is because American culture in general is more acquisitive and self-indulgent. And part of it is due to the fact that almost all of the girls have risen into the upper middle class. They've taken a step up from what their parents had — in family incomes, in the size of their homes, in the toys and accoutrements that clutter their kids' lives.

Right: The girls' hands on a pregnant Kelly. Left: Karla and Diana, both pregnant.

Karen says her fourteen-year-old son thinks nothing of asking for a $160 hockey stick, and he'll want it within minutes of eyeing it in a store. "When I was his age, I was detasseling corn, saving up money, and using the money to buy my own clothes," she says. "I'm not sure kids today understand what that was like. There were things I wanted as a kid but would never ask for. I knew there was no reason to ask, because it wasn't in the realm of possibility. My parents wouldn't get it for me anyway."

A recollection comes into Karen's head,

and she turns to Jenny. "Remember in junior high? What was the coolest magazine?"

"Teen Beat," says Jenny. "I had a subscription."

"Yes, and I'd always go to your house to read it. Every issue. I never asked my parents for my own subscription. I knew it wasn't necessary. Because, hey, I could just go to your house and read it there."

The girls talk about the definition of "spoiled."

"When I think of spoiled, I think of obnoxious and unappreciative," says Karen. "I wouldn't describe my kids like that. But they're spoiled in the sense that they have no trouble just asking for whatever they want. My son wanted a Razr phone. It's three hundred dollars. He just asked."

Karla says that in the wake of Christie's death, she has a heightened sense of the needs, moods and desires of her two surviving kids, Ben and Jackie. She knows how they feel inside — like a part of them is missing without Christie — and she knows it's naïve to think she could fill that emptiness by buying them material things. Still, she admits that she has relented at times when they wanted her to buy them something. She knows life is fleeting and she wants them to be happy and feel whole.

All the girls want their children to be happy, of course. But when they think back to their own childhoods, they realize that their parents weren't especially focused on keeping them happy and satiated. Their parents didn't just give them things. Their parents were more apt to say: "You want something? Find a way to get it and leave me out of it." As Karen sees it, there's less of that philosophy in the culture of parenting today.

She reminds the girls of the time she and Karla were in a department store fashion show. As a reward, they got a discount on clothing. "I was so excited," she says. "I had saved up my babysitting money, and I used it to buy a pair of Calvin Klein jeans, which was a real extravagance."

The girls lament that the idea of wanting, saving, buying, savoring is foreign to a lot of kids today, even kids in Ames. These days, the students at Ames High and elsewhere in Iowa might not be as hip as kids in, say, Beverly Hills, but they're still full-fledged consumers, like their peers all over America. At least that's what the girls are hearing from loved ones back home. "My niece in Iowa went to get a bra and underwear for the prom and spent seventy dol-

371

lars," says Karen.

Jane circles back to her original point. The fact that kids have more today isn't necessarily terrible, she says. But she urges the other girls, in their roles as mothers, to adopt her mantra.

She tells them a story: "A couple of summers ago, my family was out all day doing fun stuff. We went to the water park. We went out to eat. It was almost the whole day. And we got home at four o'clock and the girls were asking Justin and me, 'What do we do now?' Like they were already bored. And I'm thinking, 'Jeez! We've been having a good time all day long! What am I, a camp director?' And that's when I started saying, 'Things won't be going well in this house, and fun times won't be happening, unless we have cooperation and appreciation.' I think everything can be distilled down to those two words."

The girls stop walking to stand under a tree and take a drink from their water bottles. That's when Kelly says that maybe they should cut back on their pining for the good old days and their complaining about young whippersnappers. They're starting to sound like grouchy old ladies.

"Anyway, on some level, I think our kids do understand the issues," Jane says, and then offers up another story. At Hebrew school, her daughter Hanna was recently given an assignment. The kids were studying the Ten Commandments, and each was asked to create an appropriate eleventh commandment. Hanna came up with "Thou shalt be appreciative."

"She explained to me that people don't appreciate all the things they have, and they should," says Jane. "And I was so thrilled. I said to Justin, 'Wow, the kids heard us! We're getting through!'

"You know, it's funny, because half the time, as your kids get older, you feel like you're talking to a wall. You feel like an inanimate object that they're ignoring. But sometimes, when you're just living your life, they surprise you, and when they do, wow, it's so great."

From the moment Karla delivered Christie in 1990, and through all the children who've followed, the girls have been trading an unending procession of motherhood tales.

Often, their reports from the home front are meant merely to entertain.

In a 1999 letter to all the girls, Marilyn described her daughter, Emily, as a three-year-old optimist with "a zest for skipping" rather than walking. "On warm summer days, she likes to exclaim with delight, 'It's our lucky day!' "

That same year, Jane's younger daughter was two years old. "Sara shows a strong independent streak," Jane wrote. "She seems to have no fear except for clowns and ice-cream trucks. Our only fear is the day Sara sees a clown driving an ice-cream truck!" Meanwhile, Hanna was four years old that year, and when she got her tonsils out, she took a liking to the Vicodin she was taking for her pain. "We then had another problem," Jane wrote, "a kid who kept pleading with us, in shorter and shorter intervals, for more Vicodin — even after the doctor said she was completely healed and in no need of pain medication. Fortunately, we were able to stop just short of a twelve-step program."

Sally's daughter Lindsay won her school's spelling bee at age ten in 2001, "so now we are spelling more than we talk in our house, in preparation for the next level of competition," Sally wrote.

The girls identified their kids to each other in part by their quirks. At age three, Karla's son Ben was a loud talker. At age six, Kelly's daughter Liesl wanted hair like Jan Brady of *The Brady Bunch.* At age eight, Marilyn's son David decided to wash his Game Boy in the sink, and Marilyn had to use a hair dryer to dry it out and get it working again. Those were among the million anecdotes the girls shared with each other.

On some fronts, the girls first got involved with each other's kids prenatally. In 1998, for instance, Kelly, Karla and Diana visited Cathy's house in California. On the plane ride west, Kelly watched Diana devour a McDonald's Big Mac. "I've never seen you eat like that before!" Kelly said. "Maybe you're pregnant." Diana and her husband had two daughters at the time, and hadn't yet settled on the idea of having another child. But in L.A., the other girls convinced Diana to go to a drugstore and buy a pregnancy test. Sure enough, and to her surprise, she tested positive. So the Ames girls knew the good news — she was pregnant with her third child — before her husband did.

From the time they each got email accounts, the Ames girls have been asking each other for instant advice regarding their kids. One of them recently had questions about attention deficit disorder and teens — what are the signs? — and threw it out to the other girls. Sally and Kelly weighed in as teachers. Cathy offered nutritional advice. Everyone had thoughts.

A few days later, Jenny wrote an email to everyone about her three-year-old son, Jack, having trouble sleeping through the night. Marilyn wrote back about her own son's sleep issues, but no one else responded to Jenny's email. Finally, Jenny wrote again, "Hey, did you guys forget about me and my question?"

Jenny didn't have Jack until she was forty-one, so he is by far the youngest of the twenty-one children. Because the other Ames girls are now focused on their own preteens and teens, they've moved on from toddler issues. Jenny's follow-up email, written with mock indignation, left the girls slightly guilt-ridden, and most felt obliged to recollect how they'd dealt with nap time and sleepless nights. "You know what? I don't really remember how we got through it," Karla said.

The girls enjoy observing the ways, big and small, in which each of them chooses to make her commitment to motherhood. Karla makes sure she provides nutritious after-school snacks and meals. Marilyn keeps in mind her dad's final wishes to remember the things he did for her that made her happy, and to do those things for her own kids. Karen, who rarely misses her sons' hockey games, realizes that she is very comfortable with her decision to be a stay-at-home mother. "I know there are lots of wonderful working mothers," she says, "but for me personally, I love being at home to get my kids to school in the morning, and to be there when they get home. When we are in the car together going to hockey practice, that's a great time to talk and hear what's going on in their lives."

In Jenny's case, when Jack was an infant, she felt strongly about the benefits of nursing him. And so, at an Ames girls gathering at Diana's house in Arizona, with Jack back home in Maryland, she brought along a breast pump. The need to pump didn't stop her from joining any activities. She sat with everyone, talking and pumping away. Jane came up with her own pet name for the machine, Big Betty, which the other girls quickly adopted. They had some good laughs impersonating what they called "the milking machine," which sounded like a piece of heavy machinery.

No one told Jenny they had dubbed her device "Big Betty," and then Jane casually mentioned it in an email after the reunion. Jenny asked for an explanation.

"I kept talking about Big Betty because I think it's so cool that you are nursing, and so dedicated to pumping, which I never got the hang of," Jane replied to Jenny, cc-ing everyone else. "I also think it's cool that you were so freely pumping in the mix of things. That's just as it should be. No need for a nursing mother to miss out on the conversation."

Jenny responded: "Well, I'll be packing up Big Betty to take down to Mexico with me on vacation this Friday. I'll be pumping and dumping, as FedEx will not allow me to ship my milk from country to country. It'll break my heart pouring that liquid gold down the drain. But I'm leaving my parents with about thirty-five bags of frozen breast milk, so that ought to be a good start. The things we do for our kids!

"When Jack is older and he is screaming that I don't love him — or is that something that only girls do to their mothers??? — I'll be sure to remind him of my time spent pumping every day, three times a day, at the office, on vacation, in the middle of the night, in the wee hours. . . ."

As a girl, Jane had always assumed she'd be a working mother, and figured she'd end up as a professor. Given that she was the daughter of an anthropology professor and a social worker, it's not surprising that she got to college and narrowed her interests down to anthropology, sociology and psychology. After taking some sociology courses, however, she decided that the topics of sociology, such as solving the problems of poverty, were just too broad and unmanageable. "I was drawn to psychology, where I perceived the issues to be more specified and empirically testable," she says, sounding very much like the academic she has become. She spent several summers at Grinnell College working with live pigeons doing operant conditioning research; that's the use of consequences to modify behavior. She considered pursuing graduate work in animal learning, but instead got her Ph.D. in cognitive psychology.

When her students post comments on "Rate Your Professor" Web sites, almost all of them give Jane high marks: "Professor Nash is a very clear teacher. She uses lots of everyday examples. Very specific grader, though, so study specifics." "Best professor ever! She's super-motherly. She expects a lot from you and sets the bar high. If you like to learn, to be treated like an adult, and don't mind high expectations — take Nash!"

Jane is proud of her career, but like all of the other working mothers among the Ames girls, she calls her children her greatest accomplishment. "Time will tell, however, if we've really done our work well," she says.

Her wishes for her two daughters are specific. "I want them to become happy, fulfilled women who feel a sense of pride in themselves," she says, "and most importantly, I want them to really love each other. I always say to them, 'Friends come and go, but you always have your sister.' " Of course, that's not true for her, since she has all the other Ames girls. But she thinks her experience is something of an exception to the rule. "Friends often fade into the background," she says, "and your siblings are always in the foreground — at least in a semi-functional family."

Jane says finding a work/life balance is the greatest challenge in her life. Her job is somewhat flexible. She can take some of her work home, such as grading papers or assessing labs. Then again, when she's in the house, her girls always need her to drive or talk or whatever. "When I'm at home," Jane says, "I often feel conflicted about which hat I'm wearing, my professor hat or my mom hat."

Her husband, Justin, is very involved with the girls, and that helps. "He's patient," she says, "when I'm at the end of my rope and want to renegotiate our roles or responsibilities. But the fact remains that I'm home earlier from work than he is, so there are many tasks that fall on my shoulders in the afternoon and early evening."

The one area in Jane's life where she feels most compromised — and she has discussed this with the other Ames girls — is the time she gets to spend on herself. "I'm talking about the things that aren't about work and aren't about family."

Looking at her life, she realizes she's pretty much down to two "me time" things — running and her book group. "Both come with plenty of guilt associated with them," she says.

Jane started running in 1997, after her second daughter, Sara, was born. "I was on maternity leave, and home with a baby and a three-year-old," she says. "Before I became a runner, the day would start with a baby crying or my older daughter wanting breakfast. This seemed like a tough beginning to what was going to be a long day. So one day I decided that I would get up before everyone else and go for a walk. Then at least I would have some fresh air and would have accomplished one thing before the day began in full.

"Well, walking was taking too long, so I started running. And when I returned home, I found two kids who were dressed and fed." Her husband had stepped into the void, so to speak. And her older daughter was able to dress and feed herself.

"Now what would you have done?" Jane says. "Well, if you were like me, you would try that again the next day and then the next and then the next. All of a sudden, I had become a runner to escape what I called 'the morning mommy onslaught.' "

In her general psychology class, Jane has actually used this story as an example of "negative reinforcement."

As her daughters got older, Jane would continue to try to sneak out of the house early. "I didn't want the girls to see me leaving and giving myself what I perceived as this very selfish alone time," she says. "Yes, I can't shake the guilt. But then Justin convinced me to let Hanna and Sara actually see me going for a run, so they could witness a woman trying to stay fit — and taking time to do something for herself."

Jane hadn't exactly considered that she could be a role model for her daughters by taking time for herself away from them. It took her husband to give her that insight.

The Ames girls appreciate sharing these sorts of "aha" moments with each other.

Sally was sick a lot early in her pregnancies. One day when she was pregnant with her second daughter, she was kneeling on the floor of the bathroom, throwing up. Her older daughter, then two years old, was casually swinging the toilet lid up and down, banging it on Sally's head as she was vomiting, asking, "Whatcha doing, Mommy?"

Sally told the other Ames girls: "As she was banging away on my head, I was thinking, 'How in the world did this become my life? Throwing up while being assaulted by a toddler with a toilet lid?' "

Perhaps because she's a teacher, Sally has found lessons in the stresses of motherhood, and she has shared these with the other girls.

Her younger daughter, Katie, was a very fussy baby. "She cried for about three months straight," Sally says. One day, Sally was driving back to Ames to see her parents, her husband wasn't with her, and she was feeling overwhelmed. Katie was a baby. Lindsay was two years old.

"Katie had been crying continuously," Sally later wrote in an email to the other Ames girls. "Lindsay kept trying to keep a pacifier in Katie's mouth, to give her a bottle — just something to stop the noise. I felt so exhausted and tense. Finally, Katie fell asleep and there was blissful silence for about two minutes. Then Lindsay said, 'Mom . . . Hey, Mom . . .' I really just wanted quiet, so I gave her an exasperated, annoyed and impatient 'What is it?'

"I turned to look in the backseat and saw Lindsay looking at Katie. Then she said, 'I just think Katie is so beautiful.' I of course told her that I agreed that they were both beautiful. But honestly, I felt ashamed that my two-year-old showed so much more patience with the whole situation than I had."

As mothers, the girls also help each other by straightforwardly sharing the ways they've found to cope and then thrive.

After she quit work to stay home with Alexa, her first daughter, Diana found herself emotional for long stretches. Alexa did a lot of crying. Diana seemed to cry even more. Her husband would come home at dinnertime and he'd find her sitting on the floor of the closet, crying. "Alexa just keeps crying and I don't know how to get her to stop," she'd say. She had more experience, of course, by the time she had her other two daughters. But she has admitted to the Ames girls that until her youngest reached kindergarten, "I felt like we were completely out of control, like we were literally drowning." She told the Ames girls about a mother in her daughters' elementary school who left the kids and moved to a beach in

Mexico.

When she was overwrought or was struggling to discipline the kids, Diana would tell her husband, half seriously, half kidding: "That's it! I'm moving to Mexico!" And he'd respond: "No. You can stay here. I'm moving to Mexico!" They both made it through without moving to Mexico.

The age difference between Kelly's sons, Quin and Cooper, is just fourteen months, and when they were boys, sibling rivalry led to a lot of arguing and physical fights. "I can't deal with it," Kelly told Diana one day. "None of my teaching skills are working. We'll go to McDonald's and they'll both demand the same Happy Meal toy. Then they'll get in the minivan and they'll both want the same seat." Kelly feared her older son, Quin, might actually hurt Cooper. "Cooper lets his older brother pummel him," Kelly said. "I'm freaking out. I have no strategies." Diana had joined a parenting group, and she asked other parents there for input. When they suggested a certain book on sibling rivalry, Diana immediately sent it to Kelly as a present. "That book saved me," Kelly recalls. "It helped me realize that I wasn't a failure — that even good kids and good parents go through this." (As a teen, Cooper is six-foot-four, and his older brother, who's five-foot-ten, knows not to mess with him. "Both boys are in wrestling and play football, and now they're best friends," says Kelly.)

Marilyn felt a bit of postpartum depression after her first child was born in 1994. She was on maternity leave from her job as a career consultant. "You feel like having a baby should be great," she said, "especially when you're a first-time mother. And then, well, some of it is not so great." Her son Christopher was born in the fall, and by the time she was comfortable taking him out and about, it was winter in Minnesota — cold, icy, dark. She'd find herself driving around with Christopher, feeling sleep-deprived, nervous and grouchy.

After her other two kids were born, she sometimes felt resentful, even doing things she enjoyed. She had always loved going to the family lake house, where she had so many childhood memories. But now the idea of packing up the kids and all their belongings felt like an unpleasant chore, not an adventure. Her mother noticed that she just didn't seem like herself, and told her so.

Marilyn had worked until her third child was born, but by 2000, she had stopped working and was home caring for the kids while her husband, Chris, a business consultant, was on the road four days a week. She felt very lonely, with three kids under age six to look after, mostly by herself.

At one point, she took her kids to the pediatrician and he asked her how she was making out as a mother. She told him: "I feel like I'm raising my voice a lot more than I ever have in my life. I'm concerned about that." The doctor's response: "Well you have three little kids and a husband who's out of town a lot. It's normal to feel this way."

Still, something didn't feel right to Marilyn. She eventually went to her own doctor and was diagnosed with depression. Since then, she has taken mild antidepressants, which she says "take the edge off" and make her a more patient, more loving, happier mother. A large part of her feels very fulfilled, focusing her life, at least for now, on helping her three kids learn how to appreciate and embrace education, to find a path to more independence — and to be better people.

She has told the other girls that she calls one of her medications "the be-a-nice-mommy-instead-of-a-screaming-bitch pill." "I can definitely tell when I'm not on it," she says. "I become a 'screaming meemie.' Even the dog has the sense to run for cover."

Because Marilyn feels she has been helped, she's very open about the medications she's taking. She has warned the others that it's important to find the right dosages and the right regimen of medications. One antidepressant led her to gain twenty pounds, which isn't uncommon.

Marilyn also points out that depression can be part of the aging process, no different than high cholesterol or thyroid issues. She and her husband have jokingly changed the words to the song "The Wheels on the Bus": "The wheels on the bus start falling off, falling off, falling off, the wheels on the bus start falling off — at the age of forty!"

Marilyn believes that speaking frankly about her medications to the other girls can be a great service to them; maybe they'll see signs of depression in their own lives. "It's not an embarrassment, because it's neurological. It's not something you can control by eating right and exercise," she says. The girls are generally open about how they've helped themselves through challenging times in their lives, whether it's Cathy talking about being in therapy or Marilyn talking about taking the antidepressant Effexor. The girls are pretty matter-of-fact when they're together, and it's comforting. "I'm not the only one opening a pillbox," Marilyn says.

In recent years, women's health proponents have singled out women like Marilyn as frontline soldiers in the battles against depression. The reason is this: Though 70 percent of women in a 2004 nationwide survey said they felt "depressed, stressed, anxious or sad" in the previous twelve months, only 27 percent of them talked to their doctors about this. So who do most of them talk to? Their girlfriends.

More than 60 percent of women who have signs of depression tell their friends how they're feeling, according to this survey by the National Association of Nurse Practitioners in Women's Health. Given how women confide in each other, the organization created a program called "Girlfriends for Life: Helping Each Other Stay Healthy." The program was designed to raise awareness that friends can be crucial players in recognizing the symptoms of depression and encouraging those in crisis (or just suffering the blues) to get help. As program organizers put it: "Sometimes the only thing keeping a woman from falling over is the girlfriend right beside her."

Now that most of their kids are heading into their teens, the Ames girls spend some of their time at the reunion at Angela's trading tips on how best to connect with them. "I find they'll do a lot of good talking in the car, if you're quiet and listen to them," Sally says.

"I've read research about asking open-ended questions," Jane says. "You don't ask, 'Did you have a good day at school?' You need to say, 'Tell me about your math class.' And you've got to get them when they're fresh, right home from school. If you wait until the end of the day, before they go to bed, they're not going to share as much — or at all."

Karla talks about her son, who likes to come home from school and go sit up in a tree in front of the house to think. When he climbs down from the tree, he's often ready for conversation with Karla or Bruce.

The girls swap stories about the sorts of questions their kids ask them. Karen tells of the day her son came home from sixth grade and said the gym teacher had been enlisted to give "the sex talk" to students. "We're at the dinner table," Karen says, "and first he tells us that he saw a picture of a vagina. Then he has a question for us. He wanted to know: 'So how much comes out during an ejaculation?' " Karen was impressed that her husband figured out a way to calmly answer the question. "He got the soap dispenser, squirted a little into his palm, and just said, 'That much.'"

Kelly tells the girls about her daughter Liesl's questions. Having two older brothers, and watching them get potty trained, Liesl learned early what a penis was. Then one day at the supermarket, she wanted a candy bar and Kelly told her it had peanuts in it. "Her eyes got huge," Kelly recalls. "She said, 'Really? That candy bar has a penis in it?'" More recently, as a teen, Liesl asked Kelly: "When you and dad were married, when did you have sex?" Kelly answered: "When you were asleep." (It's a good answer, some of the other girls say, but it might just lead a kid to stay awake all night.)

Because the girls live all over the country, they also compare geographical differences in their children. The Midwest contingent gets a kick out of the fact that Diana's daughter heads west from Arizona in the summer and goes to "surf camp" on the beaches of California. And here at the reunion, they're all taken with Angela's seven-year-old daughter, Camryn, and her Southern accent. Camryn is so poised as she asks polite questions about the girls' friendships and talks about her own friends.

Meanwhile, those with older kids talk about how their offspring now give them unsolicited advice: "You're too old to wear a bikini." "You're too young to be complaining about how tired you are." "You're too judgmental, Mom!"

Diana tells a story about the ways in which daughters notice how their mother's bodies are declining. "My friend Barb in Arizona was sitting with her thirteen-year-old daughter," Diana says. "Her daughter wanted to snuggle with her, so she put her head down on my friend's chest. She kept lifting her head, putting it down. My friend asked her, 'What are you doing?' She said, 'Mom, where's your boob?' So my friend told her, 'Hold on, honey. I think it's down here.' Then she readjusted herself, pulled herself up, and all was well." The girls roar at that story.

When the girls are together, questions are raised: How do they each view themselves as parents? Are they succeeding? Are their kids thriving? Are they happy being mothers?

"Parenting is rewarding but hard," says Jane. "My heart is definitely in it, but I'd give myself a B as a parent."

The girls talk about all the bad parents in the world. "OK," Jane says, "compared to a lot of what's out there, I'll give myself an A."

Given the often frenetic nature of their parenting lives — the struggles to stay on top of everything — the girls say they've found it easier over the years to forgive their own parents' deficiencies. Karen tells a story, dating back to middle school, about the day when she needed to bring in a baby photo of herself to class. Because she was the fifth of five children in her household, there were far fewer photos of her. Her mother looked, but couldn't even find a baby photo of Karen. So she gave her a photo of her older sister, Barb.

"Mom, that's not me. It's Barb," Karen said.

"It's OK," her mother said. "You looked just like her when you were a baby."

The other girls laugh over this story, and then Cathy jokingly says, "My mom probably gave me a picture of my older brother. I'll talk about it in therapy."

The girls share stories of how they've found new reasons to appreciate their own parents now that they're adults. Angela tells about the day in 1979 when her dad came home and said he no longer would be working as the manager of the Gateway Center Hotel in Ames. (It would later become a

Holiday Inn.) He couldn't bring himself to say he'd been fired. He just said he planned to find another job. Angela knew he'd likely need to look beyond Ames, and so she began crying, telling him she couldn't leave her friends, she just couldn't! Years later, her dad told her that seeing her reaction that day, and realizing how much she loved and needed the other girls in her life, he made a decision. He'd limit his job search to Ames. It was a selfless act for Angela's dad — limiting his own career because he had put his daughter's happiness first.

Conversations about motherhood lead naturally into conversations about fatherhood, and their husbands' strengths and deficiencies.

This Ames girls' reunion is lasting almost four days. That means their husbands back home are looking after twenty children on their own. The girls think this might be beneficial for both their kids and their husbands — offering one-on-one time without motherly interference.

Diana, Jane, Angela and Sally — who between them have eight daughters and no sons — say they hope a little bit of confiding is going on between their daughters and husbands while they're cocooned here at the reunion.

These are not easy times for fathers and daughters. As diligent dads try to bond with daughters born in the 1990s, many are struggling. Across America, Daddy's little girl is growing up faster than ever — in a world of date-rape drugs and risqué clothing — and fathers often respond by ignoring danger signals or by retreating to a life focused on their sons. Even before daughters are born, many fathers feel conflicted. A 2003 Gallup poll showed that 45 percent of men would prefer having a son if they had only one child, compared with 19 percent who'd prefer a daughter — a ratio little changed since 1941. And once a girl arrives, her parents are 6 percent more likely to get divorced than if she was a boy, according to a study by researchers at the University of California at Los Angeles and the University of Rochester. Parents with three daughters are about 10 percent more likely to get divorced than parents of three sons. In homes with teenaged girls, the likelihood of divorce doubles. (The reason dads with sons are less apt to divorce: They may feel a greater need to stick around as a male role model. They're also more comfortable around boys.)

At the same time, reams of research show that girls who are close to their dads are less likely to be promiscuous, develop eating disorders, drop out of school or commit suicide.

For the most part, the Ames girls say their husbands are pretty good at connecting with their daughters, though the men will sometimes say, "You'd better go talk to your mother about that."

Like so many men, their husbands often feel most comfortable bonding through activities. "My husband and daughter play golf together," says Sally. Walking eighteen holes, a dad and daughter can discover a lot about each other.

Because most of their husbands arrived in the girls' lives after they left Ames, the men aren't especially close to each other. They are friendly and cordial, and they enjoy each other's company when they get together as a group. But they recognize that the relationships between the girls themselves are almost sacred. The men see no need to form close bonds with each other.

The girls say they completely appreciate that their husbands — every one of them, including Kelly's ex — have been supportive of their get-togethers over the years. Their husbands don't make them feel guilty about leaving the family for their reunions. "Go," they say, "and have a good time. The kids and I will be here when you get back."

Late one night during the reunion, Kelly is talking about her divorce, and Cathy, the only Ames girl who never married, throws a question out to the group: "Do you all feel as if you'll be with your husbands forever?"

All the married girls say that yes, they'll make it to the end.

And then Cathy asks, "Well, if you're in this for forever and ever, how good do you expect it to be?"

From there, a decision is made. Just for fun, the girls are going to rate their husbands. They agree to go around the room one by one using the old reliable scale of one to ten. "Today, my marriage is a ten; I haven't seen him yet," one of the girls says jokingly. Another asks: "Are we rating the man or the marriage? Because that could be two different numbers."

(To resist starting trouble in their marriages, the girls are reluctant to reveal all of their comments, and their husbands' individual scores, for inclusion in this book.)

They decide they'll rate the men on several factors, including "the quality of life he brings to my family," "how he makes me feel about myself," "how involved he is as a father," "how attentive he is" and "how attractive I still find him."

Kelly is divorced, of course, and Cathy is single, but the other eight all say that their husbands are decent men — good providers with strong work ethics, smart guys with lots of interests.

Some of the nonworking Ames girls say they appreciate that their husbands earn a good living, allowing them to stay home. That helped lift a husband's score. Some of the working women say their husbands encourage their careers — another score-booster.

Someone comes up with a straightforward line of questioning they all can contemplate: When my husband gets home from work, how do I feel? Am I glad to see him? Am I neutral about it? Or do I think, "OK, now I have to deal with him and his issues"?

One of the girls says she actually gets a little excited when her husband walks in the door. A few others say they wish they had that feeling, but they don't. "That's the time of day when I'd like some downtime, and that's when he wants to talk," one says.

"I feel excited when I see my husband driving away," someone says. (She's kidding!)

Do any of their husbands get excited when they walk in the door?

"When we get home from this reunion, they'll definitely be glad to see us," one says. "That's when they'll be able to hand the kids back to us."

Over the years, some of the girls have had slight, innocent flirtations with other men or at least have found other men attractive from a distance. They can talk about these sightings or interactions with each other far more easily than with their friends back home. If there's a man they notice is handsome at Little League or at a PTA meeting, there's no upside in mentioning it to a neighbor, who might know the man and his family. But here, in the confines of an Ames girls reunion, it's easy to share this sort of thing. They're still faithful to their husbands, but they're more comfortable here revealing whatever they've been thinking.

Cathy asks if they can picture their husbands married to anyone else. Or could they see themselves married to any of the other Ames girls' husbands? "I could picture myself having an affair with your husband," one says jokingly about a husband the girls have repeatedly mentioned as being very attractive.

The girls acknowledge some issues in their marriages. One says she sometimes feels as if all she has in common with her husband is their shared devotion to their children.

And there are the full range of annoying habits to be discussed, which lower husbands' scores slightly: "He puts his dirty clothes next to the hamper, not in it." "He never washes fruits and vegetables." "The day we're having people over is the day he decides to clean the garage." "I clean up the house and put stuff at the bottom of the staircase to go upstairs. Every time he goes up the stairs, he just walks by whatever I've put there." "When I clear the table, I'll take all the dishes to the sink. When he gets up, he takes only his dish."

"When something is lost, I want to keep looking until I find it. I'll look and I'll look," one of the girls says. "My husband gives up looking so early. That's annoying to me."

"He's a good-looking bad looker," someone responds.

Coming up with an exact score for each husband is an inexact science. "It's hard to rate husbands, because a lot depends on the day," one girl says. "Sometimes it's a ten, and then the next day it's a five."

None of the eight married women give their husbands a rating lower than six. And when they add up all of their scores and divide by eight, the average score for their husbands is an 8.2. Not bad, they decide.

When they were girls in Ames, dreaming of storybook romances and marriages, would they have been happy with the idea of an 8.2 marriage?

Truth is, as girls, they couldn't even fathom the full impact of being a wife and mother.

"I'll take an 8.2," one of the girls says. "I think that's a sign of a happy household."

As the reunion continues, Jenny is waiting for the opportune time to give everyone some special news. She hasn't had any alcohol since she arrived, and no one notices. Then during one of their dinners, she gets the attention of everyone at the table and tells them her surprise: At age forty-four, she is a couple months pregnant. Her three-year-old son, Jack, will have a sibling.

Everyone is so thrilled for her. There are hugs and congratulations all around.

Jenny, overjoyed at this later-in-life chance to have a second child, admits to a memory dating back to the weekend she got married in Ames in 1996. A bunch of the Ames girls had come into town with their children, and they were planning to get together so all the kids could interact with each other. Jenny, of course, was too busy with wedding duties to join them. But a thought was in her head that day: "I sure wouldn't be too interested in hanging out with a bunch of kids. I'm glad I don't have to go to that gathering! Who wants to be with all those kids?"

Perceptions and feelings change, of course. "My favorite thing about my life is being Jack's mom," Jenny now says. "If I knew how wonderful it would be, I would have done it earlier."

She thinks being an older mother has made her far more patient, less fearful about things like germs, more able to compartmentalize duties at home and on her job at the University of Maryland School of Medicine, where she is assistant dean of public affairs. "I think I'm a better mom because I work. I am lucky to be able to feel a strong sense of accomplishment at the office, and it's nice to have adult conversations there. I don't feel like I should be at work when I'm at home, and that I should be at home when I am at work. When I'm home, I'm totally present.

"I'm proud of the work I do, I really am, though if I didn't do it, somebody else could. But nobody can raise Jack the way I can. He's my kid and I think I can raise him best."

Jenny tells the others that longevity is in her genes, so she hopes she'll be around for her kids for a long time. (After her grand-mother died, her grandfather courted and then married his sister-in-law — Jenny's grandmother's sister. "We called her Aunt Grandma," Jenny says. "Aunt Grandma lived to be 103. So I'm hoping to live long, too.")

If all goes well with the pregnancy, Jenny will deliver a baby who will come of age in the 2020s. What issues will Jenny face as an older parent then? Will "cooperation and appreciation" still be the appropriate man-tra? Will the other Ames girls all be grand-mothers by then, giving short shrift to her emailed questions about raising teens?

The day after Jenny's announcement of her pregnancy, the girls go into Angela's backyard so photos can be taken of them all in a group with their hands on Jenny's belly. The photos are meant to mirror those taken when they were in their late twenties, hav-ing their first children.

The girls will look older in these new photos, of course, but they're infinitely wiser, too. "It'll be so wonderful to have another new life in our lives," Kelly says as she and the others take their positions in a half-moon around Jenny, literally envelop-ing her in their good wishes.

15
News from Ames

"Any news from Ames?"

Always, whenever the girls get to talking, someone will eventually ask that question. And of course, there is always news. Most of their parents are still in town, keeping them informed, sending them clippings from the *Ames Tribune,* sharing stories about births, marriages, divorces.

Sometimes, the news from home is just fluffy and amusing.

Here at the reunion, Karen offers a report about a certain woman she bumped into during a recent visit to see her parents in Ames. The woman looked stunning — her figure, her face — and Karen mentioned this when she saw Dr. Good, the dentist she used to work for. "She looked so cute!" Karen told Dr. Good. "I don't remember her being so cute." He responded: "For the right price, you can also be that cute. Even cuter."

In her hometown near Philadelphia, Ka-

The girls at their twentieth Ames High School reunion in 2001

ren knows plenty of women who've had extensive plastic surgery. "At the gym, the ones with plastic surgery do sit-ups and their boobs point toward the ceiling. They jump up and down and nothing moves. Meanwhile the rest of us are wearing two bras." On the East and West Coasts, bionic boobs are everywhere. But to think that women in Ames are lining up to have head-to-toe plastic surgery — well, that's news-worthy.

The news from Ames is not always so frivolous, of course. The girls also share reports of their parents' illnesses or setbacks in their siblings' lives or "news" they've happened upon on visits home. Several of the girls have taken their kids sledding on the hill by Ames Municipal Cemetery. While the kids sled, they've stood silently in the snow at Sheila's grave site, and then walked around, spotting names they know — teachers, classmates, parents . . . people they never realized were gone. Sometimes, the girls get their news from Ames on slabs of marble.

In recent years, it has become easier to get news coverage from home in real time. All the girls have to do is type "Ames" into Yahoo! or Google News, and the latest media reports fill their computer screens. They're then able to email interesting links to each other. It's a continuous sharing of all things Ames.

National news emanating from Ames picks up every four years because of the presidential races. The Iowa caucuses began getting attention in the national press in 1972, but the caucuses didn't become full-blown media events until after the girls left town in the 1980s.

From then on, each presidential cycle got crazier than the one before. The girls would phone home and they'd be lucky to get through. Often, their parents' phones were busy because so many campaigns were calling, inviting them to meet the candidates at teas or luncheons or cornfield rallies. "I heard from four potential presidents yesterday," Jenny's mother told her one morning, wearily, "and three so far today, but it's not even noon yet."

On his first campaign swing through Ames in February 2007, a full eleven months before the caucuses, Barack Obama told a crowd of locals that he was having trouble being taken seriously. He lamented that the media was reporting on what he looked like in a swimsuit while on vacation in Hawaii, rather than his positions on the Iraq War. According to TV news coverage that night, the Ames crowd cheered Obama wildly, which led the Ames girls to wonder about both his Iraq policies and what he looked like in a swimsuit.

Often, when Ames hits the news, the girls can't help but be reminded of each other, their families and, of course, their childhoods.

After September 11, 2001, when someone was mailing deadly anthrax to politicians and media outlets, early news reports said the anthrax was "the Ames strain." Researchers at Iowa State had been studying anthrax since 1928, and microbiologists there had more than one hundred vials of anthrax. Scores of news reports suggested that someone in Ames, perhaps working in tandem with terrorists, was responsible for the anthrax attacks. The girls had to wonder: Could it be an old acquaintance? Some weird guy they knew in high school? Eventually, it was determined that the anthrax used in the mailings couldn't have come from Iowa State. Wrong strain. False alarm.

For the girls, spread around the country, such news brought back memories of the mysteries from their childhoods, when they had classmates whose parents or grandparents had secret jobs at Ames Lab, making atom bombs.

In the mid-1990s, when some of the girls called home and asked for updates, they were told that Marilyn's father was trying to stop construction of a youth sports complex in town. The complex's soccer field was slated to be built adjacent to a site where, in the 1950s, radioactive thorium was deposited by the Ames Lab. Dr. McCormack helped organize a citizens' group that had the soil tested for signs of radiation. The group contended that test results showed the field would be dangerous for children. The Iowa Department of Public

Health argued that the field's radiation levels were within acceptable standards, and children would be no less safe there than elsewhere in Ames.

Marilyn's dad had given an impassioned speech at a public hearing. As a pediatrician, he explained that infants and growing children are highly susceptible to cellular damage from radiation. He talked about cancer risks. And then, as the city council looked on, he folded his arms together as if cradling an imaginary infant. "I've tried to make sure that the babies in this town were raised in good health," he said, "and I didn't do that to have them die on that soccer field." People in attendance that night said Dr. McCormack had tears in his eyes.

When he realized that he was suffering from the onset of Alzheimer's, he passed on leadership of the protest movement to others. He helped convince thirty-six doctors to sign a statement against the sports complex, and they also raised questions about radiation issues elsewhere in Ames. There were reasons for concern: Relatively young alumni of Ames High were dying, often of cancer, at rates that seemed high. On some streets, cancer and Parkinson's disease were visiting almost half the homes. No studies were done, so the incidences were dismissed as anecdotal. But the reports were troubling.

Even as Alzheimer's began stealing his lucidity thought by thought, Dr. McCormack kept lobbying against building those sports fields in that location. He talked about how dust would be kicked up and kids would breathe it in. City councilwoman Pat Brown, a friend of Jane's and Marilyn's families, became a vocal opponent to the sports complex. One night by phone, she received a death threat warning her to support the complex "or you'll be sorry." She needed twenty-four-hour police protection for a while after that.

"Dr. McCormack was a respected man," Brown now says, "but people didn't listen to him."

The sports complex ended up passing in city council and the soccer field was built. Thousands of children have played soccer on it each year since.

The news from Ames. So often, it left emotions swirling.

Sometimes the news from Ames was about one of the girls themselves.

One day in February 2007, Marilyn drove down to Iowa from her home in Minnesota to have dinner with Jane's parents — and to venture into the Ames Public Library. This specific library visit was a planned mission. Marilyn had finally decided to go into the microfilm room, to find the cabinet labeled "Ames Daily Tribune" and, for the first time in her life, to open the drawer that contained the film for September 1960.

Holding the box in her hands, she felt a kind of unsettling curiosity, and more than a bit of dread and sadness. What would she learn by looking at it?

She sat down, spooled the film into the microfilm reader, flipped on the switch and then turned the dial to the right. Front-page photos, movie listings and sports news from 1960 began speeding by her on the screen. She didn't stop to read anything. She was looking for the front page from September 26. The film whirred by so fast that by the time she stopped it, September 29 was on the screen. She turned the dial in reverse . . . September 28, September 27 . . . and then there it was, September 26, with the front-page headline: "Accident Fatal to Ames Boy."

It was the biggest news in Ames that day, bigger than two major stories that were bumped lower on the page. One of the bumped articles was a preview of the tele-vised Nixon-Kennedy debate, to be held

411

that night. Headlined "Much at Stake, Nixon-Kennedy Debate Tonight," the article described the debate as "an electronic suggestion of the famous debates 102 years ago between Abraham Lincoln and Stephen A. Douglas." The other big story was about President Eisenhower's arrival by motorcade for a United Nations General Assembly meeting. More than 750,000 New Yorkers had crowded the streets to greet him. That day, Fidel Castro would give an infamous four-hour speech at the UN, lambasting U.S. policies.

And yet, those two historic stories were dwarfed on the front page of *The Ames Tribune* by the large photo of two smashed cars that had met at the crossroads of four cornfields. The death of Marilyn's brother Billy had pushed everything else aside. Marilyn was here in the microfilm room because she had decided she wanted to know as much as she could about what happened that day.

Looking at that giant photo on the front page, she broke into tears, and that surprised her. She thought she was doing research, not digging into her psyche. She had never before cried for Billy, at least not that she could recall. She knew, of course, that Billy's death had led to her dad's vasectomy reversal, and to her birth, and that the accident was very well the most traumatic moment in the lives of her siblings and parents. But, as she would later tell the other girls, she had always been emotionally strong about it.

She surprised herself again, there in the library, when a memory came crashing into her head, a memory of a car accident back in Minnesota five years earlier. Her husband was driving the family car home from church on a Sunday morning. She was in the front passenger seat and their three kids were in back, along with two of her sister's kids. A car made an illegal turn at a red light and smashed into them. The airbags went off, and their car was totaled, but miraculously, nobody was badly hurt. And right then, looking at that microfilmed image of the 1960 car wreck, it occurred to Marilyn that both her son and nephew had been around the age Billy was when he died. And looking at that awful 1960 photo in *The Ames Tribune,* she thought to herself: "Maybe it was Billy. Maybe Billy put his hand down and touched the five kids in our car, and somehow said, 'No, not them.' "

Through her tears, she continued to study the microfilm version of the story about the accident. It spelled out details — that the two-car collision happened at 11:45 A.M. at the intersection of two gravel roads, that Marilyn's mother and three other siblings were seriously hurt, that tall cornstalks may have obstructed the view. The story said Billy was seven years old, though he was actually still six. His birthday was a few weeks away.

The article also gave specifics about the fifteen-year-old boy who had plowed his speeding car into the McCormacks' station wagon, and about how he had violated his "school permit," which allowed him to drive only on a direct route to school and back. The boy had been injured also and was hospitalized. His name was in the article: Elwood Koelder.

Seeing the name startled Marilyn. She'd never known the boy's name, though she was aware that her parents had long ago forgiven him. "He was just a boy himself," her mom would say. And now to finally have his name in front of her, well, Marilyn decided immediately that she wanted to find him.

She wiped away her tears, printed out a copy of that article and put the microfilm box back in the drawer. That night, over dinner with Jane's parents, she recounted her visit to the library.

"His name is Elwood Koelder, and he'd be sixty-two years old now, if he's still alive," she told them. "I'd like to talk to him."

"What will you say to him?" they asked.

"I don't know," she said. She wondered whether he felt remorse or thought about her brother each year on September 26. How had the accident affected his life?

"Maybe I'll tell him it's OK. If he's been hurting about this all these years, he can go easier on himself. I got the chance to live in this world because of what happened that day, so maybe I'm the one who should tell him this."

Marilyn has a letter in her hands that she printed out on her computer back home and brought to North Carolina for the reunion. Several of the girls are on the back porch with her, and she's explaining how the letter came to be written.

She tells them about discovering Elwood's name on microfilm and then plugging it into Google. Within seconds, she had found a small-town newspaper story from 2005 about a truck driver named El Koelder, who lived in Milford, Iowa. The story was about how he and his friends spent sixteen years trying to harvest a pumpkin large enough to win top prize at the local county fair.

Marilyn couldn't find a listing for Elwood in directory assistance, but she did find a number for a fellow pumpkin grower mentioned in the article. She called and talked to him. "I knew about Elwood from a long time ago and wonder what he's up to now," she said.

The man was chatty, telling her that Elwood worked as a truck driver, had a son who served in Iraq, and was separated from his wife. He gave her Elwood's cell phone number, but then asked, "Now, who is this again?" Marilyn gave her name and then said, "It's been a long time. I don't even know if Elwood would remember me or my family. . . ."

"I felt a little underhanded," Marilyn tells the girls, as they sit on the porch, "but I really wanted his number."

"Did you call right away?" someone asks.

"No," she says. "I figured I'd wait until the weekend, when he wasn't driving his truck. I didn't want to startle him and have him drive off the road."

Actually, three months passed before she found the courage to make the call. Her heart pounded as Elwood answered, and she began by introducing herself. Her name was not familiar to him. She asked if he was driving and wanted to pull over. He said he was in his truck, but he had a hands-free headset on his cell phone. He was fine. And so she began.

"In 1960," she said, "my family was in a car accident and I believe you were the driver of the other car. My brother, who was almost seven years old, died in that accident. . . ."

There was a pause. "Yes," he said. "I remember."

"I don't want to alarm you," Marilyn told him. "That's not why I'm calling. I guess I just want to tell you that after my brother died, things turned out well for the rest of my family. We're OK. I guess I'm contacting you because I need this closure."

He was listening. Marilyn went on. "What I'd really like to do," she said, "is send you a letter to tell you who I am, and to ask how you've been since that accident. Do you mind if I ask for your address?"

"I'd like to read your letter," he said softly, "and I will call you back after I get it." He gave her his address.

He asked her no questions. Maybe he got the sense that she wanted to begin their dialogue with the letter, not over the phone. "This may be a lot to absorb while you're on the road," Marilyn said.

"We will speak again after I read your letter," he told her. "Thank you for calling."

When Marilyn finishes telling the other Ames girls about that phone call, she pulls out the letter she wrote and passes it around. Jane and Karla read it earlier, in a back bedroom. Now the other girls are seeing it.

In the letter, she told Elwood the things she knew about the accident, how it had led to her birth, and she reassured him that her parents never blamed him. She asked him what memories he had of that day, what injuries he had endured, how his family reacted.

As the other Ames girls consider the letter, one paragraph Marilyn wrote stands out for some of them. It begins: "I wanted to write to tell you that I owe you thanks. Had it not been for the accident, I wouldn't have been born. I wouldn't have had the great childhood I had growing up in Ames. I wouldn't have the friends I made there. I wouldn't have my wonderful husband and children."

She ended her letter: "Not many people get the opportunity to communicate, in a positive way, about a life-changing accident. I would like to get a letter from you to find out how your life has been. I wonder if you've been happy, if you're happy now. I want to let you know that if you ever had or still do have any anguish over the accident, well, I think that God has a way of planning things. I am relieved that you were receptive to giving me your address when I called you. I look forward to hearing from you."

A couple of the girls tell Marilyn that it's a very moving letter, that it could bring closure, that they're eager to see if and how Elwood responds.

"My daughter says the story of how I tracked down Elwood could be a movie," Marilyn says.

"If they made a movie," one of the other girls tells her, "you'd be single, he'd be gorgeous, you'd fall in love, and you'd drive off in his truck and get married."

Six of the girls are taking a hike on a state park trail a half hour from Angela's house. Marilyn is walking with Kelly, while Jane and Karla are a little farther up the trail, discussing the letter to Elwood that Marilyn showed them earlier in the day.

"Marilyn wrote it from her heart," Jane says, "but I just couldn't get past her saying 'thank you.' Those aren't the right words. If you say them out loud, it's like saying, 'Thank you for killing my brother.' It made me angry that she said that. It bothered me.

She shouldn't be thanking him."

"I thought exactly the same thing!" Karla says. "That line jumped out at me." It felt to Jane and Karla as if Marilyn's thank-you was offering Ellwood an opportunity to say, "You're welcome."

Marilyn catches up with them, and Jane speaks to her frankly. "I found the letter a little troubling. I just didn't think 'thank you' is what you meant to say."

"No," Marilyn allows, "that isn't the message I wanted to give."

"What would have been a better way to say it?" Karla asks, and Jane considers the question as they walk through the woods.

"I guess," says Jane, "that I would have worded it something like: 'I just want you to know the full story of my family, in case you've wondered. The accident happened. We can't change that. We understand it was probably painful for you, too. And I just want to put things in context for you. I want you to know that I am a consequence of what happened. My birth is a consequence.' "

Marilyn has already put the letter in the mail. It's too late to edit out her thank-you. But she smiles at her old friend. "Context . . . consequence . . ." Perfect words. Why hadn't she shown that letter to Jane before she mailed it? It means a lot to her that Jane would parse the letter, looking out for her.

"Thank you," she says, and this time, she means exactly that.

16
THROUGH KELLY'S EYES

It's time to go to sleep, and the girls are in various bedrooms at Angela's. Kelly joins a conversation in the room Cathy, Karen and Diana are sharing, and the talk turns to hairstyles.

"All my life, I wanted beautiful long hair like yours," Kelly tells Karen, "but my hair grows very slowly and I get tired of my style. So I end up cutting it short in a fit of restlessness. Then I have to slowly grow it all out again."

The girls tell Kelly that her hairstyle hasn't changed much since high school. That surprises Kelly. In her mind, she recalls times when she had arranged her hair differently over the years. But here are her friends telling her that when they look at her, they see the same old Kelly with the same old hairdo.

Maybe that's because Kelly always looked her best in the same haircut. But she cer-

Kelly, Karla, Sally, Marilyn

tainly had her hair moments that came and went. In junior high, her mom took her to get her hair cut by a woman who had a salon in her basement. Ice skater Dorothy Hamill was the woman influencing style at the time, and Kelly was talked into getting her hair cut into that cute bob. Given her very curly hair, Kelly thought she looked ridiculous in that style. She never ventured into that basement again.

In ninth and tenth grades, she and the other girls carried big combs in the back pockets of their first designer jeans. In the summers, they used lemon juice to try to lighten their hair.

Early in high school, Kelly got her first

perm by a stylist Cathy and her mom recommended. She took Diana with her and enjoyed meeting the openly gay stylist. She had what she called "enormous eighties hair" for a while.

And then there was the time *Grease* came to a theater in Ames, and Kelly and Diana attempted to dye their hair before attending. Kelly the brunette tried to go pink, and blond Diana tried to go black. The results were iffy at best, but Kelly recalls feeling proud and radical.

In her adult life, too, Kelly had different hairstyles. But here are her old friends telling her they see her as predictable. And so Kelly makes a decision, but doesn't articulate it. She's going to grow out her hair — make a real change — and then come to the next reunion with a new look. It's past time, given the changes in her life, the divorce, her arrival in her forties. What will she look like with long hair? What will the girls say when they see her? Kelly can hardly wait for the next reunion.

At this moment, none of the others know the unexpected direction in which life will take Kelly, or what her hair will say about her when they next see her.

Kelly and her husband made the decision

to separate in 2005, right before the reunion at Diana's house in Arizona, and about a year after Christie's death. Kelly arrived early that weekend, before everyone else, and when Diana picked her up at the airport, Kelly was an emotional wreck. She hadn't yet told any of the girls she was getting divorced, and on the drive to Diana's house, she spilled everything.

Kelly admitted she enjoyed spending time with another man she knew from work. The new man was appealing, Kelly said, because he was "organized, tidy and kind, and maybe that's what I think I need right now."

Kelly was so grateful for the ways in which Diana was there for her. In Kelly's view, her old friend was being nonjudgmental. Kelly felt like, in that moment, she was finding out what it was like to have unconditional love from a friend.

On several fronts, Diana disapproved of the ways in which Kelly contributed to the breakup of the marriage.

This was the second time Kelly struggled with the concept of staying faithful in a marriage where she wasn't happy. The first time was when she'd been married for three years and her husband was traveling a lot for work. As Kelly explained it: "My affair was with a man who was handsome and carefree. He was also around, while my husband was often gone, working in another state. It lasted six weeks, and then I vowed never to have an affair again. But then I met someone after Christie's death, and I had no desire to stay faithful."

Diana listened and offered sympathetic words when appropriate, and silence when that seemed right. She kept Kelly busy with projects. Years earlier, Karla and Kelly had started a reunion tradition in which the host put together an amusing welcome gift for the others. Diana had decided that she wanted to make slippers to give the girls when they arrived at the Arizona reunion.

"Kelly, you'll help me," she said.

The slippers would be made with, of all things, Maxi Pads. A woman in Diana's church had a crafts table set up in her home, so Diana told Kelly they needed to go over there to learn the process. Each slipper would require two Maxi Pads. One would become the sole of the slipper, and the other one would wrap around the toes, forming the top of the slipper. The pads would then need to be glued together and decorated with beads, flowers and charms.

Kelly considered the whole process. "I am not a crafty person," she said. In fact, she was proud of one of her Christmas letters to the other girls that had poked fun at Martha Stewart.

"You can do it," Diana said. "It's going to be fun."

Diana took Kelly to the grocery store and they stood in the feminine hygiene aisle, discussing what types of pads to buy.

"Extra long or extra thick?" Diana wondered.

"I don't know," Kelly said.

"I'm thinking extra long," Diana decided.

Kelly was thinking: "This is totally surreal. My life is an uproar. And I'm making crafts out of Maxi Pads."

But maybe that was exactly the diversionary therapy Kelly needed. She had stepped into a foreign world, where Maxi Pad crafts enthusiasts were connecting with each other online, emailing amusing suggestions for how to describe the slippers on gift cards: "soft and hygienic," "built-in deodorant feature to keep feet smelling fresh," "no more bending over to mop up spills." At least these crafts-crazy women didn't take life so seriously.

When they returned to Diana's house, Diana put Kelly in charge of the glue gun. They started assembling the slippers, adding on plastic flowers and other baubles. It went on like that for a couple of hours; they talked, they glued, they took apart Maxi Pads. Kelly confided in Diana about wanting to be with another man. Sometime after that, she left her glue gun tipped sideways, and Diana snapped at her.

"What are you doing, Kelly? Will you watch it please? You can't leave the glue gun tipped sideways! Come on."

Kelly found herself thinking: Here was one of life's great ironies. Diana seemed to be understanding about Kelly leaving her marriage. But here she was, chastising her for a sideways glue gun. Maybe Diana's feelings about Kelly's questionable decisions were showing up on the Maxi Pad front.

As the night wore on, Kelly and Diana got so caught up in the slipper assembly line that, until the phone rang, Diana didn't realize that she'd forgotten to pick up one of her daughters at church. Diana rushed out of the house, and Kelly was left holding the glue gun.

As she worked, one of Diana's other daughters asked if she would test her on her spelling words.

And so Kelly sat there, gluing baubles on Maxi Pads, calling out words and making sure they were spelled right, all the while contemplating the end of her marriage.

The next day, the other girls arrived and

Kelly began filling them all in. Most listened, resisted being judgmental, and occasionally shared a helpful story of divorce that their siblings or other relatives went through. Like Karla, Angela had gotten divorced and remarried, and both of them were able to offer Kelly their perspective that light comes after darkness. As they spoke to her, Kelly thought to herself: "It's comforting to have people who can give you stories that make a difference when it's so bleak."

Upset and distraught over the breakup, Kelly's husband had her cell phone service stopped because he was angry at her and didn't trust her while she was at Diana's. So she was in Arizona without a phone. Then her husband wanted to talk to her so he called Diana's house several times. Unpleasant conversations were sure to ensue if Kelly took the phone, so she didn't. Her husband always got along well with the other Ames girls. He respected and liked them. "But he assumes you'll unify behind me," Kelly said, "and that's hard for him."

It was obvious that Kelly's husband was caught up in his anger and the swirling emotions he was feeling. Diana finally and firmly told him to stop calling, to just give Kelly this time alone with her friends, and he complied. Kelly was grateful that Diana took this stand. The weekend with the girls became a brief respite from so many hard issues swirling back in Minnesota.

A large part of Kelly was beside herself. But through it all, she also found herself having fun. Just being with the other girls made that inevitable. At one point, the women all put on their Maxi Pad slippers, circled up the way they did as girls, and each put one foot forward. Then they aimed their cameras downward to capture what looked like the March of the Maxi Pads. They couldn't stop laughing.

There were times that weekend when Kelly felt desperate, confused and shattered. But she also felt embraced and loved. And that sustained her.

When Kelly thinks back to her childhood dreams, to what she wanted to do or be when she grew up, she always had a clear, four-word answer in her own head. "I want to write."

She didn't always articulate that to her friends. She recalls signing up for Career Day in junior high with some of the other girls. What career should they learn more about? They decided, like so many of their female classmates, to meet with the modeling agency that had come to school. As Kelly now thinks back to that day, she realizes that she went only to be with her friends. She has an image in her head of Diana, in a tan outfit with a hat and her Farrah Fawcett hair. Diana certainly could be a model! But Kelly? She wanted to be a writer.

She was and is a terrific writer. The girls have known this since childhood. They see her writing talents in her emails to them, and in the stories she sent them from her 2000–2004 stint as a local newspaper reporter, when she took a hiatus from teaching. Now back in the classroom, she feels she is living her writing dream by teaching journalism and writing to a new generation.

In her forties, Kelly senses that the word "writer" can be defined broadly. It's about expressing emotion. It's about helping people think. It's about using words to understand herself. It's about helping other people find their own words.

Briefly in high school, Kelly thought she might want to spend some time in the military. Later, in college, she flirted with the idea of joining the Peace Corps. "Teaching definitely fills that void," she has told the other girls.

Kelly loved working as a newspaper reporter, but she returned to teaching because she missed interacting with kids, especially teaching them about First Amendment issues. She feels First Amendment rights have been restricted during the Bush years and wants her students to be more active citizens.

Many of her students call her "Zwag," rather than Ms. Zwagerman. They say she is unlike any teacher at the high school. Spend a day with her students, and they speak openly about her. "Most teachers, you can't argue with them," one boy says, "but Zwag is the kind of teacher who thinks that what you say matters. She likes to go back and forth with you. She wants that give-and-take." Says another student: "She'll mark up your paper with a red pen, and when you get it back, there's so much red you can't bring yourself to look at it. We don't like it, but we do realize that she tells it as she sees it."

As Kelly explains it: "Every red mark is an opportunity to teach."

"She's my track coach," one boy says. "She coaches me in the hurdles. Even if you win and feel you had the perfect race, she's always telling you what's wrong and how you can improve. That's not easy. Sometimes I get Zwag overdose."

Kelly has talked with her students about her relationships with the Ames girls, and they are intrigued and full of questions. In the office of the student newspaper, *The Echo,* a group of the editors are sitting around and one girl says, "It's great that Zwag has so many friends. I have one friend — that's why we're sitting here next to each other — and she's my best and pretty much only friend. I wish I had more friends like Zwag has."

These Faribault students talk about how groups of friends form in high schools today. There are the typical groupings — the druggies, the jocks, the nerds. But there are new subgroups now. At schools today, for instance, there are groups of girls who are all anorexic and sit together at the same lunch table every day, not eating. There are girls bonded together as "cutters" — their friendships bound in self-injury.

Kelly monitors her students closely, trying to stay aware of problems in their home lives, their friendships, their own fragile psyches.

Some of the Ames girls worry that Kelly is too open with her students. As she guides them through their own issues, she's not averse to sharing personal details of her own life and struggles. She's open about her own political views and her honest assessment of administrators with whom she has battled. She counts ex-students among some of her best adult friends now. They are in their twenties and thirties, and Kelly is both mentor and confidant to them. At the same time, they help her see the world from a younger perspective.

Kelly hears the other Ames girls' concerns, but in her mind, they don't quite understand her view: that she isn't just teaching journalism to her students. She's teaching them about the world beyond Faribault, Minnesota. And when a teacher and former student become friends, it's an honor and gift to both.

The other girls notice that Kelly didn't move far from Ames, that she took a traditional job as a teacher, that she is not the full rebel they predicted she'd be when they were all young. But Kelly still sees herself as strident. In fact, she thinks that in some ways, she's more of a rebel now.

Gay rights is just one of many causes Kelly has embraced as an adult that wasn't on her radar screen when she was a girl back in Ames. She is proud of a letter she received from a mother of one of her students who is gay. The letter arrived a few weeks before she headed to the reunion at Angela's.

Faribault is a mostly conservative town, of course. Kelly's brave support of the gay boy did not go unnoticed by his mother, who wrote:

I am so thankful for your presence in my son's life. Teachers can and do make a difference. Sometimes they close the doors for young minds, but not you. You challenge them. You encourage them. But mostly, you have taken the time to support and befriend my son. You have empowered him and guided him to use his voice and his pen to express himself. I know of some of your more personal conversations, and I am so proud that my son would choose a person of your caliber to confide in. It tells me that he has the ability to recognize wisdom when in his presence. Thank you for taking risks.

Kelly considers her greatest achievement to be the work she has done with students such as this boy. She also is proud of the efforts she has put into raising her kids, but knows her divorce has taken a toll. Because her three children live primarily with their father, and because she and her ex are not speaking, there have been challenges and difficulties. Her children have blamed her for the demise of the marriage, but now there seems to be a better understanding that both people in a bad marriage play a role when it fails.

In Kelly's view, she did make attempts to save the relationship.

The very week of Christie's death in February 2004, she had rethought everything. She was on leave from teaching, working at the local newspaper, and she just decided to quit the reporting job and add a year to her leave. She wanted to explore who she was and rethink her marriage.

She had been married since 1987, and she knew the relationship was floundering. Was there any way to save it? She thought she'd try. In the summer of 2004, she planned a five-week family road trip out west. She wanted to pull her family together, to show her husband, her two sons and her daughter that she appreciated them and felt blessed that they were all healthy. But the trip served only to drive home the obvious: Her marriage was over. A couple of months after the vacation, her family visited her husband's relatives. "I knew I was seeing them for the last time," she says.

Kelly tries to reflect on marriage and motherhood honestly. "I hope I've contributed in a meaningful way to my children's growth and development," she says. "Certainly, I provide the basic necessities, but I do wonder if lessons I've tried to teach them will make a difference in their lives. The jury is still out on this, with all three of them in high school. I'm holding my breath and I'm just hoping they make choices that keep them safe." Kelly assumes they'll experiment in ways that she and her friends did when they were teens. "But I had the other girls to catch me when I fell," she says, "and I'm not sure my kids have such a strong support system from their friends. My children are very influenced by their friends, and I'm not sure they have the safety net I had with the girls in Ames."

Kelly's daughter Liesl is fourteen years old and has come to recognize how crucial friends can be. "I think friends are way important — sometimes more important than family," she says. Why does she say that? "Because of divorce."

She explains that she has been able to confide in her friends about her parents' breakup because so many of them have divorced parents, too. She has bonded with several other girls over divorce. She's had one particular friend since first grade, and that girl "is really wise. She gives me lots of good advice. I feel like she helped me through everything when I was really mad at my mother over the divorce. Even though I was mad, my friend told me to hang out with my mom."

The parents of another friend have an amicable divorce, and Liesl envies that. "For Mother's Day, my friend's father made breakfast at his house and took it over to the mother's house. So they were able to celebrate Mother's Day as a family. That sounded nice."

Liesl is saddened that her parents are not at the stage where they can spend time together. And because she has begun to look so much like Kelly, she says she wonders if her dad is thinking of his negative feelings toward Kelly when he looks at her.

But overall, Liesl says things are improving. For Valentine's Day, Liesl came to Kelly's house and they ordered a heart-shaped pizza and rented some romantic movies. They talked about Liesl's long-distance boyfriend, who lives in a town that Liesl described precisely as "twenty-six minutes away." The boyfriend is always texting Liesl, and she loves getting his texts. He has promised, however, that if he ever breaks up with her, he won't do it by text, and she appreciates that.

Liesl's texting stories have reminded Kelly of her own texting adventures, post-divorce. "The first text message I ever received was from a man I dated last spring," she says. "There was something incredibly exciting and a little erotic about receiving 'thinking of you' as I was finishing the school day. I quickly taught myself how to send a text message back, and from that point on, we sent 'good morning' and 'good night' messages every day."

Kelly now trades text messages with her students — at all hours, if they have homework questions, they get in touch — and at times she has had all three of her kids in the car, and they've all been texting at once. She noticed how silent it was in the car, yet everyone was communicating.

And so Liesl's texting love life, her fears about being dumped via a text — it all resonated with Kelly. And bonding with her daughter on Valentine's Day was a thrill on other fronts, too. They vowed to each other that, at least for the foreseeable future, they'd try to spend a part of every Valentine's Day together, so they aren't just relying on the boyfriends in their lives.

Liesl said she was glad she spent last Valentine's Day with her mom. "I love her," she said, "and wanted her to know it."

■ ■ ■ ■

Like all the Ames girls, Kelly has given thought to the question of who she is now and what she wants from her life moving forward. "I want to be a strong female role model," she says. "I want to be an inspirational and motivational teacher. I want to be a parent who builds a network of love and support for my children, which includes involving my parents in their lives. I want to be a kind and caring friend."

Over the years, she has come to a realization about the Ames girls: All of them have close family ties — they're close to siblings, parents, children. "These women seem to have an extraordinary capacity for strong connections, and not just with their families and the group of us, but also with their newer friends and colleagues. Maybe through our strong friendship we have learned how to more deeply care for others."

Kelly's liberal leanings are shared by some of the other girls, but not by all. "It's therapeutic to talk politics with Cathy, Jane, Angela and Sally," she says. "Some of the others are more private, and we respect that."

Not long before the reunion at Diana's, George W. Bush was inaugurated for a second term, and there were disagreements among the girls about his record and about the war in Iraq. At one point, the conversation turned to gay marriage, and it was obvious that others weren't in agreement with Kelly's more liberal support of it. She tried to steer the conversation off of that topic because she feared it might get unpleasant. One day they all went for a hike and broke into groups. When Kelly's group returned, Cathy pulled her aside and joked, "You left me with the Republicans!"

Actually, because she lives in California, Cathy is grateful that some of the other Ames girls connect her with a part of conservative America she rarely sees anymore. She lives in the quintessential blue state. Almost all of her friends there are West Coast liberals. And yet when she sees the humanity, good intentions and mid-American values of someone like Marilyn, she says, it's as if she's getting a reminder to temper any urges to be dismissive of red-state conservatives. "Marilyn is also a face of the red states," she tells herself.

The girls are proud that they resist getting into political arguments or combative philosophical debates. That would defeat one of the reasons they get together. As Kelly explains: "When I am with them, I am reduced to someone who simply experiences joy in the moment. It is like walking into a party where everyone knows each other and everyone is having fun. My gut aches from laughing when I am with them. How often do any of us experience exhilarating moments of happiness? So consider this: Every time I am with these women, even when mourning brings us together, I am lifted up with joy."

In all sorts of ways, Kelly is happy to be in her forties now. "A lot of women in their forties look fabulous," she says. "They're working out, their bodies are fit, they take great care of their skin and hair. It's no wonder that the acronym MILF has become popular." (For those who don't know the term: Just Google it!)

As Kelly sees it, almost everything she has learned about beauty has come from the other Ames girls. "I don't spend a lot of time exploring new beauty products, and I often don't know about new trends, but every time I get together with them, I learn ways to improve my diet, my skin, my hair. I get a crash course from them on what works and what doesn't. They are truly a panel of health and beauty experts."

Maybe it's their Midwestern roots, but Kelly believes most of the other girls try to portray a look that radiates health as opposed to glamour. "I don't get manicures and pedicures," Kelly says. "I'm not overly zealous about whitening my teeth. I'm not going in for skin treatments. I am ardently against breast enhancement."

Her focus on health as opposed to glamour is her way to combat a culture in which women are still objectified and there's an unrealistic airbrushed ideal that is everywhere in the media.

Kelly has been monitoring the culture's impact on women all her life and in all sorts of ways, so she's a bit of a barometer for her friends in that respect.

When Kelly considers the woman she has become, she sees flashes of the fighting spirit she first developed back in Ames. Yes, she and the other girls benefited from the Title IX legislation of 1972, designed to end discrimination against girls in sports and educational opportunities. But Kelly also remembers the bad old days.

There was the time at fifth-grade recess when she and a few other girls decided to play soccer with the boys. A teacher came running out and angrily told the girls to quit the game. The teacher, a woman, implied that by being so physical, the girls were acting in a seductive manner when they had contact with the boys. Kelly proudly recalls how she and the other girls heard the teacher out, then chose to keep playing.

In junior high, when Kelly was student council president, she attended a meeting with teachers, parents and students to discuss ways to improve the school. One suggestion was to make sure the girls and boys had equal activities. Someone said, "Girls should be allowed to do the pole vault in track." Kelly can still remember how one of the adults laughed. "That won't work," he said. "Girls will never have the upper body strength to do the pole vault."

But there were sea changes, too, showing up in the living rooms around Ames, and Kelly now believes the impact wasn't insignificant. "During our formative teenage years," she says, "women featured on TV shows went from playing housewives to being the Bionic Woman and Wonder Woman and Charlie's Angels. The first female athletes who made an impression on us entered our lives when we watched the Olympics. They participated in sports very few of us were involved in, but at least we were seeing strong female athletes in competitive situations."

Kelly likes telling the other girls that once she began teaching, the feminist mentors in her life were her older colleagues. Encouragement from them kept her in the workplace. She had one fellow teacher named Ruth who was an ardent feminist and took Kelly under her wing. In 1995, after her third child was born, Kelly thought about leaving teaching. She had actually turned in her letter of resignation, explaining that with three children under age four, she felt overwhelmed with the duties of motherhood and needed to be home. Ruth convinced her to stay, to think about how her decision would affect her pension. "I did it," Ruth said to Kelly. "You can, too."

Ruth told her about how, as a young mother in the days before car seats, she'd tuck her baby in a laundry basket to transport her to a babysitter each day. "Women used to lose their jobs once they became pregnant," Ruth said. "They'd hide their pregnancies as long as they could."

Kelly listened and then took back her letter of resignation. "It was a way to honor the women who had been pushed out of their jobs when they became mothers," Kelly now says.

She understands and admires the other

Ames girls who choose not to work outside the house. But she says she has a special appreciation for the working women among them, for how they balance work and family.

"I once listened to a debate between working moms and stay-at-home moms," Kelly says. "Although I respect that this is a very personal choice, it's important for society to acknowledge the benefits of women in the workplace. We need to praise the women who are doing essential, valuable jobs — and not criticize them."

Kelly is proud that there are three working teachers in the group — Kelly at a high school, Sally at an elementary school and Jane at a college — and that Karen may someday return to teaching. She admires how Jenny has a high-powered job as an assistant dean of public affairs at a university and that Angela runs her own public relations company.

When Kelly's daughter Liesl has a day off from her own school in Northfield, Minnesota, Kelly invites her to drive south with her and join her for the day as she teaches at Faribault High School. "I want to model for her how happy a woman can be at work," she says.

■ ■ ■ ■

Kelly admires the back stories of how her old friends from Ames found their way in the workforce. Jane was always smart and inner-directed back in Ames, so Kelly wasn't surprised that she'd work hard to get her Ph.D. and become a professor. Angela has always been a terrific multitasker — taking on a host of projects and committees as a student at Ames High. So Kelly knew she'd make a go of it when she began building her own PR agency in North Carolina. Angela was suited to juggle a host of clients, motherhood and more.

Kelly thinks it's terrific that Diana had a full career years ago as a certified public accountant, then took time off to raise her kids and has now gone back to work twenty hours a week behind the counter at a Starbucks near her home in Arizona. Since her husband is self-employed, Diana likes that her family can take advantage of the full health-care benefits that Starbucks offers even its part-time workers. And Diana says she's having a lot of fun working as a barista — interacting with regular customers and knowing their names and their orders before they ask. She calls it great exercise for an aging brain. "Some people do Sudoku," she says. "I work at Starbucks."

Diana also likes talking and listening to her younger coworkers. She feels protective of some of the teens and twentysomethings who work with her — and she learns a lot from them, too. They give her a glimpse into the world her preteen daughters will inhabit in a few years. She's impressed by so many things about them, but she's also a bit taken aback by all their piercings and tattoos. "Their lives are exciting, though sometimes worrisome," she says, "and getting to know them gives me a lead-in to discuss issues with my kids at home." Her coworkers have asked what she'll do if her kids come home someday with body art. "Well, honestly, I hope the trend doesn't last too long," she tells them, "but I know there are much worse things they could get involved in. I'll just keep loving and supporting them."

Kelly likes the idea of Diana — who drinks hot chocolate, not coffee — spending her days at Starbucks learning from her young coworkers. It sounds like more of a kick, and appears more emotionally rewarding, than being a CPA.

Kelly also is proud of Jenny, whose earlier career was in politics. Jenny came from a family that was active in Republican Party circles in Iowa. Her grandmother was a state legislator, and her grandfather, a newspaperman, knew Ronald Reagan back when the future president was a radio sports announcer in Iowa. The two men once took a train together from Des Moines to a convention in New York, playing poker all the way.

Because of her GOP pedigree, Jenny joined the Young Republicans when she got to the University of South Carolina. In 1984, Nancy Reagan made a campaign stop at the school, and Jenny was on the committee that met her at the airport.

Jenny was in the Delta Delta Delta sorority and had heard that in her day Mrs. Reagan was, too. "It's so nice to meet you, Mrs. Reagan," Jenny said, as they shook hands. "And I just want you to know that I'm so glad you're a Tri Delt!"

Mrs. Reagan smiled and replied, "Well, I went to an all-girls school. I wasn't in a sorority. I'm not a Tri Delt."

Jenny found herself stammering, "I'm so embarrassed," and Mrs. Reagan rescued the situation by saying, "Well, is it still nice to meet me?"

After graduation, Jenny went to Washington, D.C., and worked as a receptionist at the National Republican Congressional Committee. Then, in 1986, she got a job as

449

an aide to an Ohio Republican in Congress, Donald (Buz) Lukens. It was an exciting time to be young, learning about how government works, dealing with constituents and hanging out after work with other young Republican staffers.

"In a House office, the staffers are like a family," Jenny would explain to Kelly and the other girls. "There are only six of us, and it's close quarters. We're all in our twenties, and it's almost like Buz is the dad and we're all the kids."

At first, she described the congressman to the others as "a perfectly nice old guy." He was in his fifties then and divorced. Jenny found it interesting that no matter how unattractive, fat or churlish a politician might be, there were always "congressional groupies throwing themselves at these guys, mostly women in their thirties and forties."

Buz was a politically incorrect throwback, and in the 1980s, people like him were still common at the Capitol. He called Jenny and the other young female staffers "honey." He put his arm around everyone. "He's very touchy-feely," Jenny said, "but he's harmless and he cares about all of us."

Then Congressman Lukens was caught paying $40 to a sixteen-year-old girl to have sex with him. The encounter was secretly taped by an Ohio TV station. After that made headlines, a House elevator operator accused him of fondling her.

A firestorm followed, and there was even a photo in the congressional newspaper, *Roll Call*, illustrating the fact that Lukens and his staffers were under siege. The photo showed the hand of a Lukens staffer sticking out from behind a partially closed door to the congressman's office. Between the fingers was a sign that read: "No comment." That hand was Jenny's.

Lukens would end up resigning, and it was left to Jenny and her colleagues to pack up his belongings. He was too depressed to help. Congress had been his life and now he was ruined. Jenny worried she'd come into the office one morning and find him dead. (He would later go to jail for nine days.)

Once he was gone, Jenny and the other staffers held on to their jobs for a couple of months; there were still constituents' needs to attend to. But Jenny found herself unable to get another job on Capitol Hill. "It's awful," Jenny told some of the other Ames girls. "All the other offices have shunned not just the congressman, but those of us on his staff. We're pariahs. We're unhirable. No one will even interview us."

Jenny worked as a temp for a while and

eventually got a job at the Business Round-table, an association for corporate chief executives. In those years, Kelly would take her students to visit Washington for national journalism conventions, and she'd meet up with Jenny in fancy hotel lobby bars and listen to updates on her career and love life. Eventually, Jenny ended up in her job as an assistant dean at the University of Maryland School of Medicine.

The picture of Jenny in Kelly's mind was always the image of the smalltown girl she was back in Ames, driving around in that old World War II–era jeep her dad had bought her. Now, in Washington, Jenny seemed so sophisticated and glamorous, advising Kelly on the transit system, the best hotels, the sites an average tourist wouldn't know about. She wore heels and a suit, while Kelly was in tennis shoes — a teacher from the Midwest touring the Capitol with wide-eyed students.

Jenny took Kelly to her office, and Kelly thought she seemed so worldly. Around her cubicle, Jenny displayed photos of her family and friends — so Ames had a presence — but the work Jenny was doing just seemed important. For the Business Roundtable, Jenny was working on a public-service ad campaign aimed at asking legislators to fund programs that help American children be more competitive in math and science.

While Kelly was impressed with Jenny's work, Jenny viewed her old friend as so much further along in life. Kelly already had children. And here she was, visiting Washington, leading a group of fresh-faced students from Minnesota, a busload of kids who depended on her and looked up to her. To Jenny, Kelly seemed like the more developed adult.

It was intriguing how Jenny and Kelly viewed each other. For her part, Jenny felt as if she'd arrived at her success without having a clear game plan. When she was a child, her mother was very busy with community and charity projects, but she was almost always in the house when Jenny got home from school. "I always thought my role in life was to be a mom and serve the community," Jenny says. "It wouldn't have occurred to me that I'd be the sort of working woman I am now. Who would I have seen in Ames who is like me now?"

Jenny feels circumstances turned her into who she is. "When I got to Washington, where it felt like seven women to every man, I realized I had to change my plan. I looked around and said, 'Well, there's no one here I want to marry who wants to marry me, so

I'd better go with Plan B.' And that's when I decided I'd better be serious about what I'd be when I grew up." (As things turned out, Jenny didn't end up marrying until 1996. She and her husband, involved in their marriage and careers, waited eight more years before having a child.)

After marveling at Jenny's career trajectory, Kelly is impressed by the ease with which Jenny has now segued into late-in-life motherhood.

"Although any of the women would be wonderful role models for my daughter, Liesl," Kelly says, "I've really been drawn to Jenny over the past few years. Several times, I have held her hands during sad moments — including at Christie's memorial service — and each time I was surprised by how small and fragile they seemed, and yet how strong they are."

Since her divorce, Kelly has tried to look at her life as it is, to appreciate the light and deal with the darkness. "I never imagined a life where I would feel so alone," she says, "that I would be a mother but not have my children with me all the time, that I could have lovers but not have someone as a constant in my life."

On the positive side, here at the reunion

at Angela's, she shares with the other Ames girls her observations about all sorts of wonderful moments in her life back in Minnesota. She tells Sally about a man she has dated. "He's used to petting animals," Kelly explains, "and when I'm on the couch watching a movie with him, he'll pet my neck. Oh my God, I love that! It's like heaven to have a man pet your neck. You put your head in his lap and he's just stroking. The whole movie!"

Kelly tells the others that she holds in her heart her memories of that weekend reunion at Diana's, when the girls were all there for her, a militia in Maxi Pad slippers. She thinks back to the long walks she took in the Arizona desert air with Angela and Sally, and how willing they were to think deeply about what advice they had for her. She recalls the flight back to Minnesota with Karla, and how Karla offered her home as a safe place to stay if Kelly ever felt she needed that. Kelly thanks them all for that.

Kelly tells the girls that her daughter is completely intrigued by their relationships. In one of Angela's bedrooms, while Kelly is getting dressed for dinner, her cell phone keeps buzzing. It's Liesl, texting her.

One of Liesl's first text messages reads: "I can't wait to see you Wednesday!"

Another says: "When I see you Wednesday, what do you want to do?"

And then Liesl comes up with a plan. "Mom, we'll have ice cream and you'll tell me everything about the weekend. I can't wait to hear about all of it!"

"Liesl knows exactly why we're all down here together," Kelly tells the other girls over dinner, "and she's excited for the details."

She plans to tell Liesl the specifics of the weekend — where they went for dinner, how they went for hikes, the sort of conversations they had until early in the morning. But those are just the particulars. What Kelly really hopes Liesl will pick up in her retelling is a feeling of how deep the bonds between women can get.

She's not sure what exact words she'll say, but Kelly the wordsmith would like her daughter to know this:

"Having these women in my world has meant not only acceptance, but radiant joy and laughter that knocks me right out of my chair. Through our darkest moments, we have lifted each other up. In every moment of grief we've shared, our laughter is a life vest, a secure promise that we will not go under."

17
MYSTERIES
AND MEMORIES

It is just after breakfast on the final day of the reunion, and Jane tells the other girls that she has noticed something: They're showing up in her dreams a lot more lately.

Maybe it's the fact that, through email now, the girls seem to be in closer contact than at any other time in their adult lives. Maybe it's because of her daughter's bat mitzvah project involving Christie or her deepening bonds with Karla. She also suspects that, because they have been sharing stories for this book, long-buried memories and questions have been floating into her subconscious.

In the mornings, she doesn't have clear recall of these dreams, or any real sense of what they might signify. She just knows she has spent part of her night in Ames with old friends. Later on some mornings, when she's out running, she also finds herself thinking about the girls and the roles they've served in her life.

For all of the Ames girls, even in their waking hours, there is a dreamy quality to some of their memories of their lives together — especially those involving mysteries and unanswered questions.

As the years have passed, however, they've found the courage to make contact with certain people or to ask questions they didn't ask when they were younger. And so some old mysteries can be at least partially resolved. This is especially true on two fronts, one involving Marilyn, the other involving Sheila.

On August 1, 2007, the I-35 Bridge in Minneapolis collapsed during evening rush hour, sending about a hundred vehicles into the Mississippi River and onto its banks. Thirteen people died, 145 were injured, and because more than 140,000 vehicles had crossed the bridge that day, it felt as if a terrible lottery had hit the residents of the Twin Cities. Who was unlucky enough to be on the bridge at exactly 6:05 P.M.?

After the collapse, area residents fielded millions of phone calls and emails from their friends and relatives across the country, all asking: "Are you OK?" As Minnesotans, Karla, Kelly and Marilyn heard from the

458

other Ames girls in the hours that followed; the others shared their concern and then relief that they were safe. But Marilyn was most moved by the very first email she received after the collapse. It came from Elwood Koelder, the other driver in the 1960 accident that killed her brother.

She still hadn't met him or had their long-awaited full conversation. But she was touched by his unexpected email. "Just a quick note," he wrote, "checking that none of your family has been involved in this catastrophe."

Marilyn wrote back that her family was fine, and that she appreciated hearing from him. It was meaningful to her that Elwood had chosen a tragedy like this as an opportunity to show concern for the family scarred by that long-ago tragedy involving him.

After that, Marilyn did get on the phone with Elwood to follow up on the letter she had written to him. She later recounted the conversation in an email to the other Ames girls. It felt surreal speaking to him, she said, but also cathartic.

"I told Elwood what I always say to my kids: 'There's a difference between an accident and on purpose.' If Elwood had killed Billy intentionally, I don't know that I would be interested in contacting him. But it was an accident, and he was just a child himself."

Elwood told Marilyn that he was on his way home from church the morning of the accident. He said he doesn't remember the actual collision — how fast he might have been going, how the cornstalks obstructed his view, anything. At the moment of impact, he was thrown from his car, ended up underneath it, and passed out. When he came to, he heard his horn blaring and tried to get up, hitting his head on the undercarriage of the car. The horn continued unabated, so he made his way to the hood, opened it, and pulled on some wires, and finally it went silent. That's when he saw the McCormacks' destroyed car, some of its occupants still inside, and felt an awful kind of adrenaline racing through his body.

Dr. McCormack was already out of the car, and Elwood helped him lift Billy out of the front seat. Elwood recalled what Dr. McCormack said to him: "Thank you for your help. I'll take it from here." (After learning of Elwood's recollection, Marilyn and her family saw it as a quintessential Dr. McCormack response. It was just the sort of gentle direction he'd use to guide a nurse, an EMT or his own children.) Over the years, Elwood said, he has wondered to himself: "Is there anything else I could have done to help that boy?"

Elwood spent a week in the hospital, recovering from a concussion. He also had a knee injury. Because he was driving on a permit that allowed him to travel only to and from school, he was charged with not having a valid driver's license. When his case was reviewed, however, his family argued that the fifteen-year-old boy had driven to church Sunday school the morning of the accident, so in essence he was on his way home from "school." The court fined him just $25 and the case wasn't pursued any further. The McCormacks never chose to file a civil suit.

"When he told me about the $25 fine, that was the only part of his story that twisted a knife in me," Marilyn wrote in her email to the girls. "I had to repeat to myself: This was an accident. He didn't do this on purpose."

Elwood told Marilyn about his family — three daughters, a stepson who is an army staff sergeant, grandchildren. He talked about his work as an Iowa-based truck driver, delivering doors and countertops to retail outlets such as Home Depot, and he said he was reeling from the high price of

461

gas. He said he hoped to meet Marilyn in person the next time he drove through Minnesota.

After the phone call, Marilyn's older sister, Sara, decided to write to Elwood also. She shared her letter with Marilyn, since she thought it might be cathartic for Marilyn also to have a record of Sara's recollections of that day and her memories of Billy.

She began by thanking Elwood for his concern after the I-35 Bridge tragedy, then shared with him a few images of Billy. (He died just before his seventh birthday, when Sara was five.) Sara recalled being a preschooler and wrestling with Billy in the hallway early one morning. Her father, still in bed, called out to them: "Billy and Sara, are you two dressed yet?" "We were completely naked," Sara wrote to Elwood, "but Billy replied with a resounding 'Yes!' It was a unique concept to me that one could lie, but I followed his example with an equally enthusiastic 'Yes!!!' before we scampered off to put on our clothes."

Sara told Elwood about one of her father's favorite memories of Billy: "When Dad returned from work each day, Billy would laugh so hard that he would sometimes fall on the floor." Sara also wrote of how, after the accident, adults would say things to her that felt a bit off the mark. "I recall a well-meaning woman who said, 'God needs your brother more than your family did.' Even though I was young, I thought, 'It was simply an accident. The God I know wouldn't take a child away from a family for his own needs.' "

Sara wanted Elwood to know that "the crossing of your path with ours gave my siblings and me the opportunity to learn more about our parents' philosophies of life. Dad said that many people offered him condolences after the accident. He also told us about a custodian at the medical clinic who lost his son at about the same time. The boy had been playing in a construction hole, and the dirt caved in on him. 'People may have known me better because I was a physician,' Dad said, 'but my pain was no greater than his.' Dad kept speaking to the custodian about his son's death, because he knew others would move on and stop asking.

"Dad was clear and gentle when communicating with parents of a child who had died. He would ask about their marriages, whether they had left their child's room untouched, and if they still expected to see their child run into the kitchen at breakfast time. 'I know it is like rubbing salt into wounds when I ask you about your child,' Dad would say, 'but I want you to be able to speak about your child with laughter and joy, rather than pain. I will keep meeting with you until that happens.' "

Sara wanted Elwood to understand also how grateful she was to have Marilyn as her sister. "I always regarded Marilyn as a special present to me from my parents," she wrote. In explaining the trajectory of the McCormacks' lives after the accident, Sara also said that the family came to say "I love you" more frequently. "We try not to lose sight of the extraordinary importance of family and friends."

For his part, Elwood now says he was "blown away" the first time he heard from Marilyn, and he welcomed news of her existence. It was overwhelming to him to learn that she was born after her dad's reversed vasectomy. Speaking one day by cell phone as he drives his truck, he says that getting to know Marilyn and her family has served to ease his mind. Billy has been part of his life for forty-seven years. "I've thought about that little guy," he says. "And now, knowing that a new life came into the world for the one that went out, well, it's a miracle, is what it is."

Elwood says he has been moved and

impressed by what Marilyn has told him about her friendships with the other Ames girls. It's sobering, he says, to think that Marilyn's identity as a doctor's daughter and her place in this group of friends were in certain ways informed by her brother's death and her feelings of not wanting to disappoint her grieving parents. "You never know what will happen to you because of what happened to someone else," Elwood says. "You just never know."

Around the same time that Marilyn was tracking down Elwood, the Ames girls were also reestablishing ties with Sheila's family.

They had gotten word that Sheila's younger brother, Mark, had a four-year-old son with a rare form of cancer. A Caring Bridge Web site had been set up to share health updates, and the girls visited it and left messages to let the Walsh family know that little Charlie was in their thoughts.

Kelly, Sally and Karla had seen Sheila's mom a couple of years earlier at the memorial service for Cathy's mother. But for most of the others, this was their first contact with the Walsh family in many years. Visiting the Caring Bridge site, of course, reminded the girls of all those months when Christie was writing about her cancer journey. It was hard for Karla, especially, to read about Charlie, but her note to the Walshes was upbeat: "I'm sending positive energy to all of you. Know that Sheila's friends are praying for your family."

The other girls also left notes of encouragement, identifying themselves to Charlie as "friends of your Aunt Sheila." "You are a very handsome boy, and oh so brave," wrote Angela. "I went to school with your Aunt Sheila and think of her often." Marilyn wrote: "Keep smiling, champ!"

Sheila's mom, Sheila's sister and two of her brothers had moved to Kansas City, Missouri, and they were touched to see all the comments on Caring Bridge from Sheila's old friends. It had been a long time.

One afternoon, on the spacious back deck of Mark's upscale suburban home, he and his mom, along with his sister, Susan, and brother Mike, agreed to speak for this book about their feelings regarding the other Ames girls, and to share their memories of Sheila. (A third brother, Matt, lived out of town.)

Mrs. Walsh admitted that she was disappointed because most of the other Ames girls didn't stay in touch after Sheila died. "They just literally deserted me," she said. "They never came around. Never. It would have been nice if they had." But she is forgiving because she understands that they were also grieving and were unsure how to respond or what to say to her.

She saw those who attended Sheila's funeral. "Yes, some of them came, but you know, they were grieving within their group." She doesn't recall them coming up to her; if they did, it was brief. "It's OK. They were young."

(For their part, the Ames girls recall feeling a bit slighted at the memorial service. Ushers asked them how they knew Sheila, and when they said they were her friends from childhood and high school, they were directed to a side pew. Susan's and Sheila's college friends were seated more prominently. When people are grieving, and their emotions are so heightened, they notice such things.)

Sheila's family described her as being completely devoted to the other Ames girls. If someone made a crack about, say, the weight of one of her friends, Sheila would respond sharply. "She was intensely loyal," said Susan. "If you were in her inner circle, she would jump off a cliff for you."

The Walshes smiled and laughed over many of their memories of Sheila. They remembered when she and some of the other Ames girls did neck exercises, twisting and stretching their necks so they wouldn't get wrinkles.

Susan said she and Sheila were sometimes very close, and other times, there was distance — or they fought. Though they were only eighteen months apart, they traveled in different circles of friends, especially as they got older. Sheila had told the other Ames girls that it was hard to live in Susan's shadow, because Susan was so beautiful and accomplished, and got along better with their mom. Susan now understands some of the dynamics. "I was a rule-follower," Susan said, "and Sheila wasn't."

They shared a room, and Susan has sweet memories of late-night conversations and of games they played as little girls. One was a convoluted "how hot are you now?" game they'd play by adjusting the settings on each other's electric blankets.

"There's something about losing a sister," Susan said. "It's like losing a part of yourself. In a lot of ways, she made me feel good about myself." She added: "Each of us has put our memories of Sheila in a sort of protective, separate compartment, deep down inside somewhere." It was emotional for them to be talking again so openly about her.

Sheila was headstrong. When Mrs. Walsh took the girls clothes shopping, she said, "Susan had this tall, thin figure and was easy to fit. Sheila was harder. And she always wanted something that didn't look good on her. So shopping trips could be ruined."

The family was often reminded of how close Sheila was to Dr. Walsh. Mark said that as an early teen, he used to go on a five-mile race with his father, and Sheila sometimes pedaled along on her bike. The first time he outran his father, Sheila was very upset. "She was actually crying," Mark said. "She asked me, 'How'd you beat him with those little legs of yours?' She just had this bond with him. She was Daddy's girl."

"She knew how to work him," said Susan.

"To Sheila, he was a softy," Mrs. Walsh added.

As a dentist, Dr. Walsh had a reputation of being very gentle when he put his hands in a patient's mouth. He often had that same gentleness in how he dealt with his children, especially Sheila.

Susan and Sheila were in the same sorority at the University of Kansas — when Sheila was a freshman, Susan was a sophomore. For her twentieth birthday, Susan received $100 from her dad. He died two days later at age forty-seven of a heart attack, and Susan ended up using the $100 toward plane tickets for her and Sheila to go home for the funeral. On the plane that day, they both were very quiet, their faces pale, their eyes red from crying. Two young men on the plane noticed these two pretty, red-eyed girls and tried to hit on them. "Hey, what have you two been doing?" one of them asked.

"They assumed we were stoned," Susan said. "It's weird, the things that you remember about moments like that."

After Dr. Walsh died, Sheila was grieving for herself, but also very concerned about how her mother was faring. "She was just so empathetic," Mrs. Walsh said. "And she was such a good listener."

Mrs. Walsh said she never went on a date after her husband died. She was too busy trying to raise five children on her own. She smiled at one memory of the weeks after Dr. Walsh's death. She was with a friend in her bedroom, trying to figure out how much the family would have to live on after factoring in Dr. Walsh's life insurance payout and any remaining proceeds from his dental practice.

"Oh my gosh," she said to her friend after she finished her calculations. "We're only going to have five hundred dollars a month. The mortgage is more than that!"

The women looked at each other. "I can't believe that son of a bitch would leave you with just five hundred dollars a month," her friend said.

Mrs. Walsh did some more figuring. She never was too good at math. Turned out, Dr. Walsh had made sure the family had $5,000 a month to live on. Because he sensed that he'd die young, like his father, he had made sure everything was in place.

When Sheila went to Chicago in January 1986 to work for a semester interning as a child life specialist at a hospital, her brother Mark didn't really know what that job was. Now that his son was receiving cancer treatment, he understood. Child life specialists offer emotional support, education and resources to families. They are trained to ease young patients' fears. They look out for their siblings. "When Charlie is going to have a procedure, something where they need him awake and they're going to hurt him, the child life specialist comes in with dolls or toys and distracts him. It helps. Sheila just loved kids, so I can really see her doing that."

Sheila loved the job and loved living in

Chicago. Her family noticed a growing maturity about her. She was living in housing provided by the hospital, making new friends, and was also spending time with Bud Man, her old friend the Budweiser employee from Iowa. He was then living in Chicago.

Her family got the call that she had been in an accident early on a Sunday morning in March. It appeared she had fallen, they were told by someone at the hospital, and had suffered a subdural hematoma. That's a traumatic brain injury in which blood collects between the outer and middle layers of the covering of the brain. It is caused by the tearing of blood vessels. Sheila was in a coma, but she was stable and doctors believed she would recover.

Mrs. Walsh flew to Chicago, and when she got to the hospital, Sheila was in bed. There was no visible injury from the fall. She looked peaceful, like she was sleeping. Doctors said she still had brain activity.

"Has she said anything?" Mrs. Walsh asked a nurse.

"She spoke just once," the nurse said. "The only thing she has said was 'My dad is coming to get me.'"

The nurse didn't know anything about the family history, or that Sheila's father had died four years earlier. Sheila had arrived at the hospital unconscious.

Mrs. Walsh was stunned to hear what Sheila had said. But over time, the family has taken comfort in knowing those were Sheila's last words. "I believe our dad was coming to her to say it's OK, it's time to go," said Susan. "It helps us to think they are together."

Sheila lived for another two days, never regaining consciousness. By the end, when the family was told she had no brain activity and wouldn't recover, they decided to donate her organs. Sheila had never mentioned that she'd want to be an organ donor, but given who she was, how she loved people, and how she always had this urge to help others, well, it was clear to the family that she'd agree with their decision. Her liver went to a dentist's wife, which Mrs. Walsh felt was a fitting nod to her husband's profession. Liver transplants were often unsuccessful in the 1980s, however, and the woman didn't survive.

The family was told that Sheila's organs went to seven people, but they were given no names. They read in the newspaper about a woman who was a teacher in Iowa City and received a heart/lung transplant the day after Sheila died. They assume that

Sheila was the donor. This woman also didn't survive long.

Someone received Sheila's corneas, and the family likes to think that the recipient is still living and enjoying the view. "Sheila had beautiful eyes," Susan said. "Really beautiful eyes."

After Susan arrived in Chicago on the Monday Sheila died, she and her mother tried to learn what had led to the accident. They talked to her friend Bud Man, who was understandably distraught. He said he and Sheila had been downtown in a bar, drinking. They had met some people there. Sheila and Bud Man got in a little argument and she said she was leaving.

The people she met in the bar invited her to go to a party at a two-story brownstone elsewhere in the city, and she left with them.

Mrs. Walsh and Susan went to look at the house and talked to people in the neighborhood who had heard about the incident. The story the neighbors told was this:

Something happened at a party inside that house that made Sheila uncomfortable or upset. She got a little freaked out, the Walshes were told, felt she needed to get away and decided to go out on the balcony and then jump the short distance to the roof of the garage next door. She made it to the garage roof fine, but then she tried to climb onto the fence adjacent to it so she could get to the ground. She slipped and hit her head when she fell to the ground.

She was always kind of clumsy, Susan said, and it certainly didn't help that it was dark, about 2 A.M. on a Saturday night, and that she'd been drinking.

When Mrs. Walsh and Susan stood by that fence, they could still see blood from where Sheila had hit her head. The police report was bare bones: A young woman slipped climbing off a fence, hit her head, and was taken to the hospital.

The Walshes were never able to find and talk to anyone who was actually inside that house that night. In their grief, they didn't really try too hard. It was hard even to concentrate on the specifics of the incident.

And so the mystery of what made Sheila leave that gathering — and by the balcony, not the front door — was never solved. Perhaps it wasn't as sinister as people might think, said Mark. "It wouldn't have taken much for her to go off. Someone might have just said something and she got upset." Susan's take: "I don't think she was being chased. I just think she realized she was in a situation she shouldn't be in and she was trying to leave."

Bud Man felt terribly guilty that he'd let Sheila leave him that night. The Walshes were understanding. They said Sheila could be impulsive. "Once Sheila made up her mind," said Mrs. Walsh, "there wasn't much you could do." The fall and the way her head hit the ground "was bad luck, basically," Susan added.

For years, the family found it hard to talk about the details of how Sheila died. That's why the Ames girls, and most everyone else in town, never really heard the full story.

Just as the Ames girls speculate about what Sheila might be up to now had she lived, her family has also thought through the same what-ifs.

"I'd have been worried about who she'd marry," said Mrs. Walsh. "She didn't always make the best choices." But as Mark sees it: "At the end of the day, she would have found the right guy and she'd be happily married with kids." Added Susan: "I like to think she'd be living here in Kansas City with us. Maybe it wouldn't have started out that way, but she'd come to be with us."

Whether she'd have built a career as a child life specialist, she'd surely be a great presence in the life of her ill nephew Charlie. The family described him as a boy who is spunky, fun-loving, hardheaded and determined. He reminded them of Sheila.

At the North Carolina reunion, the girls are recalling their favorite experiences with Sheila.

One memory: During high school, Sheila drove this little beat-up yellowish/greenish car. At lunchtime, students were allowed to leave school and get something to eat, as long as they were back before the bell rang. They had exactly thirty-five minutes. So some of the girls would run out to Sheila's car, and she'd speed them over to Taco Time on the other side of the train tracks that cut through Ames. Lunch at Taco Time could be a great risk because if a long train happened to pass through, and they were stuck waiting behind the gate, they'd be late returning to school.

That's part of what made it exciting going out for lunch; they were at the mercy of traffic lights, passing trains, the lines at Taco Time, Sheila's driving. "We'd be laughing so hard, trying to eat lunch as we raced down Lincoln Way," says Cathy. "It was a race against time, always!"

After talking about the fun times, the conversation turns to the fact that they didn't stay in touch with the Walshes after

Sheila died. "They probably think we forgot about her and went on our way," says Karen. "They don't know how much she meant to us."

"We were twenty-two years old when she died," says Jenny. "It's not like we were fully functional adults. We thought we were so young and invincible, and when Sheila died, it was such a shock. We didn't have the life experiences that we have now, the sense of what's the right thing to do, how to deal with grief. It would be so different if one of us died now. We'd know how to respond. We'd have more understanding." Jenny says it's not an exaggeration to say she thinks of Sheila every day.

Each of the girls has her own specific memory of how she learned about Sheila's death, and of going (or not going) to the funeral.

Karla, who couldn't afford to fly in from Arizona, recalls that Jenny was mad at her for not coming. Meanwhile, Kelly and Diana recall driving together to the funeral from the University of Iowa in Iowa City. On the ride, they got into a heavy discussion about heaven and hell. "I didn't have a strong sense of there being a heaven and Diana did," says Kelly, "and she was so angry at me. For more than an hour on the

Sheila leads the Ames girls.

road, I don't think we even spoke."

The girls who attended the funeral recall how they stood at the grave site after the memorial service. It was mid-March, but given Iowa's weather, it was still extremely cold. "When it was over, everyone left — the family, the adults — and we stood there," Sally says. "I remember it was a very powerful moment, just standing there. It must have been ten minutes. We didn't say anything."

As the girls talk about Sheila, a few of them hatch an idea. What if they pooled some money — they've got resources now that they didn't have when they were younger — and established a scholarship at Ames High in Sheila's memory? It could be given to a female student who was kind to everyone, who was well liked — someone who was a good friend to other girls.

The winner shouldn't be selected by teachers or administrators, the girls decide. "She ought to be nominated by her friends," Karen says.

The girls are completely enthusiastic about creating a Sheila Walsh Scholarship. They picture this new generation of Ames girls thinking about the qualities which define a good friend.

They say they'd love to meet the winner of the scholarship: what a terrific and giving girl she'd likely be. No doubt someone just like Sheila.

18
NORTH OF FORTY

On the way back from dinner in Raleigh, the girls are traveling in two cars, one following the other. Suddenly, the first car makes an abrupt U-turn. Did they take a wrong turn? Did someone forget something back at the restaurant?

"What's going on?" Marilyn wonders in the second car.

A cell phone rings in car number two. A few of the girls in the first car, driven by Angela, are calling to say they have made a decision. They've spotted a sexy lingerie store on the side of the highway and they're pulling into the parking lot. They want to look around. Maybe they'll find something fun.

There are a few groans in the second car. Some of the girls are tired. Some are just feeling their age. They have no great urge to go browsing in a lingerie store.

The two cars pull side by side into the

The tobacco field behind Angela's house, 2007 (left to right): Diana, Jane, Karen, Marilyn, Karla, Sally, Kelly, Jenny, Angela

store's parking lot and the girls talk to each other through open windows. Kelly, Diana and a few others say they're up for going in. But the rest aren't especially interested. The majority vote no.

"OK," says Angela. "We'll just go back to my house."

The cars drive away, and Kelly says something about "wet blankets" and "party poopers." Even the girls who were intrigued by the idea of going inside this naughty store surrendered awfully easily. "You're big talkers," Kelly says, "with granny underwear in your suitcases."

The days of piling into cars and going to cornfield keggers feel long ago for these women. They can't picture themselves exactly in that same party-time, adventure-seeking frame of mind they had back in high school. Some of what's at play here is just maturity. A woman in her forties doesn't have the same sense of fun as a girl in her teens. But much of it, of course, is also the result of where life has taken them. The laughs still come in huge bursts. But in adulthood, there have been a lot of sobering moments, too — a lot of emotion-stirring places they've been together. Those images are often clearest in the girls' heads.

Two years after Christie died, for instance, Diana flew into Minnesota, and she and Kelly stayed at Karla's house on a night Bruce was out of town. Diana and Kelly slept in Christie's room, which had remained little changed from the day she last slept in it. Her doctors had allowed her to come home for her fourteenth birthday, so she could be with her family, and that was her final night in the bedroom.

Karla had preserved the room pretty much as it was; she hadn't rearranged anything. She told Kelly and Diana that there was no comfort in seeing that empty bedroom every day, but she couldn't bring herself to alter it.

Diana and Kelly didn't talk much about Christie in the bedroom that night. Each of them wondered if they'd feel Christie's presence, but they didn't articulate this. "I was both afraid and honored to be staying in her room," Kelly told Diana the next morning. "I guess I wanted Christie's spirit to visit me, to tell me she was OK."

On a different trip, Cathy and Sally slept in Christie's room when visiting Karla, and they had that same sense of wanting to feel a connection to her. The room was dominated by a large and lovely poster-sized photo of Christie with her best friend, Jessie. The poster, a gift from Jessie, hung over the bed and included the words "Friends Forever" in big type. And so the room spoke about both loss and friendship.

Karla confided in the other girls about her "sad time" — starting with the Christmas holidays and continuing through Christie's birthday on January 9 and the anniversary of her death, February 20. Karla explained how her family tried to remember Christie in upbeat ways. They had taken her to P. F. Chang's, a Chinese restaurant, for her last birthday. So Bruce, Karla, Ben and Jackie returned to the restaurant on the January 9 after Christie died. They had dinner and then went back to their house for home-made Funfetti cupcakes, which were Christie's favorite, just as they had on her birthday.

The Ames girls continued to be impressed and moved by how supportive Bruce was of their friend Karla. Karen couldn't get out of her mind the day of the funeral, when Jane held Bruce's hands and said to him, "This must be the hardest day of your life." Bruce paused, then responded, "No, the hardest day was the day Christie was diagnosed." In his answer, the girls felt as if they'd gotten a look into the depth of his pain and his love for Karla. The hardest day of his life had been ongoing.

The girls considered Bruce to be one of the most giving husbands they had ever observed, and that was well before Christie was sick. There was one gathering years earlier at Karla's house. Bruce volunteered to sack out on the family's boat with the kids for a couple of days so the Ames girls could have the full run of the house. Then he spent a day driving them all around in the boat — pointing out landmarks, making everyone lunch, getting them all drinks. "He's a one-in-a-million guy," Karen liked to say.

Bruce, while nursing his own grief, also knew to give Karla space and time, and to support her as she struggled to find coping rituals. For a long while, Karla would touch Christie's ashes on the mantel before going to bed, just to say good night. She said she liked talking about Christie, but struggled to focus on "the happy years." Too many harder memories crowded things out. There were too many reminders around the house, on the street, around the community.

People would nonchalantly ask, "How many children do you have?" and Karla would usually say "three," and explain. To avoid questions, a few times she said, "two," and then felt too guilty afterward. "It's not fair to Christie not to mention her," she told the other girls.

The decision to move out of Minnesota crystallized for Karla when she was in bed one February morning, three years after Christie's death. It was President's Day, the kids had off from school and Bruce was at work. Their daughter Jackie crawled into bed with Karla and started talking about one of the horses that the family owned. They kept horses in a stable thirty-five minutes from their house. "Wouldn't it be great if I could wake up every morning and kiss my horse on the nose?" Jackie said to Karla. "I could just roll out of bed in my pajamas and go give a big kiss."

Bruce's family had land in Bozeman, Montana. His great-grandfather was the homesteader there in the late 1800s, and there was a barn right on the property. Karla figured the time had finally come: Why not just move there?

"Call your dad," Karla told Jackie. She dialed Bruce, he voted yes also, Ben did the same, and the decision was made. Yes, it would be painful to leave Christie's bedroom, and all those memories, good and bad, behind. But it could be the best thing for Karla, Bruce, Jackie and Ben. And the horse might just like being kissed first thing in the morning.

"Part of me can't imagine leaving Minnesota, and living in a place where people never knew Christie," Karla admitted to Marilyn and Sally one day when they came to visit. She told them of a bracelet Jackie wore with Christie's initials: CRB. Jackie had the bracelet on one day when she was at a medical appointment, and a woman working in the office asked, "What does CRB stand for?"

"It's for my sister," Jackie told her.

And the woman said, "Oh, yeah. That's

right. You had a sister who died." The woman said nothing else, just moved on to the next item of business. "A lot of people are nervous or don't know what to say," Karla later told her friends. "But I really felt for Jackie in that moment. It's hard for kids, when people just gloss it over, when they don't really acknowledge her loss."

In Montana, where no one knew Christie, there might be even more glossing over, Karla said. Moving there could be hard for the family in ways they couldn't even fathom. And yet a strong part of Karla knew the decision to go was the right one for her and her family. And in her heart she knew: Christie would understand.

"After losing her," Karla said, "we've been learning not to wait until tomorrow to do anything."

In their forties, several of the other girls also opted to take an inventory of their lives and to embark on new journeys. Cathy made plans to cut back on her work as a makeup artist and to focus more on screenwriting. Marilyn thought she'd get into singing and acting in community theater, tapping back into talents she'd nurtured earlier in her life. Karen felt herself getting closer to a return to teaching, and that wasn't all that

was new for her. As she liked to put it, jokingly: "If tomorrow's Monday, I'm starting
a new diet!"

In middle age, the Ames girls' interests
took turns they never would have predicted
earlier in their lives. Angela, for instance,
who had built a successful public relations
business in North Carolina, decided to start
a second business, Finality Events.

It would be a special-events planning
company to help people create "unique life
celebrations" to help them remember those
who've died. She was motivated by the loss
of her mother in 1995 and her brother in
1999, and by watching Karla cope with
Christie's death in 2004. In the case of her
mom and brother, especially, she felt they
didn't get the life celebrations they de-
served. "The minister who tried to talk my
brother out of being gay ended up being
twenty minutes late for the service," Angela
told the other Ames girls. As a business
model, she figured she was on to something:
Baby boomers would want a memorable
way to be remembered when they died.

Finality Events would help families identify the unique aspects of a loved one's life
to commemorate. Her staffers would write
a "life remembrance story" that would be
more than an obit. She planned to market

the service to people who may have turned away from organized religion. She hoped to get it started in 2009.

Meanwhile, Diana felt surprisingly fulfilled in her forties, and that included her decision to take the job at Starbucks. She had always admired her mom's career as a dietician, and she went to college knowing she would also have a serious career. She moved to Chicago to get the big-city experience she never had growing up in Ames, and she enjoyed being a CPA. But at age thirty-one she had her first daughter, and she soon experienced feelings she'd never anticipated. She went back to her job, but spent the day worrying about her baby. After work, she'd drive eighty miles an hour to pick her up. She soon quit her job and was an at-home mother for thirteen years. "Marriage and family were never high on my list of priorities when I was in my twenties," she'd tell the others. "Isn't it funny how those two things are now the center of my life?"

As her three daughters got older, she was happy to find the job at Starbucks. The hours were good, there wasn't a lot of stress, and the fact that her whole family could get medical insurance through Starbucks was a major perk. Plus, most every customer came from a different line of work, which Diana found intriguing. "I see life beyond Mommydom," she told Kelly. "It's just the right job for right now."

Diana also started thinking more clearly about ways in which "giving back" could be a part of her daily life. As she put it: "Every little step you take in showing kindness, volunteering at school and church, listening to others and sharing a smile at Starbucks — I think that all helps the world."

She became more passionate about the environment. She helped set up a recycling program at her Starbucks. She began driving a hybrid vehicle, a Prius. And she dreamed of someday living in a green house.

By their mid-forties, women know they're at a crossroads. They are still holding on to their younger selves, but they can also see their older selves pretty clearly.

"I'm proud of my gray hairs," Cathy tells the other girls gathered at Angela's. "Every four weeks, I say, 'I'm proud of you!' And then I cover them up."

"I certainly see my life divided into sections," Kelly says. "I was a daughter in my parents' home for two decades, until I graduated from college. Then I got married and was a wife and mother for twenty years.

I think the next stage of my life involves loving people without necessarily living with them."

Middle-aged women also start to have a clear sense that their friendships with other women likely will be the longest lasting relationships of their lives. There are about 12 million divorced women in the United States, a figure that has doubled since 1980. There are another 12 million widows, and as baby boomers pass on, that number is expected to rise sharply.

The Ames girls certainly see the need for female friendships when they consider their mothers' generation. Women over age sixty-five outnumber men in that age group three to two. By age eighty-five, there are only four men for every ten women. Karla's mom has been a widow since 1990. Marilyn's mom lost Dr. McCormack to Alzheimer's years before he died in 2004. Both Karla and Marilyn see that their mothers' bonds with female friends have been vital and sustaining through the years. If a woman doesn't want to burden her children with her emotional and companionship needs when she's older, it's vital to nurture female friendships.

The Ames girls feel so lucky to have each other that they feel less pressure to make their other friendships as deep as possible. The friends the Ames girls have made later in life, outside the group, often have been important to them, but there are limitations. "My husband asked me if I missed the friendship I had with Marilyn, that intense junior-high friendship," says Jane. "No, I don't have anyone in my life like that now. In junior high I so wanted a best friend. I don't need that now. I don't need someone else to make me whole. I have a family. I feel whole as a part of that.

"My friends back home are important, but I don't get to see them much. I joke with my close friend at work about our phone relationship. We talk on our way to and from work."

Kelly says that for a while she had what she calls a "bad friend," a woman who joined her when she went to nightclubs to listen to music and dance. They sometimes lived on the dark side — drinking too much, being too wild — and so they were "bad" together, Kelly says. The friendship ended over Kelly's disapproval of the woman's behavior and her inability to trust her. Her relationship with the woman left her all the more grateful for her bonds with her Ames friends.

Cathy says she got a midlife taste of the

limits of friendship. She had been getting closer to a woman in Los Angeles; they'd spent a lot of time together, and Cathy was carving out time to be there for this woman. Then Cathy's mother died, and this woman never even acknowledged the loss. "Not a text message, not a call," says Cathy. Four months went by without the woman mentioning anything.

Cathy was hurt and angry. In therapy, she talked about how she should be grieving for her mom, but she was angry at this woman — "and angry at myself for believing that someone would show up for me when it turned out she wouldn't. I realized she would never be the kind of person who'd be there for you when you were down, even though all she had to do was say, 'I'm thinking of you. I'm here if you need me.' "

In therapy, and already in her forties, Cathy realized she was discovering something important. "The lesson was that this was about me. I was projecting on her what I needed her to be. I had to accept her limitations."

Cathy has continued her relationship with the woman, but sees her far less frequently. "I never said anything to her about how I felt," Cathy says. "I took it as my lesson."

And, obviously, this experience left her all

the more grateful that she had the Ames girls in her life.

In their forties, the Ames girls have discovered reasons why their relationships with each other often seem easier than some of their relationships outside the group. Perhaps, they say, it is because over the years, they have come up with unspoken or barely acknowledged ground rules that seem to work.

They don't brag about their husbands' jobs or incomes.

They talk about their children's achievements, but not in a gloating way. They root for each other's kids, just as they root for each other.

They make every effort to be with each other for key events in their lives: weddings, serious illnesses, funerals.

If they have disagreements among themselves, if they have negative opinions about each other, if they have things that need to be hashed out, it all remains in the group. They don't go to their husbands with their complaints. They don't tell their friends outside the group.

One upside of being in their forties, the girls say, is that they feel like they've grown beyond a lot of things. They're beyond a cutthroat kind of ambition, they're far less competitive, they've lowered their expectations of others, and they're learning to find satisfaction in just living. They're seeing what feels good: something as easy as just being together, talking on Angela's porch.

19
THE GAME

It's getting late on the final night of the reunion, and Angela has a surprise activity for everyone. She invites them off the back porch and over to the area of her backyard where she has lit the logs on a large outdoor fire pit. Chairs have been arranged into a circle around the fire.

"Everyone get comfortable," Angela says. "It's time to answer a few questions."

She pulls out a cloth bag. Inside of it are twenty pebbles, all with numbered stickers on them. The numbers correspond to fill-in-the-blank statements that Angela has typed up on a sheet of paper folded on her lap. Each of the girls will reach into the bag and pick a number.

"It's a great game," Angela says. "Just answer honestly. We have enough pebbles for two rounds. It's going to be fun."

"Maybe it's a good thing we're drinking wine," someone says.

Angela shakes the bag and holds it in front of Diana, who reaches in and picks out the pebble with the number 14 attached. Angela looks at her list, finds 14 and reads: "When I tell people where I'm from, they say _____."

Diana's first thought is that she is "from" Scottsdale, Arizona, where she now lives. "Sometimes I don't tell people I'm from Scottsdale," she says, "because they'll say 'Snotsdale?' So I just say I'm from Phoenix."

The girls notice, of course, that she didn't say she was "from" Ames. What was she thinking?

"Oh, yeah, of course, I tell people I'm from Iowa," Diana says. "And that's when they say, 'Idaho?' "

"When I lived in South Carolina, so many people were provincial and had never left the state," says Jenny. "I'd say 'Iowa' and they'd say 'Ohio?' "

Karen says that where she lives, outside Philly, "people think Iowa is cold and wet. They ask, 'So what is there to do there?' "

"People in Minnesota don't really like Iowa," adds Kelly. "I didn't know that until I moved there."

"In Minnesota, they say the best thing to come out of Iowa is Interstate 35," says Angela.

I-35 and then, of course, all of the Ames girls.

Next it's Sally's turn. She picks pebble 2: "The angel on my shoulder keeps saying _____."

"I guess my mom is the angel on my shoulder," she decides. "Some people say, 'What would Jesus do?' I find myself thinking, 'What would JoAnn do?' And I guess JoAnn on my shoulder tells me to be less judgmental."

"I literally had this angel on my shoulder saying, 'Don't do it,' " Kelly says, "and then I did it."

"Did what?" Diana asks.

Kelly just smiles and everyone laughs.

Marilyn picks the pebble numbered 15: "None of you know it, but in my twenties I _____."

"None of you know it," she says, and pauses, "but when I was in college, I slept with some boy on a cruise ship — the Norwegian Cruise Line — in the Caribbean."

In response, there is something of a group gasp, and several girls start asking questions at once. "If everyone is quiet, I'll tell you," Marilyn says. And then she shares the story of how her older sister was the ship's doctor, she went along for the cruise, met some

The lineup today (left to right): Karla, Sally, Karen, Diana, Jenny, Cathy, Kelly, Marilyn, Jane and Angela

boy, and that's what happened.

Jane gets pebble 12: "You think you know me, but _____."

"You think you know me," she says, "and that I'm a pretty together person. I'm together on my job. But I'm actually a very sensitive person. I have one friend back home who is confrontational sometimes. That's hard for me. Please don't ever yell at me. I don't like being yelled at."

Karen picks pebble 6: "In ten years I'll be _____."

"Fifty-four," she says, "and an empty nester, and possibly teaching again. I had a job offer for this coming year, but I turned it down. It was a Quaker preschool where my kids went to preschool. My oldest son is going into high school, my second son is in middle school. There are too many changes in our lives right now. It wasn't the right time to go back. But in ten years? I think I'll be teaching."

Jenny pulls pebble 15 from the bag: "None of you knew it, but in my thirties I _____."

She thinks for a moment. And then she smiles. "None of you knew it, but I went to Egypt and had a romance with a sheik."

The other girls start buzzing. "A romance with a sheik?" Karla says, trying to picture it.

Jenny explains. It was back when she was single and worked for the congressman. The congressman was on the foreign affairs committee, and this Egyptian sheik came over on business. He asked Jenny to come to Egypt for a job interview. She was always adventurous and figured even if she didn't take the job, it'd be an experience. The sheik flew her to Egypt first class, had a chauffeur meet her at the airport, and then he put her up in a fancy hotel suite. He took her on his private plane so they could rendezvous with his yacht in the Red Sea.

"Was it oil money?" the girls want to know.

"I'm not sure," Jenny says.

"Did you know the sheik's intentions?" the girls ask.

"I was a girl from Iowa," she says. "I thought I was going for a job interview. I believed him."

"I hope he showed you a damn good time," Kelly says.

"He showed me a good time, he did," Jenny says. "I was supposed to be there for a week and I stayed for two. But I also had the feeling that I should do what he wanted or I might not get back home. It wasn't like I was kidnapped. It's just that women were subservient there, and I just had this sense about it all."

"Was he cute?" Karen asks.

"He was," Jenny says. "He was probably about forty-four. But he seemed so much older than we are now. It turned out to be a wonderful time, honestly."

Angela has a question. "What did you tell your parents?"

"That I went for a job interview," Jenny says, and everyone laughs.

Round two. It's Diana's turn again. She picks pebble number 11: "The most appealing famous man is _____."

"Dead or alive?" she asks.

"Try one dead and one living," someone says.

She opts for John F. Kennedy and Johnny Depp.

The other girls start naming names: George Clooney, Bono. Karen likes Jon Bon Jovi because he's still married to his high-school sweetheart. Sally mentions Mike Rowe, host of *Dirty Jobs* on the Discovery Channel. (It's fitting. Of all the girls' husbands, Sally's has the most physical job. Back in Iowa, he's a project supervisor for a company called Hog Slat, which builds hog confinement units.)

Kelly says she likes Kenny Loggins. She enjoyed his 1998 book about the secrets to an undying love, written with his wife, who happened to be his former colon therapist. Kelly says she resisted the easy ways to dismiss the book: that the enema-giving Mrs. Loggins "knew Kenny inside and out," or that the couple had no prescriptions for marriage and romance, considering their 2004 divorce. Kelly says she understands that not all love lasts forever, but that doesn't mean it never existed.

Jane picks her second pebble: "In thirty years I'll be _____." "

"I'll be seventy-four years old," she says,

"and taking wild trips all over the world. With Justin."

"You notice she involved Justin," Karen says, "That's good."

Karla picks pebble 3 out of the bag: "I'll move back to Ames when _____."

While Karla is thinking, no one says, "when hell freezes over." And Karla soon has an answer. "I'd move back if my mother got ill and needed me," she says. Some of the others agree; they'd consider moving back to help their parents.

And then Cathy says, "I'll move back when all of you move back." It's such a perfect answer that the girls actually applaud. "We should get one big house and we'll all live there together," says Karen. Angela adds: "Or we should just build the Shit Sisters Retirement Community."

Now it's Karen's turn, and she picks pebble 1: "The last time I cried was _____."

"Well," she says, "we've all cried this weekend." Everyone starts to enumerate — at the table over there, at two in the morning last night, in the living room the first day, when Marilyn said the blessing before dinner . . .

And then Karen gives her answer. "I cried with Cathy, talking about when her mom died, and how much I regret that I didn't

504

make it in for the funeral," she says. "We cried with Karla over Christie. I cried with Jane when she talked about her daughter's bat mitzvah. I cried with Marilyn when she talked about her brother Billy, and the accident, and that letter she wrote."

"So you didn't cry that much this weekend," Diana says, and everyone laughs.

"Could we count how many times we laughed this weekend?" someone asks.

Karla says she has laughed so hard that she's uncomfortable. "I get tired of laughing so much when we're together," she says. "I know it's time to go when my cheeks hurt."

The cloth bag is handed over to Kelly, who picks out pebble 19: "You all think I'm _____ but really I'm _____."

Kelly takes a breath while she thinks for a moment. Someone says maybe they should have gotten the pebbles in advance. They could have formulated answers.

"No," Kelly says. "That would have felt like homework. I like doing it this way. Thinking on the spot."

The backyard is silent except for the crackling fire, as Kelly formulates her answer in her head.

She repeats the phrase from pebble 19. "You all think I'm . . . but really I'm . . ."

And then slowly, drawing out her words, she says, "You all think I'm only interested in sex . . ." The others laugh.

"Now you're going to feel bad for laughing," Kelly says, and starts again. "You all think I'm only interested in sex, but really . . . I'm interested in finding relationships as special as the ones all of you have."

She pauses, then delivers the longest response of the evening.

"Having watched Karla and Bruce and their incredible relationship, I am searching for something equally as meaningful in my life. I left a bad relationship because I saw how Karla had a really good relationship. And I wanted that, too. That's the truth.

"I saw I had only a shadow of a loving, happy connection with my husband. Some people are content to live that way. I decided I was not, especially after seeing Karla's marriage and family, and seeing what a healthy home life looked like. And every time we are together and Karla confirms that her marriage is a ten, I feel like I have validation to find something like that in my life. In fact, all of your marriages are really up there. Your relationships are strong. And I feel like I deserve that."

"You do," says Karla.

"You go, girl," Diana says.

"And, Diana, I've seen you and Bob over the years. I've seen what he does for you. That's another ten. I want that, too, in my life." Kelly has gotten slightly tearful. Jenny reaches out and takes her hand, a kind and sisterly impulse that swells Kelly's emotions even more.

"And I know you think I'm just crazy," Kelly says, "and that I'm not finding the right guys and I'm just looking for fun. But really, I am looking for something as wonderful as what you all have. That's all I want. Something that simple, that wonderful, that easy."

"I hope you find it," Karla says softly.

"I know I will," Kelly says. "Part of me feels like I'm on my way there. I know it's somewhat disturbing to watch me get there." Everyone laughs. "And it's a little bit frightening, because I have a lot of fun finding my way. But you guys have confirmed for me that I need to keep doing what I'm doing. I need to keep searching, looking, trying . . . and that I'll get there. I will. Anyway, I thank all of you."

Some of the other girls wipe away their own tears. And then a few take turns hugging Kelly. They stand by the fire for a few more minutes, then one by one head into the house to get ready for bed. In the morning, the reunion will be over, and everyone will need to head off for the airport.

20
THE WOMEN
FROM AMES

It is before dawn on Monday morning, and the Ames girls rouse each other, dress pretty quickly, zip up their suitcases, and then gather in Angela's large kitchen for their final cups of coffee together.

No one says they wish the reunion would last any longer. They're not exactly talked out — there's always more to say — but they're all pretty ready to get back to their children, husbands and current lives.

As the sun rises, they take a final look at the tobacco field beyond Angela's back porch, and then they pile their suitcases into a minivan and a car and head for the airport. Their conversations on the ride are slightly subdued. That's how it gets sometimes at the end of their gatherings. Some of them find themselves lost in their thoughts.

At the security checkpoint, they share their final hugs. Everyone is turning this way and then the other way, embracing, clutching hands. Kelly, Karla, Sally and Marilyn will fly together to Minneapolis; Sally will drive south to Iowa from there. The others all head for their own gates: Diana to Arizona, Jenny to Maryland, Karen to Philly, Jane to Boston. Cathy will fly to Kansas City to see her dad. Angela will drive home and finish cleaning everything up.

Within hours of their return to their own homes, they are again trading emails. They profusely thank Angela for her hospitality, they recollect the highlights of the weekend, they speculate about who should host the next reunion. They also remind each other to keep everyone posted on all the unresolved issues they talked about over the past few days.

As is always the case after they get together, they find themselves contemplating the meaning of their bonds to each other. This reunion, they agree, is just another step on a journey of friendship that should take them until the end of their lives. "Someday, when we're old women, we'll be able to sit together and look back at these richly detailed lives," Kelly writes. "Even the most common of us have had these journeys. In one way or another, we have every woman's story."

And those stories continue.

In September 2007, three months after the reunion, Kelly sent an email to all the other girls. "I just got off the phone with my health care provider, giving me test results," she wrote. "Her last words to me were to surround myself with loved ones tonight. You are the first people I am telling. I have breast cancer. I will immediately go through more testing to determine what stage I am at. All I know at this moment is that it is lobular carcinoma. I have no history of breast cancer in my family. My daughter will never be able to say that.

"My hands are shaking. So is my heart."

It was crushing news for the other girls. Karla immediately called Jane. "I had to make a cup of tea, sit down and process it all," Karla told her. "I'm scared for her."

The other women had similar feelings, but they responded as if they were soldiers on a joint mission. Marilyn promised to drive down and be with Kelly any time she needed a companion at an appointment. Karla offered to share all the medical knowledge she'd gathered during Christie's illness, and reminded Kelly to get a flu shot and to have her kids do the same. Cathy told her there are great wigs out there "despite what you may have seen on Britney Spears. You can get a human hair wig for just a few hundred bucks, and they'll cut it on you. I'd be happy to go shop for one and send you what I think would look good."

Jenny wrote: "How I wish we lived closer, so that we could hug you with our arms rather than our words. And now I'm going to switch into work mode." Thanks to her job at the medical school, Jenny had lots of advice to offer: "Go to a university medical center, because they see the most cases and are most up-to-date on treatments. If you do decide to use a community hospital, find out how many cases of lobular carcinoma they treat annually. If that number is low, you MUST go elsewhere for your treatment. You also will want someone to go with you to appointments, at least at the outset. Frequently, patients are so overwhelmed with emotion, and all the treatment plans and options, that it helps to have a family member or friend who can be there to take notes and help ask questions."

This has been the way things have gone between the Ames girls as adults. Love. Support. Advice. Action. What's the problem? What's the solution?

Kelly told the other girls that their support "lifted my spirits to unimaginable heights." She shared with them how her daughter Liesl broke into tears upon hearing the news, and slept with her that night. "She made me promise never to go out without my wig if I experience hair loss. I threatened to go to all her events bald and wearing tank tops that would emphasize if I only have one boob." Kelly kept her sense of humor, joking about the possibility of meeting "hot doctors" at her appointments.

Her tumor was about the size of a squished softball, and an MRI also indicated that the cancer had spread to her lymph nodes. Her doctor suggested four or five months of chemo, followed by surgery. "I want chemo to shrink this thing and destroy any rogue cells that have broken away from the warm womb in my breast," Kelly told the other girls. She had thought doctors would recommend immediate surgery. "I expected to have this 36DDD breast gone by next week, so I'm experiencing a weird sort of relief that I'll be intact for a while — although that means hauling around this damn tumor. Stay tuned. . . ."

Kelly talked to her students, to brace them for her altered appearance. She and her students agreed that a wig might look silly on her, so she decided to wear hats. Surgery wouldn't come for another six months, Kelly told her students, "so I'm celebrating my body in its current form while I can. I'm not angry or despondent about what is happening, at least not yet. I'm grateful for the time and the ability to fight this."

The other Ames girls decided to send Kelly flowers on the days she'd be getting chemotherapy. On her first day of treatment, they sent roses. "The roses are extraordinary," Kelly told them a few days later. "Unusually large creamy blossoms tinged with pink. They are slowly opening this week, and they just keep getting more beautiful. I truly feel surrounded by your love and concern."

During her initial rounds of chemo, Kelly felt achy and light-headed, as if she had the flu. It was manageable, though she knew the effects would be cumulative. She vowed to try to just take everything day by day.

Kelly was mostly upbeat, but one day she confided to the girls that she had yelled at one of her sons and felt miserable about it. "Liesl was around to pick up the pieces, and she consoled me and just kept saying, 'Sorry, sorry, sorry.'"

For her second round of chemo, the Ames girls sent Kelly a fall bouquet — yellow, white and deep red flowers. When her mother asked who had sent them, Kelly was too choked up to speak.

Her hair started coming out in handfuls, so she got a buzz cut. "I'm in good spirits, gals," she wrote in an email, "although the hair situation is bothering me more than I expected. It will take guts to walk into class tomorrow with a new, butch look. I'm just hoping I don't have a weird, lopsided head. My right ear does stick out more. Oh well . . ."

By spring, chemo had reduced her mass to the size of a marshmallow. Still, she knew she'd eventually need surgery, and there was also a tiny spot on her lung which would need to be monitored.

For one of her last treatments, the other Ames girls sent spring flowers in a lovely basket. "Never doubt the power of phone messages, cards or emails when someone is going through a tough time," Kelly wrote when saying thank you. "Even the briefest messages have reminded me that I am never alone. Some people find that sort of comfort in God; for me, my friends are ever-present."

Kelly's graphic design students were making posters as part of their course work, and so, partly to remind them that they can overcome their own adversities, Kelly had a color poster created with two photos of herself. The first photo had been taken at the reunion at Angela's; smiling slightly, she is wearing a tank top, has all her hair, and looks terrific. In the second photo she is in a similar tank top, she has no hair, but her smile is broader. It's a powerful image, striking and brave. The poster, titled "Soul Power," included a quote from Marcus Aurelius, the Roman emperor and philosopher: "If you are distressed by anything external, the pain is not due to the thing itself, but to your estimate of it; and this you have the power to revoke at any moment."

The other girls all weighed in on the poster. "You look beautiful!!!" wrote Karla, who also offered advice to Kelly to help her with muscle cramping caused by her treatments. "Christie had the same problem. I swear, I try to forget most of it, but the important stuff I should recall. Anyway, be sure to get a potassium supplement from your oncologist. It will make a difference."

Kelly thanked everyone for their kind comments about her poster, but she wrote back to them: "I certainly don't consider myself beautiful right now. I hate looking at my face in the morning; I look so naked until I put on eyeliner, pencil in eyebrows and add a little color to my cheeks. I try to focus on radiating confidence and positive energy. Maybe that actually is beauty. That is what I wanted to get out of the poster. When we got together at Angela's, I was so concerned with how I looked. I felt like my skin had too many flaws, my teeth weren't white enough, my stomach was too poochy, my hair wasn't glamorous. Now, I look at the photos we took down there and I marvel at how beautiful my eyebrows and eyelashes were. I had two breasts at that time that I should have adored, instead of stuffing them into a high-powered Victoria's Secret bra. I should have been thrilled I simply had healthy teeth and a mouth and throat without sores."

She ended by telling the other girls: "Enjoy yourselves right now. Take a moment today to be grateful for all your body parts. Really celebrate your body and your health. So much can change in a few months."

In April, an MRI showed that Kelly's tumors were gone, but concern remained that cancer cells were still present. Her oncologist and surgeon both recommended a mastectomy, but Kelly talked them into removing only tissue that had been affected. It would be a two-step process that could preserve her breast.

Kelly was honest with her friends. "I

believe there's a strong chance of cancer returning," she said. "It is likely I have cancer cells resistant to treatment that have traveled through my body and are tucked in some fertile spot, biding their time until there are enough of them to make their presence known — and wage war." She said she tried not to focus on that possibility — such thoughts are "not helpful," she kept telling herself — and instead tried to think positively.

The other girls understood her reluctance to have a mastectomy, and were supportive. As Jane summed things up: "I think she feels that if the cancer is just going to come back in three years, she might as well have a breast until then."

Kelly posted her profile on the dating site eHarmony.com, explaining that she'd like to be an example of how a woman with breast cancer can remain sexy. Always the writer, she found it cathartic to compile clear-eyed reports of her dating experiences:

"I've had two lovers since my lumpectomy. My first was a man I'd been with for 18 months. He'd been with me all through treatment. He was supportive and didn't seem to mind when I lost my hair, including my eyebrows and eyelashes. But the first night I stayed with him after my surgery, he refused to look at my breasts. I felt humiliated. I felt ugly. I felt unlovable. Our relationship ended that night.

"My second lover was a man I met through eHarmony. His brother recently died of cancer, and this tenuous connection is why I trusted him. Although he claimed he wasn't bothered by the scars on my chest, I was afraid of his reaction to my breast, so I asked if I could keep my bra on. Although there had been lots of chemistry when we first met, the same passion didn't carry into the bedroom. Once again, I blamed my breast, and once again, I felt unattractive."

A year after the reunion at Angela's, the girls ended up getting together in the Berkshire Mountains of Massachusetts. Jenny's family belonged to a time-share program, and so they were able to stay in two condo units not far from a lake, a spa, a Shaker village and a Norman Rockwell museum.

Before her cancer, Kelly had wanted to show up at this reunion with long hair, to show everyone how ready she was for a new look and a new life. Now as fate had it, she had a new, unwanted look. Her hair had begun to grow back after the chemo, but it was thin and close to her scalp.

The girls told Kelly that she looked radiantly healthy. They complimented her on her tan. They said she looked more fit than ever before in her life. But Kelly confided in Diana: "When I look at my reflection, it just doesn't feel like me. The person who looks back is so very different than who I was one year ago."

Kelly joked with the other Ames girls about her dating experiences, but resisted telling them too much about her insecurities regarding her body. As she later explained it: "I didn't tell them that I am working hard at getting all parts of my body fit so that a lover might decide that nice legs or a firm bottom will compensate for ugly breasts. I didn't tell them that I needed to keep my bra on when with a man. I knew they would all say to me that my body is beautiful no matter what shape or size. I wondered if they understand that if I had a longtime partner, I wouldn't be at all ashamed of my breast. Perhaps I would have even agreed to have a mastectomy. But since I'm dating, it feels like I have to market myself, and so breasts are, I'm ashamed to admit, important.

"Now that my left breast is misshapen from my lumpectomy, I have discovered how difficult it is to walk the talk. It's one thing to intellectually know that breasts shouldn't be so idealized in our society. But it's quite another thing to present to the world a body that has slightly deformed breasts, and might someday be without breasts."

In the Berkshires, the girls again did a lot of hiking. (Some would trek to the top of Jiminy Peak Mountain, because that was the only place they could get cell phone service to call home.)

At one point, Karla and Kelly were hiking next to each other.

"I think the fresh air is really great for me," Kelly said. "It has to be beneficial for my health."

Karla agreed. And that brought a thought into Kelly's head. She wondered aloud how Karla and Christie were able to stay healthy when they were cooped up day after day in the hospital. Karla told her that parents at the hospital had talked of wanting an area where they could go for fresh air. "But we agreed it couldn't be up on the children's floor," Karla said, "because that was eight stories up. If there was an outdoor balcony, the parents would all want to jump."

Karla told the story in an upbeat way with a slight smile, and everyone laughed. But Kelly noticed that when the laughter subsided, it just felt as if everyone wanted to cry.

Karla and her family had moved to Montana as planned, and she spent the year overseeing the building of a new home on a gorgeous piece of land that Bruce's dad generously gave them. Bruce was promoted to general manager of his company, which manufactures equipment for the telecommunications industry. That meant he had to spend part of the week in Minnesota, plus a few weeks a year at the company plant in Costa Rica. Karla missed him when he was gone, and vowed to travel more with him when the kids got older. But for now, she had embraced living in Montana, and had thrown herself into the building of the house.

"I loved our home in Edina so much," she wrote to the girls, "but this one is going to be great. The views alone are incredible, and the architect maximized them in her design." She liked the community and the people she met in Bozeman. She loved being able to go skiing and hiking as a family. Jackie and Ben had enrolled in a new school and were doing wonderfully academically. And Bozeman felt awfully safe, she said. The most noteworthy "crime" in the local police report was someone "mooning" out a car window.

Karla felt great joy in watching her kids riding their horses as they cantered around the property. Ben and Jackie were the fifth generation in the family to live on that land, and Karla also loved to see them walking up and down the gravel roads — beautiful kids set against such natural beauty. When Bruce was home, he'd have coffee with Karla on the deck every morning, after which he'd "commute" to his office right there in the house. It felt pretty romantic sometimes.

Nothing was forgotten, of course. Karla was in Montana on the day that would have been Christie's eighteenth birthday. "It was a hard one," she wrote.

Back in Minnesota, Edina High School remembered Christie at its graduation ceremony by setting out a vacant chair with a single rose on it. "What a kind gesture," Karla wrote to the other girls. "It meant a lot to us."

A few weeks later, Kelly happened to find herself in Edina, meeting a man set up through eHarmony. She and her date were walking to a restaurant for ice cream, and Kelly realized that the last time she had been in this restaurant was on her birthday two years earlier, with Marilyn and Karla. Just then, by coincidence, Karla called.

"Can I call you back?" Kelly asked her.

After the date was over, Kelly drove over to Karla's former house, parked on the street out front and put the top down on her convertible. A memory came into her mind of the day she came by this house to pick up Karla before the fortieth birthday gathering at Jenny's. Christie was out front in her soccer uniform, her hair, short and fine, blowing in the breeze, a smile on her face as she waved good-bye and told her mother to have a great time with her friends.

Kelly pulled out her cell phone and called Karla's house in Montana.

"Guess where I am?" Kelly asked.

The two of them ended up talking about Kelly's health, the other Ames girls, life in Montana, Kelly's date.

"I'm trying to take an intellectual approach," Kelly told her. "I want to be smart about dating. I don't want to be like a man and think with my penis." To reiterate her point, Kelly found herself speaking loudly into the cell phone: "I'm not going to think with my vagina this time!"

At that moment, a man was walking by and heard every word she said.

When he passed, Kelly told Karla: "This

guy — I'm guessing he's a former neighbor of yours — well, he just gave me the strangest look. Guess that's life with the Shit Sisters, huh?"

Both of them laughed. Then things felt more subdued as Kelly found herself looking at Karla's former house and just remembering.

Jenny ended up losing the baby she was carrying at the reunion at Angela's. Especially given her age, the miscarriage was a blow. Would she be able to get pregnant again?

Some of the other Ames girls assumed she might not try, but she did, and she showed up at the Berkshires reunion with a surprise: She was pregnant. Several of the girls were in tears when they saw her. They wanted to plan a shower for her, but Jenny asked them not to jinx anything. She said she wasn't preparing the baby's nursery. She wasn't thinking about names. She wanted no gifts until after the baby was born.

Kelly asked if she could put her hand on Jenny's stomach while the baby moved, and Jenny welcomed that. "I did this when you were pregnant with Jack, and we were staying at Marilyn's for Christie's memorial service," Kelly reminded Jenny. Jack turned out to be such a terrific kid, and so Kelly hoped for a similar blessing this time for Jenny.

The pregnancy was indeed uneventful, and at age forty-five, Jenny gave birth to a beautiful and healthy baby girl. The baby was named Jiselle.

In October 2008, Angela in North Carolina had her own unwelcome news. She, too, had breast cancer, and it was a particularly aggressive form. It was the same type of inflammatory breast cancer that took her mother at age fifty-two.

"The cancer has not moved outside of my breast and the lymph node under my arm pit," Angela wrote to the other girls. "My chemo starts next week. My oncology team is also treating Elizabeth Edwards, who could go anywhere in the country for care, but has stayed here. So I do feel as if I have an A-team of professionals, and feel so blessed that somehow I ended up with them. Thanks for your friendship and love."

All the girls responded quickly, with love, advice and humor. (Marilyn joked: "I hope we don't become the Sisterhood of the Traveling Hats.")

Kelly made plans to fly to Maryland and stay with Jenny, and then they'd drive down to North Carolina together to be with Angela. They timed the visit for the period — ten to fourteen days after the first treatment — that Angela would need to shave her head. Kelly thought it was important for her daughter, Liesl, and Angela's daughter, Camryn, to see their mothers go through cancer treatment with their friends. "That view of life is certainly a gift we can provide our girls," Kelly told Angela. Jane talked to a nurse she knew in Massachusetts, and she suggested that perhaps eight-year-old Camryn could be shown photos of Kelly without hair, so she'd see that the hair will grow back.

On learning of Angela's cancer, Kelly sent an especially heartfelt note to her:

I am reaching out to you across miles and miles, and I am holding your hand — both hands. I am proof that you will come out on the other side of treatment and you'll be more vivacious, more healthy and more loving than you have ever been. In the next months, all the colors of the world will become brighter as your life takes on new meaning.

Kelly then alluded to the next Ames girls reunion.

I am standing before you and saying with absolute certainty that next summer we will again climb mountains together. And if you become weary, I will carry you. When we both start to stumble, our sisters will be there, walking beside us, ready to catch us and help carry us up that mountain.

As you go through this deeply personal journey, there will not be one moment when you are alone; not one moment when you are without unconditional love. We are always with you, Angela, always beside you. Your sister, Kelly.

There's a Spanish proverb: "Tell me who you're with, and I'll tell you who you are."

The story of the girls from Ames will have many more chapters, of course. To end here is arbitrary, because each year will bring new interactions, new reasons for reflection, new insights into who they are. There will be losses ahead, they all know that, but there will be great joys, too. And they have no doubt that they will be there for one another always, whatever happens. That now goes without saying.

There was a photo taken at Jane's house back in Ames in 1981, their senior year of high school. In the snapshot, every one of the eleven girls was smiling. In the back row stood Karla, Cathy, Sally and Karen. In the middle row: Jane, Angela, Marilyn and Sheila. Seated on the floor: Diana, Jenny and Kelly. They had no idea that day where their lives would take them, or that they'd bring twenty-two children into the world, or that they'd all remain so central to each other's life. On their faces, there was no indication that the ride would not always be easy, that they'd have disappointment and great grief. Just full-on smiles. Adult life awaited them.

During the reunion at Angela's in North Carolina, they posed on the back porch steps for a photo replicating that 1981 picture. All of them took the same positions, with only Sheila's spot unfilled. This time, their smiles were even broader. They touched each other even more effortlessly. They looked even happier. And why not?

In this moment, 1,163 miles from Ames and half a lifetime later, not much had really changed. There was much to be grateful for. They still had each other.

The Ames girls, 1981.
Top row: Karla, Cathy, Sally, Karen.
Middle row: Jane, Angela, Marilyn, Sheila.
Bottom row: Diana, Jenny, Kelly.
(The book cover photo shows the girls in the same position today.)

ACKNOWLEDGMENTS

When the Ames girls and I began this project, there was no road map. I knew of no man who had ever tried to immerse himself inside the friendship of eleven women. For their part, the girls had never had a journalist asking them such intrusive questions.

We mostly had a lot of fun, though at times, honestly, there were tense moments and hurt feelings. I pushed on certain fronts, making some of them uncomfortable or unhappy. Reading diaries or letters given to me by several of them, I'd learn details about the others that they hadn't intended to share. That led to debates within the group.

I watched the girls hash things out, issue by issue, and they'd almost always rally together into a united front. Though the book project became a test of their friendship, their great loyalty to each other always seemed to win out, and their friendship emerged as strong as ever. I thank them for everything they did, individually and collectively, to see this through to a finished book.

I am also grateful to their parents, siblings, spouses, children, former classmates and others in Iowa who graciously shared their memories and insights. Thanks to Lynn and Larry Zwagerman, Bernie and JoAnn Brown, Neala and Chuck Benson, Ingrid and Hugh Brady, Hanna and David Gradwohl, Hank and Kathy Bendorf, Barbara Derby, Sylvia McCormack, Meg and Vaughn Speer, John Highland, Warner Jamison, Justin Nash, Bruce Blackwood, Chris Johnson, Peggy Towner, Mary Calistro, Lynne Scribbins, Jeff Mann, Darwin and Jolene Trickle, Kevin Highland, Greg Brown, Jeff Benson, Steve Gradwohl, Polly McCormack, Jim Derks, Nancy Derks, Jim Cornette, Tom McKelvey, Jeff Sturdivant, Steele Campbell, Meg Schneider, Mark Walsh, Sunny Walsh, Mike Walsh, Susan Blowey, Liesl Schultz, Hanna Nash, Elwood Koelder, Carole Horowitz, Chuck Offenburger, Merle Prater, Pat Brown, Jahanshir Golchin, Dick Van Deusen, and Kelly's students at Faribault High School. Special thanks to Marilyn's sister, Sara Hoffman, who offered wonderful advice throughout the reporting and writing.

At Gotham Books, I am indebted to Bill Shinker, who enthusiastically embraced the concept of this book, and to Lauren Marino, who truly nurtured it. After Lauren read an early draft of *The Girls from Ames,* she sent me a sixteen-page, single-spaced memo of suggestions that was an absolutely beautiful essay about friendship; my wife even cried reading it! I am also grateful to Lauren and Bill for their support when I took a break from this book in order to coauthor *The Last Lecture.*

Others at Gotham who deserve thanks for all their efforts: Brianne Ramagosa, Beth Parker, Adenike Olanrewaju, Lisa Johnson, Susan Schwartz, Melanie Koch, Ray Lundgren, Julia Gilroy, Sabrina Bowers, Sarah Bergren, and Rick Willett.

I am supremely grateful to my agent Gary Morris for his friendship, his sense of humor about everything, and his advice and support at every step. Thanks also to Gary's colleagues David Black, Susan Raihofer, Leigh Ann Eliseo and David Larabell.

I am grateful to Randy Pausch for all his good wishes regarding *The Girls from Ames.* He knew I had set this book aside to work on *The Last Lecture,* and he was supportive when I returned to it. Thanks to Jai Pausch, too, who read short excerpts from this book early on and was encouraging.

Thanks to photographer Teness Herman and videographer Scott MacKinnon. At *The Wall Street Journal,* thanks to Neal Boudette, Mike Radakovich, Mike Miller, Eben Shapiro, Robert Sabat, Ernie Sander, John Blanton, Kelly Timon, Krishnan Anantharaman, Glenn Ruffenach, Roe D'Angelo, Alan Murray, Marshall Crook, Lee Hawkins, Kate Linebaugh, Mike Spector and John Stoll.

Of course, there aren't enough words to thank "The Girls from West Bloomfield" — my wife, Sherry Margulis, and daughters Jordan, Alex and Eden — who showed me their great love and patience as this book came together. Likewise, I am grateful for the loving support of my parents Harry and Naomi Zaslow; in-laws George and Marilyn Margulis; and siblings Darrell and Sherri Zaslow, Lisa and David Segelman, and Randy and Debby Margulis.

Among friends who offered advice or read early drafts: Beth Kujawski, Jay Boyar, Mitch Gerber, Gayle Goodman, Hilary King and Miriam Starkman.

I want to acknowledge Pam Schur and her friends in Illinois, who first set me on this road to writing about friendship in the *Chicago Sun-Times* more than two decades ago. And I thank the hundreds of women who wrote to me in response to my *Wall Street Journal* columns about friendship. Their warm and heartfelt emails helped me realize the power of women's friendships and led me to write this book.

As for the Ames girls themselves: I hope they all know how much I've come to admire them, and how extremely grateful I am that they shared themselves within these pages. At the reunion at Angela's house, they invited me to join them in one photo taken in the tobacco field out back. I was a bit emotional standing there with them, and I will treasure that photo. It's a picture of me with friends.

To learn more about the Ames girls,
or to share stories of your own
friendships, visit
www.girlsfromames.com

ABOUT THE AUTHOR

Coauthor of the international bestseller *The Last Lecture,* award-winning journalist **Jeffrey Zaslow** writes the *Wall Street Journal's* "Moving On" column, which has inspired several *Oprah* segments. He has also written for *Time* and *USA Weekend.* Zaslow lives in Detroit with his wife and their three daughters.

The employees of Thorndike Press hope you have enjoyed this Large Print book. All our Thorndike, Wheeler, and Kennebec Large Print titles are designed for easy reading, and all our books are made to last. Other Thorndike Press Large Print books are available at your library, through selected bookstores, or directly from us.

For information about titles, please call:
(800) 223-1244

or visit our Web site at:
http://gale.cengage.com/thorndike

To share your comments, please write:
Publisher
Thorndike Press
295 Kennedy Memorial Drive
Waterville, ME 04901